CHICKEN SOUP
FOR THE
CHRISTIAN SOUL

101 Stories to
Open the Heart and Rekindle
the Spirit

Jack Canfield
Mark Victor Hansen
Patty Aubery
Nancy Mitchell

Health Communications, Inc.
Deerfield Beach, Florida

www.hci-online.com
www.chickensoup.com

We would like to acknowledge the following publishers and individuals for permission to reprint the following material. (Note: The stories that were penned anonymously, that are in the public domain, or, that were written by Jack Canfield, Mark Victor Hansen, Patty Aubery or Nancy Mitchell are not included in this listing.)

Love Your Enemy. Reprinted with permission from *Guideposts* Magazine. ©1972 by *Guideposts*, Carmel, NY 10512.

There Are No Coincidences. Reprinted by permission of Warren Miller ©1996 Warren Miller.

Where's the Baby Jesus? Reprinted by permission of Jeannie S. Williams. ©1984 Jeannie S. Williams.

Trouble at the Inn. Reprinted with permission from *Guideposts* Magazine. ©1966 by *Guideposts*, Carmel, NY 10512.

Ten Cents. Reprinted by permission of Jeanne Morris. ©1997 Jeanne Morris.

In God's Hands a World of Mittens. Reprinted by permission of *The Post-Standard.* ©1996 *The Post-Standard.* All rights reserved.

(Continued on page 398)

Library of Congress Cataloging-in-Publication Data

Chicken soup for the Christian soul: 101 stories to open the heart and
  rekindle the spirit / Jack Canfield . . . [et al.].
       p.   cm.
    ISBN 1-55874-503-3 (hardcover)   ISBN 1-55874-501-7 (trade paper)
    1. Christian life.   I. Canfield, Jack, date
  BV4515.2.C45   1997
  242—dc21   97-19433
                                                                 CIP

©1997 Jack Canfield, Mark Victor Hansen, Patty Aubery and Nancy Mitchell

ISBN 1-55874-501-7 (trade paper)—ISBN 1-55874-503-3 (hardcover)

Publisher: Health Communications, Inc.
          3201 S.W. 15th Street
          Deerfield Beach, FL 33442-8190

Cover re-design by Andrea Perrine Brower
Stained glass cover image from the First Baptist Church of Fort Lauderdale, Florida,
  Dr. Larry Thompson, Senior Pastor. Stained glass created by Statesville Stained Glass,
  Statesville, North Carolina.
Cover photo by Gerhard Heidersberger

With love we dedicate this book
to the millions of people who have read our
previous books and to the 7,000 people who sent
us stories, poems and quotes for possible inclusion
in *Chicken Soup for the Christian Soul.*
While we couldn't use everything you sent in,
we were deeply touched by the heartfelt intention
to share yourselves and your stories with us
and our readers. Love to you!

Finally, brethren, whatever things are true, whatever things are noble, whatever things are just, whatever things are pure, whatever things are lovely, whatever things are of good report, if there is any virtue and if there is anything praiseworthy—meditate on these things.

Philippians 4:8

Contents

vii

3. ON PARENTS AND PARENTING

4. ON FAITH

8. OVERCOMING OBSTACLES

Acknowledgments

Chicken Soup for the Christian Soul has taken over two years to write, compile and edit. It continues to be a true labor of love and faith for all of us, and we would like to acknowledge the following people for their contributions, without which this book could never have been created:

Peter Vegso and Gary Seidler at Health Communications, for continually supporting us and giving their all to keep the *Chicken Soup* factory cooking. Thank you, Peter and Gary. We love you more than you'll ever know!

Our families, who continue to give us the space, love and support needed to produce such wonderful books. We especially appreciate your support when it looks like it will never come together, but with your belief and encouragement, it always does. You have been Chicken Soup for our Souls day after day after day!

Heather McNamara, who once again spent countless hours editing stories, searched endlessly on the Internet for authors and stories, and last but not least, kept us grounded and sane through the last days of editing the final manuscript.

Patty Hansen, who is always there with the answers when we can't find them. She also continues to find the "gems" and supports us along the way.

Marsha Donohoe and Sharon Linnéa, who read the

entire manuscript, edited each and every story, rewrote several pieces and gave us advice when we needed it. We appreciate both of you more than you will ever know.

Diana Chapman, whose support never ends, and who was not only the first reader to send in her feedback, but submitted many wonderful stories for inclusion as well. Whenever we need a certain kind of story in a rush, she is always there to help find the perfect one.

Taryn Phillips Quinn, the editor of *Woman's World* Magazine, for sending us great stories and for advising us on many issues we needed help with. Thanks, Taryn. You are a gem to work with.

Jonathan Moynes who served as our "human dictionary" in times of need while Nancy and Patty completed the project at home. Thanks Jonathan!

Joanne Duncalf, who sent us numerous great stories that she had collected from around the world, and who had seven of her friends read our final manuscript, while she continually traveled back and forth from the United States to Bosnia to keep her commitment to the children of Bosnia.

Christine Kimmich, who read the entire manuscript and contributed numerous Scripture passages and prayers for inclusion.

Kimberly Kirberger and Linda Mitchell, who read thousands of stories, searching for the "perfect 10's" to create the best book possible, and who continuously offered moral support whenever we needed it.

Leslie Forbes, the latest staff member to join the *Chicken Soup* family, who spent weeks reading, categorizing and evaluating stacks of stories. You are an outstanding addition to our group.

Veronica Romero, for continuously taking care of the day-to-day operations of The Canfield Training Group, so Jack, Patty and Nancy could stay focused on writing and editing. We also appreciate Veronica's words of wisdom, just when we thought we were going to go crazy, reminding us that God never gives us anything we can't handle!

Rosalie Miller, who tended to the unanswered phone calls and day-to-day duties that we were unable to handle in the last months of the project.

Teresa Spohn, who managed Jack's and Patty's schedules and allowed them the time to write and edit!

Lisa Williams, for taking good care of Mark and their business, so he could be dedicated to the task of traveling the world and making people aware of our books; and for scheduling time for Mark so he could help finish this book.

Trudy Klefstad at OfficeWorks, who typed the first draft of the entire book in record time and with very few errors. Thanks a lot!

Anna Kanson, the manager of rights and permissions at *Guideposts,* who continually goes out of her way to help us create the best books possible by giving us invaluable guidance, sending us incredible stories and evaluating every story we send her.

Katherine Burns, the manager of rights and permissions at *Reader's Digest,* who generously gives us her time and provides us with the information needed to locate hard-to-find authors.

To our other coauthors—Patty Hansen, Diana von Welantz Wentworth, Barry Spilchuk, Marci Shimoff, Jennifer Reed Hawthorne, Martin Rutte, Maida Rogerson, Tim Clauss, Hanoch and Meladee McCarty, Marty Becker and Carol Kline—who continuously sent us stories for inclusion and gave us lots of moral support when we needed it.

Elinor Hall, who assisted in the production of *Chicken Soup for the Woman's Soul,* for funneling stories our way when they were better suited for this book.

Larry and Linda Price, for running the Foundation for

Self-Esteem and the Soup Kitchens for the Soul project with impeccability, so that we could focus all our energies on finishing this book.

Christine Belleris, Matthew Diener and Allison Janse, our editors at Health Communications, for their generous efforts in bringing this book to its high state of excellence. Terry Burke, the vice president of sales and production at Health Communications, who is always available with words of encouragement.

To the over 7,000 Christians who submitted stories, poems and other pieces for consideration; you all know who you are. While most of the pieces were wonderful, they just didn't fit into the overall structure of this book. However, many will be used in future volumes of *Chicken Soup for the Soul*. We will be publishing such books as *Chicken Soup for the Grieving Soul, Chicken Soup for the Parent's Soul, Chicken Soup for the Expectant Mother's Soul, Chicken Soup for the Kid's Soul, Chicken Soup for the Laughing Soul and Chicken Soup for the Country Soul,* among others.

We also want to thank the following people who read the first rough draft of over 200 stories, helped us make the final selections and made invaluable comments on how to improve the book: Diane Aubery, Jeff Aubery, Susan Burhoe, Diana Chapman, Nancy Clark, Marsha Donohoe, Joanne Duncalf, Jo Elberg, Thales Finchum, Leslie Forbes, Beth Gates, Patty Hansen, Anna Kanson, Kimberly Kirberger, Carol Kline, Marianne Larned, Sharon Linnéa, Donna Loesch, Heather McNamara, Ernie Mendes, Rosalie Miller, Linda Mitchell, Monica Navarrette, Dorothy Nohnsin, Cindy Palajac, LuAnn Reicks, Veronica Romero, Catherine Valenti, Diana von Welanetz Wentworth, Rebecca Whitney, Martha Wigglesworth, Maureen Wilcinski and Kelly Zimmerman.

And the following people who contributed in other important ways:

Randee Goldsmith, our product manager for *Chicken Soup for the Soul,* who continually supports the series with a high level of expertise. We love and appreciate you Randee!

Arielle Ford, our publicist, who continually thinks up new ways to market our *Chicken Soup for the Soul* series and gives us invaluable feedback. Kim Weiss and Ronni O'Brien at Health Communications, Inc., who keep us on radio and television so we can get the word out, and who constantly keep us motivated with words of encouragement and inspiration. Irene Xanthos and Lori Golden, for making sure our books reach the widest audience possible. Teri Miller Peluso, who is always available for our every need.

Because of the immensity of this project, we are sure we have left out the names of some people who helped us. For that we are sorry, but we are nonetheless grateful for the many hands that made this book possible. Thank you all for your vision, your caring, your commitment and your actions. We love you all.

Introduction

We feel truly blessed to have been able to create this book. It has been a true labor of love for us, and like all divinely inspired projects, it has given us back much more than we have put into it. From the moment it was conceived, we have felt the power of love flowing through us and the divine hand of God directing us in our every step. Right from the beginning we have been experiencing miracles—from opening the Bible to just the right Scripture we needed, to finding the nephew of a writer we couldn't locate on the Internet! Our most fervent hope is that you will receive as much from reading this book as we did in compiling, editing and writing it.

Since the original *Chicken Soup for the Soul* book was published in 1993, we have been collecting and editing stories for *Chicken Soup for the Christian Soul*. Readers like yourselves have sent us over 7,000 stories, all of which we have read and been touched by. The 101 stories that you have in your hands are the result of endless reading and rereading, looking for just those stories that would touch your soul at the deepest and most profound level. Once we had the book narrowed down to the best 200, we asked a panel of over 40 Christian friends to pick their favorite 101 stories. As a result, we believe we have selected stories that are universal in their appeal and compelling in their impact.

We believe these stories will deepen your Christian faith and expand your awareness of how to practice your Christian values in your day-to-day life—both at home, at work and in the community. These stories will open your heart so that you may experience and express more love in your life. They will deepen your compassion for others and inspire you to greater acts of charity and philanthropy. They will lead you to forgive others for their trespasses and yourself for your shortcomings. They will encourage you to stand up for what you believe in and to believe in what you stand for. And, perhaps most important, they will remind you that you are never alone or without hope no matter how challenging and painful your circumstances may be.

Read what some of our previous readers have said about how deeply they have been touched by the stories in the *Chicken Soup for the Soul* books:

I received your third book while recovering from lupus in the hospital. I now have a better and more positive outlook on life. . . . Every story, in its own way, has taught me something.

Hong-Chau Tran, Age 21

I am successfully surviving fully blown AIDS. The prison chaplain loaned me your book Chicken Soup for the Soul, *and I have to admit, I've never read anything quite so uplifting and enjoyable. The stories were real. They were inspirational.*

Anonymous

One morning I woke up to find my face half paralyzed with Bell's Palsy. The duration is usually three weeks to three months. Halfway through Chicken Soup for the Soul, *my face began to regain motion. When I got voted "Best Smile" in Senior Class, I could not help but think of this book and the profound impact it had on my life.*

Kyle Brown

My dad read stories from Chicken Soup for the Soul *at the dinner table. After a few stories we laughed, we cried and were touched. That night my family became closer than ever.*

Vanessa Sim, 7th grade

I wanted to end my life at 14 years old. I've had that feeling for 10 years. Now—after reading your books—I promise myself to never feel that way again!

Anonymous

I am currently serving a four-year sentence. My dog-eared copy of Chicken Soup for the Soul *has been making the rounds of my 121-man dorm. Without exception, these gang-banging, hard-nosed, tough guys are all moved, sometimes to tears, by one story or another.*

Anonymous

So from our hearts to yours, we offer you *Chicken Soup for the Christian Soul.* As you read these stories, we pray that you experience the same love, inspiration, encouragement and comfort that they brought to us. We pray that your heart be opened, your spiritual and emotional wounds be healed and your soul be overflowing with boundless joy! We send you our love, and we ask that God may bless you!

Jack Canfield, Mark Victor Hansen,
Patty Aubery and Nancy Mitchell

1

ON LOVE

Love is patient and kind. Love is not jealous, it does not brag, and it is not proud. Love is not rude, is not selfish and does not get upset with others. Love does not count up wrongs that have been done. Love is not happy with evil but is happy with the truth. Love patiently accepts all things. It always trusts, always hopes, and always remains strong.

1 Cor. 13:4-7

Love Your Enemy

It is far better to forgive and forget than to resent and remember.

Anonymous

It was in a church in Munich that I saw him—a balding, heavyset man in a gray overcoat, a brown felt hat clutched between his hands. People were filing out of the basement room where I had just spoken, moving along the rows of wooden chairs to the door at the rear. It was 1947 and I had come from Holland to defeated Germany with the message that God forgives.

It was the truth they needed most to hear in that bitter, bombed-out land, and I gave them my favorite mental picture. Maybe because the sea is never far from a Hollander's mind, I liked to think that that's where forgiven sins were thrown. "When we confess our sins," I said, "God casts them into the deepest ocean, gone forever. And even though I cannot find a scripture for it, I believe God then places a sign out there that says, 'NO FISHING ALLOWED.'"

The solemn faces stared back at me, not quite daring to

believe. There were never questions after a talk in Germany in 1947. People stood up in silence, in silence collected their wraps, in silence left the room. And that's when I saw him, working his way forward against the others. One moment I saw the overcoat and the brown hat; the next, a blue uniform and a visored cap with its skull and crossbones. It came back with a rush: the huge room with its harsh overhead lights; the pathetic pile of dresses and shoes in the center of the floor; the shame of walking naked past this man. I could see my sister's frail form ahead of me, ribs sharp beneath the parchment skin. *Betsie, how thin you were!*

The place was Ravensbruck and the man who was making his way forward had been a guard—one of the most cruel guards.

Now he was in front of me, hand thrust out: "A fine message, *Fräulein!* How good it is to know that, as you say, all our sins are at the bottom of the sea!"

And I, who had spoken so glibly of forgiveness, fumbled in my pocketbook rather than take that hand. He would not remember me, of course—how could he remember one prisoner among those thousands of women?

But I remembered him and the leather crop swinging from his belt. I was face-to-face with one of my captors and my blood seemed to freeze.

"You mentioned Ravensbruck in your talk," he was saying. "I was a guard there." No, he did not remember me.

"But since that time," he went on, "I have become a Christian. I know that God has forgiven me for the cruel things I did there, but I would like to hear it from your lips as well. *Fräulein*"—again the hand came out—"will you forgive me?"

And I stood there—I whose sins had again and again needed to be forgiven—and could not forgive. Betsie had died in that place—could he erase her slow terrible death simply for the asking?

It could not have been many seconds that he stood there—hand held out—but to me it seemed hours as I wrestled with the most difficult thing I had ever had to do. For I had to do it—I knew that. The message that God forgives has a prior condition: that we forgive those who have injured us. "If you do not forgive men their trespasses," Jesus says, "neither will your Father in Heaven forgive your trespasses."

I knew it not only as a commandment of God, but as a daily experience. Since the end of the war I had had a home in Holland for victims of Nazi brutality. Those who were able to forgive their former enemies were able also to return to the outside world and rebuild their lives, no matter what the physical scars. Those who nursed their bitterness remained invalids. It was as simple and horrible as that.

And still I stood there with the coldness clutching my heart. But forgiveness is not an emotion—I knew that too. Forgiveness is an act of the will, and the will can function regardless of the temperature of the heart. *Jesus, help me!* I prayed silently. *I can lift my hand. I can do that much. You supply the feeling.*

And so woodenly, mechanically, I thrust my hand into the one stretched out to me. And as I did, an incredible thing took place. The current started in my shoulder, raced down my arm and sprang into our joined hands. And then this healing warmth seemed to flood my whole being, bringing tears to my eyes.

"I forgive you, brother!" I cried. "With all my heart."

For a long moment we grasped each other's hands—the former guard and the former prisoner. I had never known God's love so intensely as I did then. But even so, I realized it was not my love. I had tried, and did not have the power. It was the power of the Holy Spirit as recorded in Romans 5:5: "... because the love of God is shed abroad in our hearts by the Holy Ghost which is given unto us."

Corrie ten Boom

There Are No Coincidences

If we confess our sins, he is faithful and just and will forgive us our sins and purify us from all unrighteousness.

1 John 1:9 NIV

For three days a fierce winter storm had traveled 1,500 miles across the North Pacific from Alaska, packing gale-force winds and torrential rains. In the Sierra Nevadas to the east, the snow was piling up and would offer great skiing once the storm had passed.

In the foothills of the Sierras in the town of Grass Valley, California, the streets were flooded, and in some parts of town, the power was off where trees had blown down. At the small church, the heavy rain and high winds beat against the windows with a violence that Father O'Malley had never before heard.

In his tiny bedroom, O'Malley was laboriously writing Sunday's sermon by candlelight. Out of the darkness, the phone in his office rang, shattering his concentration. He picked up the candle, and with his hand cupped in front of it, ambled down the hall in a sphere of dim flickering light.

As he picked up the phone, a voice quickly asked, "Is this Father O'Malley?"

"Yes."

"I'm calling from the hospital in Auburn," said a concerned female voice. "We have a terminally ill patient who is asking us to get someone to give him his last rites. Can you come quickly?"

"I'll try my best to make it," O'Malley answered. "But the river is over its banks, and trees are blown down all over town. It's the worst storm I've seen in all the years I've been here. Look for me within two hours."

The trip was only 30 miles, but it would be hard going. The headlights on Father O'Malley's 20-year-old car barely penetrated the slashing rain, and where the winding road crossed and recrossed the river in a series of small bridges, trees had blown down across the river's banks. But for some reason, there was always just enough room for Father O'Malley to make his way around them. His progress was slow and cautious, but he continued on toward the hospital.

Not a single vehicle passed him during his long, tense journey. It was way past midnight, and anyone else out on a night like this would also have to be on an emergency mission.

Finally, in the near distance, the lights of the small hospital served as a beacon to guide O'Malley for the last 500 yards, and he hoped he had arrived in time. He parked behind the three other cars in the parking lot to avoid as much wind as possible, slipped into the right-hand seat and awkwardly wrestled his way into his raincoat before stepping out into the wind-whipped deluge.

With his tattered Bible tucked deep inside his overcoat pocket, O'Malley forced the car door open, stepped out and then leaned into the wind. Its power almost bowled him over, and he was nearly blown away from the hospital entrance.

Once inside, the wind slammed the hospital door shut behind him, and as he was shaking the water from his coat, he heard footsteps headed his way. It was the night nurse.

"I'm so glad you could get here," she said. "The man I called you about is slipping fast, but he is still coherent. He's been an alcoholic for years, and his liver has finally given out. He's been here for a couple of weeks this time and hasn't had one single visitor. He lives up in the woods, and no one around here knows much about him. He always pays his bill with cash and doesn't seem to want to talk much. We've been treating him off and on for the last couple of years, but this time it's as though he's reached some personal decision and has given up the fight."

"What's your patient's name?" O'Malley asked.

"The hospital staff has just been calling him Tom," she replied.

In the soft night-light of the room, Tom's thin sallow countenance looked ghostlike behind a scraggly beard. It was as though he had stepped over the threshold and his life was already gone.

"Hello, Tom. I'm Father O'Malley. I was passing by and thought we could talk a bit before you go to sleep for the night."

"Don't give me any of that garbage," Tom replied. "You didn't just stop by at 3:30 in the morning. I asked that dumb night nurse to call someone to give me my last rites because I know my deal is done and it's my turn to go. Now get on with it."

"Patience," said Father O'Malley, and he began to say the prayers of the last rites.

After the "Amen," Tom perked up a bit, and he seemed to want to talk.

"Would you like to make your confession?" O'Malley asked him.

"Absolutely not," Tom answered. "But I would like to just talk with you a bit, before I go."

And so Tom and Father O'Malley talked about the Korean War, and the ferocity of the winter storm, and the knee-high grass and summer blossoms that would soon follow.

Occasionally, during the hour or so before daylight, Father O'Malley would ask Tom again, "Are you sure you don't want to confess anything?"

After a couple of hours, and after about the fourth or fifth time that Father O'Malley asked the same question, Tom replied, "Father, when I was young, I did something that was so bad that I've never told anyone about it. It was so bad that I haven't spent a single day since without thinking about it and reliving the horror."

"Don't you think it would be good for you to tell me about it?" O'Malley asked.

"Even now, I still can't talk about what I did," Tom said. "Even to you."

But as the first gray light of dawn crept into the room and began to form shadows, Tom sadly said, "Okay. It's too late for anyone to do anything to me now, so I guess I might as well tell you."

"I worked as a switchman on the railroad all my life, until I retired a few years ago and moved up here to the woods. Thirty-two years, two months and 11 days ago, I was working in Bakersfield on a night kind of like tonight."

Tom's face became intense as the words began to tumble out. "It happened during a bad winter storm with a lot of rain, 50-mile-an-hour winds and almost no visibility. It was two nights before Christmas and to push away the gloom, the whole yard crew drank all through the swing shift. I was drunker than the rest of them, so I volunteered to go out in the rain and wind and push the switch for the northbound 8:30 freight."

Tom's voice dropped almost to a whisper as he went on. "I guess I was more drunk than I thought I was because I pushed that switch in the wrong direction. At 45 miles an hour that freight train slammed into a passenger car at the next crossing and killed a young man, his wife and their two daughters.

"I have had to live with my being the cause of their deaths every day since then."

There was a long moment of silence as Tom's confession of this tragedy hung in the air. After what seemed like an eternity, Father O'Malley gently put his hand on Tom's shoulder and said very quietly, "If I can forgive you, God can forgive you, because in that car were my mother, my father and my two older sisters."

Warren Miller

Where's the Baby Jesus?

I will honor Christmas in my heart and try to keep it all the year.

Charles Dickens

A nativity scene without the baby Jesus?! I have one proudly displayed at home each Christmas. For me, it's a reminder of a past holiday when I purchased the broken set.

I was bitter and disheartened that year because my parents, after 36 years of marriage, were getting a divorce. I could not accept their decision to part, and I became depressed, not realizing they needed my love and understanding more than ever.

My thoughts were constantly filled with childhood memories—the huge Christmas trees, the gleaming decorations, the special gifts and the love we shared as a close family. Every time I'd think about those moments, I'd burst into tears, knowing I'd never feel the spirit of Christmas again. But for my children's sake, I decided to make the effort, joining the last-minute shoppers.

They pushed, shoved and complained as they grabbed

from shelves and racks. Christmas tree lights and ornaments dangled from open boxes, and the few dolls and stuffed toys sitting on the nearly emptied shelves reminded me of neglected orphans. A small nativity scene had fallen to the floor in front of my shopping cart, and I stopped to put it back on the shelf.

After glancing at the endless checkout line, I decided it wasn't worth the effort and had made up my mind to leave when suddenly I heard a loud, sharp voice cry out.

"Sarah! You get that thing out of your mouth right now 'fore I slap you!"

"But Mommy! I wasn't puttin' it in my mouth! See, Mommy? I was kissin' it! Look, Mommy, it's a little baby Jesus!"

"Well, I don't care what it is! You put it down right now! You hear me?"

"But come look, Mommy," the child insisted. "It's all broken. It's a little manger and the baby Jesus got broked off!"

As I listened from the next aisle, I found myself smiling and wanting to see the little girl who had kissed the baby Jesus.

She appeared to be about four or five years old and was not properly dressed for the cold, wet weather. Bright, colorful pieces of yarn were tied on the ends of her braids, making her look cheerful despite her ragged attire.

Reluctantly, I turned my eyes to her mother. She was paying no attention to the child but was anxiously looking through the marked-down winter coats on the bargain rack. She was also shabbily dressed, and her torn, dirty tennis shoes were wet from the cold, melting snow. Asleep in her shopping cart was a small baby bundled snugly in a thick, washed-out yellow blanket.

"Mommy!" the little girl called to her. "Can we buy this here little baby Jesus? We can set him on the table by the couch and we could—"

"I told you to put that thing down!" her mother interrupted. "You get yourself over here right now or I'm
gonna give you a spankin'. You hear me?"

Angrily, the woman hurried toward the child. I turned
away, not wanting to watch, expecting her to punish the
child as she had threatened. A few seconds passed.

No movement, no scolding. Just complete silence.
Puzzled, I peeked again and was astonished to see the
mother kneeling on the wet, dirty floor holding the child
close to her trembling body. She struggled to say something, but only managed a desperate sob.

"Don't cry, Mommy!" the child pleaded. Wrapping her
arms around her mother, she apologized for her behavior.
"I'm sorry I wasn't good in this store. I promise I won't ask
for nothin' else! I don't want this here little baby Jesus.
Really I don't! See, I'll put him back here in the manger.
Please don't cry no more, Mommy!"

"I'm sorry too, honey!" answered her mother finally.
"You know I don't have enough money to buy anything
extra right now, and I'm just crying 'cause I wished I
did—it being Christmas and all—but I bet come
Christmas mornin', if you promise to be a real good girl,
you just might find them pretty little play dishes you
been wantin', and maybe next year we can get us a real
Christmas tree. How about that!"

"You know what, Mommy?" the child asked excitedly.
"I don't really need this here little baby Jesus doll anyhow!
You know why? 'Cause my Sunday school teacher says
Jesus really lives in your heart! I'm glad he lives in my
heart, aren't you, Mommy?"

I watched the child take her mother's hand and walk to
the front of the store. Her simple words, exclaimed with
excitement, were echoing through my mind: "He lives in
my heart."

I looked at the nativity scene and realized that a baby

born in a stable some 2,000 years ago is a person who still walks with us today, making his presence known, working to bring us through the difficulties of life, if only we will let him.

"Thank you, God," I began to pray. "Thank you for a wonderful childhood filled with precious memories, and for parents who provided a home for me and gave me the love I needed during the most important years of my life. But most of all, thank you for giving us your son."

Quickly, I grabbed the various pieces of the nativity scene and hurried to the check-out counter. Recognizing one of the clerks, I asked her to give the doll to the little girl who was then leaving the store with her mother, and explained that I would pay for it later. I watched the child accept the gift and then give baby Jesus another kiss as she walked out the door.

The little broken nativity scene reminds me every year of a child whose simple words touched my life and transformed my despair into new assurance—and joy!

The baby Jesus is not there, of course, but every time I look at the empty manger I know I can answer the question, "Where's the baby Jesus?"

He's in my heart!

Jeannie S. Williams

Reprinted with permission from Bil Keane.

Trouble at the Inn

For years now whenever Christmas pageants are talked about in a certain little town in the Midwest, someone is sure to mention the name of Wallace Purling. Wally's performance in one annual production of the nativity play has slipped into the realm of legend. But the old-timers who were in the audience that night never tire of recalling exactly what happened.

Wally was nine that year and in the second grade, though he should have been in the fourth. Most people in town knew that he had difficulty in keeping up. He was big and clumsy, slow in movement and mind. Still, Wally was well-liked by the other children in his class, all of whom were smaller than he, though the boys had trouble hiding their irritation when Wally would ask to play ball with them or any game, for that matter, in which winning was important.

Most often they'd find a way to keep him out but Wally would hang around anyway—not sulking, just hoping. He was always a helpful boy, a willing and smiling one, and the natural protector, paradoxically, of the underdog. Sometimes if the older boys chased the younger ones away, it would always be Wally who'd say, "Can't they stay? They're no bother."

Wally fancied the idea of being a shepherd with a flute in the Christmas pageant that year, but the play's director, Miss Lumbard, assigned him to a more important role. After all, she reasoned, the Innkeeper did not have too many lines, and Wally's size would make his refusal of lodging to Joseph more forceful.

And so it happened that the usual large, partisan audience gathered for the town's yearly extravaganza of crooks and crèches, beards, crowns, halos and a staged filled with squeaky voices. No one on stage or off was more caught up in the magic of the night than Wallace Purling. They said later that he stood in the wings and watched the performance with such fascination that from time to time Miss Lumbard had to make sure he didn't wander onstage before his cue.

Then the time came when Joseph appeared, slowly, tenderly guiding Mary to the door of the inn. Joseph knocked hard on the wooden door set into the painted backdrop. Wally the Innkeeper was there, waiting.

"What do you want?" Wally said, swinging the door open with a brusque gesture.

"We seek lodging."

"Seek it elsewhere." Wally looked straight ahead but spoke vigorously. "The inn is filled."

"Sir, we have asked everywhere in vain. We have traveled far and are very weary."

"There is no room in this inn for you." Wally looked properly stern.

"Please, good innkeeper, this is my wife, Mary. She is heavy with child and needs a place to rest. Surely you must have some small corner for her. She is so tired."

Now, for the first time, the Innkeeper relaxed his stiff stance and looked down at Mary. With that, there was a long pause, long enough to make the audience a bit tense with embarrassment.

"No! Begone!" the prompter whispered from the wings.

"No!" Wally repeated automatically. "Begone!"

Joseph sadly placed his arm around Mary who laid her head upon her husband's shoulder and the two of them started to move away. The Innkeeper did not return inside his inn, however. Wally stood there in the doorway, watching the forlorn couple. His mouth was open, his brow creased with concern, his eyes filling unmistakably with tears.

And suddenly this Christmas pageant became different from all others.

"Don't go, Joseph," Wally called out. "Bring Mary back." And Wallace Purling's face grew into a bright smile. "You can have *my* room."

Some people in town thought that the pageant had been ruined. Yet there were others—many, many others —who considered it the truest of all Christmas pageants they had ever seen.

Dina Donohue

Ten Cents

I am only one,
But still I am one.
I cannot do everything,
But still I can do something;
and because I cannot do everything,
I will not refuse to do the something that
I can do.

Edward Everett Hale's pledge to the
Lend-a-Hand Society

"Miss! Over here!"
"Waitress, could you check on my order?"
"Could you bring the baby some more milk?"
I sighed and pushed the hair back from my eyes. That gray February lunch hour found the restaurant where I worked packed with people anxious to escape the snow turned to rain. There was even a large standing crowd waiting for tables. I was already exhausted, I had a splitting headache and it wasn't even 12:30! How was I ever going to make it through the day?

I'd been plenty grateful to get this job the year before. As a suddenly single mom with two small children to support and little in the way of education or skills, it had been a godsend to be hired by a better-than-average restaurant close to a famous hospital in our city.

As the "new kid" at the restaurant, I had been started off with the worst station, a small room at the back of the building. It was a long way from the front entrance and equally far from the kitchen, so service there was unavoidably slower than in the front dining area. The room held two large tables and several tiny ones by the windows. As a rule, most of the customers exiled to the back were either single women dining alone or large families with children who were expected to be loud and demanding.

After nearly two years and several new hirees, I was still "stuck" with the back room. Usually I didn't mind. The view from "my" windows revealed a steep ravine, heavily wooded on both sides, which cradled a small stream at the bottom. It was a surprisingly beautiful spot to find hidden away in a large city. With that view, I could relax during off hours and find a moment of peace.

But today was one of those days when I longed for one of the front stations. Although I was pushing myself to keep up with the demand, I was steadily losing ground because of the hazard of getting through the mob between my tables and the kitchen. This was made more difficult by the fact that both my large tables were filled to overflowing with extra chairs and high chairs that blocked the aisles.

I stopped for a moment and glanced around to see what were the most urgent of the many things demanding my attention.

That's when I saw her. She was seated at the farthest table, jammed into a corner, her enjoyment of the view hampered by the unappetizing remains of someone else's meal in front of her. She appeared to be about 70 years old, with white hair, a deeply lined face, and hands that testified to a lifetime of hard work. She wore an old-fashioned navy straw hat, and a cotton housedress under a shabby brown coat that appeared inadequate for the weather. She sat quietly, with an air of dejection and an expression of terrible sadness.

I hurried over, and as I cleared the table, I began a monologue—scolding the hostess for not telling me the woman was waiting and complaining about the busboy for not clearing the table. "He'll get no dessert tonight for that kind of work!" I added.

She smiled to tell me she knew I was joking, but the smile did not reach her eyes.

"It's all right," she said. "I live on a farm and out that window it almost looks like home."

"I'd love to live in a pretty place, too," I said, but she was not interested in continuing the conversation.

All she had ordered was a cup of tea. I made sure her tea was hot, and told her I hoped she'd come back when we weren't so busy. Then the voices around me called for my attention:

"Waitress! Where is my coffee?"

"Over here! It's been 20 minutes since we ordered!"

And I was back on the treadmill, even farther behind.

When I looked over again, the old woman was gone. I couldn't help but wonder what had made her so terribly sad.

A few moments later I heard my name called and I looked up to see her pushing her way through the crowded aisles. "I have something for you," she said, and she held out her hand. I put down the plates I was carrying and dried my hands so she could give me a dime.

She didn't know that most waitresses here laughed at people who left only small change for a tip. Then I thought about how far she had to come, pushing her way through the crowd just to give me her money, and how she probably couldn't afford even that little bit. I smiled and said, "You really didn't have to do that." She answered, "I know it isn't much, but you went out of your way to be nice to me. I just wanted you to know that I appreciated it."

Somehow my simple "thank you" didn't seem adequate, so I added, "and God bless you."

Her response was sudden and unexpected. She grabbed my hand and started to cry. "Thank you, Lord," she sobbed. "You knew how much I needed to know there was another Christian nearby."

Leaving the dishes where they sat, I led her to a chair and said, "Tell me what is wrong, and if there is any way I can help."

She shook her head and answered in a rush. "There is nothing anybody can do. I brought my husband here for an operation. They thought it was a hernia but now they tell me he has cancer and I don't know if he will survive the operation. He is 72 and we have been married over 50 years. I don't know anyone here to talk to and the city feels like such a cold and unfriendly place. I tried to pray over it but I couldn't seem to find God anywhere around here."

She managed to stop crying. "I almost didn't come in here because it looked so expensive. But I just had to get out of the hospital for a while. When I was looking out the window in back, I tried praying again. I asked Jesus to show me just one other Christian so I would know I wasn't alone and that he was listening."

Still holding her hand I said, "Tell me your husband's name and I will pray for both of you every day for a week."

She smiled and responded, "Please do. His name is Henry."

With that she stood up and left. I went back to work with renewed energy. Somehow I didn't feel tired any more. For some reason, none of my other customers complained about the delay. I knew that God had conspired that the two of us meet and help each other. I was happy to offer her my prayers. And I hoped she knew she'd given me far more than 10 cents.

It was suddenly an absolutely beautiful day.

Jeanne Morris

The Night the Chimes Rang

It is better, much better, to have wisdom and knowledge than gold and silver.

Prov. 16:16

Once, long ago, a magnificent church stood on a high hill in a great city. When lighted up for a special festival, it could be seen for miles around. And yet there was something even more remarkable about this church than its beauty: the strange and wonderful legend of the bells.

At the corner of the church was a tall gray tower, and at the top of the tower, so people said, was a chime of the most beautiful bells in the world. But the fact was that no one had heard the bells for many years. Not even on Christmas. For it was the custom on Christmas Eve for all the people to bring to the church their offerings to the Christ child. And there had been a time when a very unusual offering laid on the altar brought glorious music from the chimes far up in the tower. Some said that the wind rang them, and others that the angels set them swinging. But lately no offering had been great enough to deserve the music of the chimes.

Now a few miles from the city, in a small village, lived a boy named Pedro and his little brother. They knew very little about the Christmas chimes, but they had heard of the service in the church on Christmas Eve and they decided to go to see the beautiful celebration.

The day before Christmas was bitterly cold, with a hard white crust on the ground. Pedro and his little brother started out early in the afternoon, and despite the cold they reached the edge of the city by nightfall. They were about to enter one of the great gates when Pedro saw something dark on the snow near their path.

It was a poor woman, who had fallen just outside the city, too sick and tired to get in where she might have found shelter. Pedro tried to rouse her, but she was barely conscious. "It's no use, little brother. You will have to go alone."

"Without you?" cried the little brother.

Pedro nodded slowly. "This woman will freeze to death if nobody cares for her. Everyone has probably gone to the church now, but when you come back, be sure and bring someone to help her. I will stay here and try to keep her from freezing, and perhaps get her to eat the roll I have in my pocket."

"But I can't leave you!" cried his little brother.

"Both of us need not miss the service," said Pedro. "You must see and hear everything twice, once for you and once for me. I am sure the Christ child knows how I would love to worship him. And if you get a chance, take this silver piece of mine and when no one is looking, lay it down for my offering."

In this way he hurried his little brother off to the city, and winked hard to keep back the tears of disappointment.

The great church was a brilliant place that night; it had never looked so beautiful. When the organ played and the thousands of people sang, the walls shook with the sound.

At the close of the service came the procession with the offerings to be laid on the altar. Some brought jewels, some heavy baskets of gold. A famous writer laid down a book he had been writing for years. And last of all walked the King of the country, hoping with all the rest to win for himself the chime of the Christmas bells.

A great murmur went through the church as the King took from his head the royal crown, all set with precious stones, and laid it on the altar. "Surely," everyone said, "we will hear the bells now!" But the cold wind was all that was heard in the tower.

The procession was over, and the choir began the closing hymn. Suddenly the organist stopped playing. The singing ceased. Not a sound could be heard from anyone in the church. As all the people strained their ears to listen, there came softly—but distinctly—the sound of the chimes in the tower. So far away and yet so clear, the music seemed so much sweeter than anything ever heard before.

Then they all stood up together and looked at the altar to see what great gift had awakened the long silent bells. But all they saw was the childish figure of Pedro's little brother, who had crept softly down the aisle when no one was looking and laid Pedro's little piece of silver on the altar.

Raymond McDonald Alden

In God's Hands a World of Mittens

Kindness is Christianity with its working clothes on.

Anonymous

Helen Bunce hadn't been to church all year. Her joints were stiff with arthritis and her bones so brittle they could snap, but what was harder to bear was the thought of being separated from her ailing husband, Karl, for even an hour or two.

Yet on the third Sunday of Advent last year, she went. It was time to dedicate the mitten tree at Emmanuel Congregational Church in Watertown, and time to reveal a decades-old secret.

Since 1949, one woman had knitted dozens of pairs of mittens and matching hats that hung on the pine tree at the front of the church each Christmas, so many of them the tree's branches were laden as if with a heavy snow. But the woman insisted on remaining anonymous. Except to her family and a circle of friends, she was known only as "the mitten lady."

And so when the mitten lady's identity was revealed
that morning, Helen Bunce, 86 years old, sat quietly in her
wheelchair, her daughter holding her hand. The members
of the congregation began to applaud, then rose to their
feet and gave her an ovation that lasted a full five minutes, able at last to thank the mitten lady in person for her
many good works.

It was the last time she went to church. Helen Bunce
died on Saturday. Karl cried when his family told him she
was gone. He wouldn't eat or drink, and he had nothing
to say. The family kept a vigil, and on Monday, 86 and sick
for many years, he died.

"That's why he died when he did," said their daughter,
Helen McDonald. "He had to be with her."

They had been together since 1928. It was summertime,
and a girlfriend invited Helen Finney to come to a youth
group meeting at Emmanuel. The girls were standing on
the steps of the church when a young man came walking
down Hamilton Street, wearing a white turtleneck,
whistling "My Blue Heaven."

"I'm going to marry that man," Helen told her friend.
Three months later she did. They were married in the
church where their three children would be married,
where 11 grandchildren would be baptized, where in 1978
they repeated their wedding vows to celebrate their wedding anniversary. It was the same church where Helen
would hear a Sunday morning children's talk that gave
her a mission in life.

The custom of the mitten tree began in 1949. Church
members would collect mittens and hats, decorate a tree
with them, then give them to poor children. Helen's best
friend knew she knitted, and so she asked her if she
would contribute. The first year, Helen made 25 sets of
mittens and hats.

The Reverend Graham Hodges, who came to Emmanuel

in 1956, talked to the children about the mitten tree one morning. He told them how children in Europe lined up to receive mittens from relief workers in the years following World War II. As the workers came to the end of a line one day, a little boy held out his cold hands to them. But by then they had run out of mittens.

"The moral was, the need is unending." said Hodges. "We needed another pair for that little boy."

Helen Bunce took the talk to heart. She could not forget about that little boy and his cold hands, and so each year she tried to knit more. In each of the past 20 years she easily exceeded 100 sets of mittens and hats. Every one of them bore a handwritten tag attached with a gold safety pin: "God Loves You and So Do I."

When she had reached her goal for the year, she knitted two more sets, one for a little girl and one for a little boy, the children at the end of the line. Those she hung on the mitten tree herself, or gave to one of the grandchildren to hang, a reminder of why she knitted, and whom she knitted for.

The knitting never left her side. She knitted as she dozed off. She knitted as she rode in the car. Her daughter Helen laughs when she remembers her mother sitting in the back seat of the car, so scared by a snowstorm she prayed out loud: "Lord, you have to get us home safe. I have to get these mittens done."

When Karl became ill with Parkinson's disease and went to a nursing home in Alexandria Bay, his wife sat with him every day, from 8:00 in the morning until 8:00 at night. She would take a Thermos of coffee, a sandwich and her knitting. Her own health began to fail, and they moved together to the Samaritan Keep Home in Watertown. When the pain in her back became too much for her, she taught herself to knit lying down.

Helen followed one rule in her knitting: never finish one project without starting the next.

As soon as one Christmas passed, she began working toward the next year. She completed perhaps a dozen sets this month and last. Every time she finished a hat or a mitten, she cast the stitches for her next project on her needles, so her knitting would always be ready to pick up.

"She felt as long as she was knitting those mittens, the Lord wouldn't take her," her daughter said.

Helen had told her family she wanted to be buried with her knitting needles. Her daughter remembered that on Saturday. She went back to her mother's room, planning to retrieve the needles that would be holding a final, unfinished project.

She found a pink and white hat that had been completed, and then she saw the needles. Her mother had bound them neatly with a rubber band and stuck them in the skein of yarn, empty. Helen McDonald is certain of the reason: her mother had known her work was done.

Barbara Stith

I have glorified Thee on earth:
I have finished the work
which Thou gavest me to do.

John 17:4

THE FAMILY CIRCUS ®   By Bil Keane

Fingers like mittens better 'cause they don't get lonely in them.

Reprinted with permission from Bil Keane.

Susan's Gift

*We must not only give what we have;
we must also give what we are.*

Cardinal Mercia

So far, so good, Susan thought with a smile, as she checked off another name on her list. The 51-year-old pharmaceutical consultant had spent weeks tracking down former classmates to invite them to a high school reunion. Plans for a thirtieth reunion had never materialized, so Susan had decided, "Why not have a thirty-third?" She'd undertaken the whole project herself, and every day she grew more excited about seeing old friends again.

There was one person she was particularly interested in reconnecting with: Bennett Scott. She'd recently learned from another classmate that Bennett was gravely ill. He'd suffered from kidney disease for years, and now he was on dialysis every day, waiting for a transplant.

I hope he gets a new lease on life soon, Susan thought, as she dialed his number. Her old friend needed a guardian angel, and although Susan didn't know it yet, she would be that angel.

When Bennett had first arrived at their South Carolina school, Susan had hardly noticed him. She was a cheerleader with many friends, and he was shy and sensitive, the new kid in town. But their paths soon began to cross. Both sang in the school chorus, worked on the newspaper and practiced under the same piano teacher. Together, they were voted "Most Talented" in seventh grade, and in high school, they shared the title "Most Likely to Succeed."

Their lives seemed intertwined, and as a result they became close friends, singing duets together and seeking each other out in the hallways and lunchroom. "I do hope you won't forget me," Susan had written in Bennett's yearbook—but after graduation, as often happens, they'd gone their separate ways.

Decades later, Susan was divorced and living in Stevensville, Maryland. Her life was filled with friends, travel and a job she loved. Bennett had settled in New Jersey with his wife, Sarah, teaching at a college and raising two kids.

Now, he was in danger of losing it all. Susan took a deep breath as his phone began to ring.

"It's so good to hear from you," Bennett exclaimed. "I wouldn't miss the reunion for anything." They chatted about their jobs, families and future plans—but Bennett never once mentioned his illness, and Susan didn't want to pry.

But after she hung up, Susan couldn't get him out of her mind—or the ache out of her heart. *It's not fair,* she thought wistfully, *he has so much to live for.* She recalled the pride in his voice when he'd told her about his 27-year-old daughter Mindy and his 23-year-old son Stephen, and his dreams of traveling with Sarah someday.

She was flooded with memories of another man whose life had been cut short by kidney disease—a man she'd planned to marry. Susan hadn't been able to save her fiancé and neither had his doctors. Sometimes her heart still broke for what might have been.

Bennett deserves to take that trip, Susan thought fiercely. *He deserves to give his daughter away at her wedding and bounce grandchildren on his knee. Bennett's family should be able to throw him a huge retirement party. And Sarah should have the chance to waltz with him during many more anniversary parties.*

Suddenly, Susan was redialing Bennett's number. "Listen," she told him, "I know you're sick, and I just happen to have an extra kidney I'd like to give you."

For a moment, Bennett was too stunned to reply. *I haven't even spoken to her in years,* he marveled to himself. *Yet, she's offering me a second chance at life.*

But as moved as he was, Bennett couldn't accept it. "Thank you," he finally replied. "But I couldn't ask you to do that for me."

"You're not asking, I'm offering," Susan protested. "And I'm not doing it just for you. I'm doing it for your family, too."

Still, Bennett couldn't bring himself to accept. In the months before the reunion, Susan repeated her offer over and over, and each time Bennett politely refused.

Then, just before the reunion, Bennett became so sick he was confined to a wheelchair. Doctors told him that without a transplant, he'd die within a few months.

Horrified, Susan redoubled her efforts. "Please let me help!" she begged. At last, Bennett agreed.

Susan arranged to be tested the day after the reunion. She knew the odds were slim that she'd be a match; tests had already shown that Sarah, Bennett's wife, wasn't. Susan also knew that the surgery would be painful and somewhat risky. But somehow, seeing her friend and his wife hugging and singing together at the high school reunion, she felt hopeful. *Please let me be a match so they can always be together,* she prayed, as the couple tearfully whispered their thanks.

Susan's heart pounded as doctors drew her blood, and she could hardly breathe when the lab called with the results: she was a match!

"It's incredible," Susan was told by the doctors. "We rarely see such a close match, even between siblings."

Susan tingled all over as she called Bennett with the news. *God must be working through me,* she thought. *That's why our paths crossed again this year. It was meant to be.*

Months later, they gripped hands before the surgery. Susan's groggy words when she awoke five hours later were, "How's Bennett?" Doctors told her the transplant had been a success. *Thank you God,* she thought.

When she visited Bennett at the hospital, he exclaimed, "I feel better already!" Then his eyes filled with tears. "How do you thank someone for giving you back your life?" he asked.

"Just take good care of my kidney!" Susan replied, wiping away tears of her own.

Eva Unga
Excerpted from *Woman's World Magazine*

The Goodest Gift

The great acts of love are done by those who are habitually performing small acts of kindness.

Anonymous

Every December, as I take out the Christmas decorations, I also take out the memory of a Christmas 20 years ago in a small town in central Maine and the gift that one little girl gave to another. In a world where Christmas is ever more glittery and commercialized, it reminds me that the true spirit of the season lies in giving, and receiving, from the heart.

Winters seemed to be colder back then, and school days dragged slowly by. At my small school, we had two classes for each grade. My class was for the children who got good grades. Most of us wore nice clothes and our parents were in the PTA. Those in the "slower" class didn't get good report cards. Most of the kids were poor. We attended the same school year after year, and by fourth grade we all knew who belonged in which class. The one exception was the girl I shall call Marlene Crocker.

I still remember the day when Marlene was transferred

to the "smarter" class. She stood by the teacher's desk that morning in a wool skirt that hung down below her knees. Her sweater was patched, but her face was wide and hopeful.

She was not at all pretty except for her intelligent-looking brown eyes. I had heard Marlene was a good student, though, and I wondered why she hadn't been in the "smarter" class all along. As she stood waiting for the teacher to assign her a seat, for a moment I imagined that I might become her friend and we would talk together at recess. Then the whispers began. "She's not sitting beside me!" someone sneered.

"That will be enough," the teacher said firmly, and the class turned silent. No one would laugh at Marlene again—at least not when the teacher was in the room.

Marlene and I never talked together at recess as I'd first imagined. The boundaries that separated us were too firmly drawn.

One late autumn day, Mom and I happened to be out driving along a wooded back road. It was one that we seldom took because Mom said it wasted gas. I was busy chattering away when suddenly, out the window, I saw a tar-paper shack so tiny that it would have fit inside our bathroom. The shack was set far back in a big field littered with rusted car parts. Across the yard stretched a long clothesline, beneath which stood a little girl who looked at us as we sped past. It was Marlene. I raised my hand to wave, but our car had already passed her. "That poor little girl," my mother said, "hanging out clothes and it's going to rain."

Once the snow came that winter, it seemed as though it would never stop. As Christmas drew near, my spirits were as high as the snowdrifts as I watched the pile of presents grow beneath our Christmas tree. At school, a few days before our school Christmas party, we passed around a hat in class to pick the name of a classmate for whom we'd buy a gift. The hat went around, and the names were drawn. Finally, the hat came to Marlene. One boy leaned forward, closer than anyone had ever been to Marlene, and hooted as he read her slip of paper. "Marlene got Jenna's name."

I began to blush furiously as I heard my name. Marlene looked down at her desk, but the teasing went on until our teacher stopped it. "I don't care," I vowed haughtily, but I felt cheated.

The day of the party, I marched to the bus reluctantly, carrying a nice gift of Magic Markers for the person whose name I had drawn. At school, we ate the Christmas cookies our mothers had baked and drank our grape drink. Then the presents were handed out, and the wrapping paper went flying as everyone tore into them.

The moment I had been dreading had arrived. Suddenly it seemed as though everyone was crowding around. Sitting on my desk was a small package wrapped neatly in tissue paper. I looked over at Marlene. She was sitting alone. Suddenly overcome by the need to protect Marlene from the mocking of my classmates, I seized Marlene's gift, unwrapped it and sat there, holding it hidden in my hand.

"What is it?" a boy hollered, when he could stand it no longer.

"It's a wallet," I finally answered.

The bell rang and the buses came and someone said to Marlene, "Did your old man make it from the deer he shot?"

Marlene nodded and said, "And my ma."

"Thank you, Marlene," I said.

"You're welcome," she said. We smiled at each other. Marlene was not my friend but I never teased her. Maybe when I got bigger, I would ride my bike over there and we could talk and play. I thought about that as I rode the bus home. I tried not to think of what Marlene's Christmas would be like.

Years went by. I went on to high school and college, and lost contact with most of my childhood schoolmates. Whenever I struggled with math problems, I recalled the way Marlene had always breezed through hers. I heard rumors that Marlene had dropped out of school to help her mother with the younger children at home. Then I heard that she had married young and started having babies of her own.

One day, I came across the white doeskin wallet I had received at that Christmas party long ago. Funny how, of all the gifts, I'd kept this one through the years. I took it out and studied its intricate craftsmanship. Beneath the top flap, I noticed a small slit holding a tiny piece of paper that I had never seen before. Sitting in my comfortable home, I read the words that Marlene had written to me years before. "To my best friend," they said. Those words pierced my heart. I wished I could go back, to have the courage to be the kind of friend I'd wanted to be. Belatedly, I understood the love that had been wrapped inside that gift.

There are a few things that I unpack every year at Christmastime—an old wooden crèche, shiny balls for the tree and a Santa figurine. I take the wallet out, too. Last year, I told my small son the story of the girl who had given it to me. He thought about it and then he said, "Of all the gifts, that was the goodest gift, wasn't it?"

And I smiled, grateful for the wisdom that let him see that it was.

Jenna Day
Submitted by Patricia Bradford

Why?

"On the street I saw a small girl
cold and shivering in a thin dress,
with little hope of a
decent meal.
I became angry and said to
God:
'Why did you permit this?
Why don't you do something
about it?'
For awhile God said nothing.
That night he replied, quite
suddenly:
'I certainly did something
about it.
I made you.'"

Author Unknown
Submitted by Sister Mary Rose McGeady,
Covenant House

God's Own Son

As Mary rocks her baby boy
She's filled with sadness, filled with joy
She looks upon that tiny face
And sees the hope of every race.

Her heart is filled with a mother's glow
And she never wants to let him go.
She'll see him run and laugh and play
And longs to keep him safe each day.

His life won't be an easy one,
His destiny hard, as God's own Son.

Mary sees the miracles he'll perform,
The lepers healed and free from scorn.
The lame will walk, the blind will see.
She sees his love will set us free.

And then she sees him on a cross.
She feels his pain and feels our loss.
She knows his life must come to this.
She sheds a tear and gives a kiss.

His life won't be an easy one,
His destiny hard, as God's own Son.

So as Christmastime draws near
And we are all so "busy" here,
With shopping, baking, trees of green
Let's ask, what does this really mean?

Let's take a moment from the fuss,
And think of all their gifts to us:
A mother's love, a baby boy,
Peace and comfort, love and joy.

For he was born for everyone,
His destiny, God's only Son.

Kathleen Weber

The Christmas I Loaned My Son

Let us not be satisfied with just giving money. Money is not enough, money can be got, but they need your hearts to love them. So, spread your love everywhere you go; first of all in your own home. Give love to your children, to your wife or husband, to a next-door neighbor.

Mother Teresa

Is there any place where we can borrow a little boy three or four years old for the Christmas holidays? We have a nice home and would take wonderful care of him and bring him back safe and sound. We used to have a little boy, but he couldn't stay, and we miss him so when Christmas comes. —N. Muller

As I read the above appeal in our local newspaper, something happened to me. For the first time since my husband's death, I thought of grief as belonging to someone else. I read and reread the letter to the editor.

Some months before, I had received word from Washington that my husband had been killed in the service overseas. Grief-stricken, I had taken my little son and had moved back to the tiny village of my birth.

I'd gone to work to help support my son and time had helped to erase a few scars in my heart. But there were special times when the ache would return and loneliness would engulf me—birthdays, our wedding anniversary and holidays.

This particular Christmas, the old pain was returning when my eyes caught the appeal in the newspaper column.

We used to have a little boy, but he couldn't stay and we miss him so . . .

I, too, knew what missing was, but I had my little boy. I knew how empty the sparkle of Christmas is unless you see it in the joyous eyes of a child.

I answered the appeal. The writer of the letter was a widower who lived with his mother. He had lost his beloved wife and his little son the same year.

That Christmas, my son and I shared a joyous day with the widower and his mother. Together, we found a happiness that we doubted would ever return.

But the best part is that this joy was mine to keep throughout the years and for each of the Christmases since. You see, the man who wrote the letter, months later, became my husband.

Mrs. N. H. Muller

Jewel

The IV's red light glowed in the early darkness, its beeping like a heartbeat, like the beat to Bette Midler's hit song about heroes, "Wind Beneath My Wings," that was playing softly from a radio in the nurses' station down the hall.

I had heard that popular song's lyrics dozens of times in my head over the weekend, late at night as I lay on a cot in the University of Massachusetts Medical Center and looked at my daughter Jewel.

Think it's strange for a 37-year-old man to have a two-year old girl as his hero? You don't know Jewel.

She's in remission now and odds are the leukemia will never come back. About 80 percent of the kids who get the most common childhood leukemia never relapse.

It's been a year full of hope—a year that brought a new baby daughter to our home—but it's been a rough year, too, a year punctuated by weekly trips to the clinic and a half dozen longer stays in the hospital. The first months of chemotherapy made all of Jewel's hair fall out. Some of the drugs made her hyper, some made her sleepy.

Through it all, there has been one constant—Jewel, who prays to "Baby Cheezits up in the sky" and who

loves Babar cartoons and family hugs, has borne her illness with a heroic grace. I can't imagine any adult dealing
with it as well. I know I haven't.

Jewel has been in the hospital for the last five days with
an infection from the catheter in her chest. Her temperature rocketed from 98.6 degrees to 105 degrees in about
five minutes when the bacteria in the catheter flushed
into her blood. Jewel shook like a leaf as I screamed for a
doctor. She, of course, handled it better than her old man
and lay there saying, "I'm good, I'm good."

Last summer, Jewel battled the doctors and nurses who
examined her. She was too young to understand why she
had to be stuck with so many needles, she didn't understand her antagonists were actually angels of mercy striv-
ing to make her better. I will never forget the look in her
eyes when I helped the nurses hold her for yet another
blood test and she howled and her dark eyes screamed,
"How can you, my protector, betray me?"

But she forgave me every time, kissing me with a loud
smack—"moh"—and dancing when I played my harmonica.
As the year went by, she gained an understanding about
the extrinsic portions of her illness—the need for trips to
the clinic, the catheter, the chemotherapy, the shots. The
knowledge has made her wise beyond her years—and
confident. What a talker she is. Sometimes she'll sit in the
front window of our house, yelling at the top of her lungs
to the older kids playing in the street.

"Beth, come play with me. Margy, come get me."

One day, I asked Dr. Newburger why so many children
who get acute lymphoblastic leukemia survive when so
many adults who get the same disease don't.

"Bottom line," he said, "we're not as tough."

Jewel's brother, Rocky, is nine. His summers should be
all baseball and fishing and tree forts and Nintendo, not
wondering about sickness and death.

About a month after Jewel was diagnosed with leukemia, Rocky and I were driving. Rocky was sitting in the front seat next to me, a bundle of skinny arms and legs in a Red Sox cap, looking at a purple sunset sky over a long, green field of corn.

I was telling him about the possibility of a bone marrow transplant. I was telling him that if it came down to it, he might be the perfect match for Jewel, how his bone marrow might save her life.

"Would it hurt?" he asked without looking away from the window.

"Yeah," I said.

"A lot?"

"It might hurt quite a bit."

"I don't want to hurt."

We drove on in silence, onto the highway.

"I'll do it," Rocky said suddenly, quietly. "I would die for my sister."

For the first time in a long time, I knew the tears welling up in my eyes weren't for sadness. And I knew, no matter what, leukemia was going to have one hell of a fight on its hands beating our family. There are too many little heroes in it.

Paul Della Valle

The Day Joe Hill Came to Stay

It is kindness in a person, not beauty, which wins our love.

Anonymous

It was a day of pink azaleas and white dogwoods in April, 1935 and Willie Ann "Babe" Hill lay dying. She needed to rest and couldn't. She worried about what would become of her nephew Joe.

This was the Great Depression in Lincolnton, North Carolina, a town of 4,000 people in the segregated South, where everyone knew each other by face if not by name. Joe Hill was 15 years old, retarded and black. His Uncle Henry didn't have it in him to care for Joe and he knew of no one else to turn to in their community.

So Henry Hill went to Marvin and Mattie Leatherman, who lived in a white neighborhood off Main Street and had helped him before. Willie Ann used to clean the Leathermans' house and Joe sometimes mowed their lawn.

Marvin Titus Leatherman—"M.T." to colleagues—was a lawyer who would reach into his pockets to pay court fees for poor clients and who counseled against divorce.

Mattie Leatherman was the neighborhood "angel of mercy," the mom who baked birthday cakes for the children of others, the neighbor who nursed the sick.

Henry pleaded with them. "Babe said she can't die until she finds somewhere to send Joe. She doesn't want him sent off to some institution where he won't have somebody to look after him."

Mattie reassured him. "You tell her to go in peace to the Lord. God has made a place for Joe, and he'll put him in it."

The next day, there was a knock on the Leathermans' door. Mattie peered past the sheer curtains and there stood Joe Hill. Beside him, a rusty metal cot.

Mattie hadn't meant she'd take him in. Yet there he stood. Marvin told his wife there was only one thing to do. If they didn't take him in, Joe might die.

They built a house out back, painted it white like the big house. Barely 9 by 20 feet, it had room for everything he needed. A bed, a dresser and a kerosene heater.

It was Joe Hill's house, and he was proud.

The Leathermans had one child of their own, Marguerite. Though Joe was 10 years older, he and Marguerite grew up together, opening presents on Christmas, blowing out birthday candles, and going for Sunday drives with the family. Little Marguerite called her parents "Mama" and "Daddy" and Joe took to calling them that, too. He was like a child, and they taught him by example and affirmation.

Saturday nights, Marvin sat beside Joe and taught him the same Bible lessons he would teach the next morning at First Baptist Church. The rules of white society might not let Joe through the church door, but Marvin was determined he would not suffer because of it.

Marvin tried to walk his life according to Matthew 25; "For I was hungry, and you gave me food; I was thirsty, and you gave me drink; I was a stranger, and you took me in."

They settled into a routine that lasted more than 45 years. Promptly at 7:30 each weekday morning, Marvin strode off to his law office half a mile away. Here was the dean of Lincoln County lawyers, the former county attorney and state senator, cutting a distinguished figure down Main Street. Always a few paces behind, Joe Hill, struggling to keep up, smiling a big smile and flinging his right arm in greeting.

"Hello, M.T.!" neighbors called out. "Hello, Joe!"

While Marvin worked in his second-floor law office, Joe went downstairs to Turner's clothing store or to the Western Auto. He'd sit in a chair for hours, dozing off if he sat too long, getting up to help if something needed lifting. As much as Marvin was a fixture at the county courthouse, so was Joe on Main Street.

One brisk morning in January 1981, Marvin walked to his office with Joe close at his heels. Marvin set to work; Joe Hill began his rounds. Marvin then went to the local diner for his usual hamburger and cottage cheese. The waitress brought a cup of coffee. A few minutes later, she turned back. The cup was tipped over. Marvin could not speak. A stroke had silenced him. Marvin was bedridden, but Joe kept up his rounds alone for months.

One day when he got home from Clemons Barbershop on the evening of October 3, 1981, he opened the front door to find extra people in the house.

"He's gone," said Marvin's daughter, Marguerite Reid. Marvin had died from another stroke.

Joe hid in the kitchen, confused and disoriented. The next day, a neighbor found him sitting on the front steps, tears streaming down his cheeks, his brown eyes bloodshot.

"Daddy's gone," he said. "What am I going to do?"

The week after they buried Marvin, Joe moved into the big house with Mattie. He fixed her breakfast in the mornings, iced tea in the afternoons, and fried chicken on

Sundays. She grew weaker with each passing year and the time finally came to move in with her daughter.

"I can't manage both of them," Marguerite told her husband, Dr. Leary Reid.

"Yes, we can," he said. "God will walk us through it . . . Joe Hill is a part of our family. He has never known anything else. We can't turn our backs on him now."

They built him a little bedroom in their house, barely 8 feet by 10 feet. It had room for everything he needed: a bed, a dresser and a bulletin board for family pictures.

It was Joe's room, and he was happy.

A year and a half later, on December 30, 1991, Mattie died quietly in her sleep. She was 90 years old. Joe, 72.

"Mother's gone to be with Jesus," Marguerite told him. "But don't you worry. We'll take care of you."

And they did.

Elizabeth Leland

The Beautiful Color of Love

What color is God,
Asked the child with skin so fair
Is he white like me,
Does he have light hair

Is God dark like me,
Asked the child with skin of golden hue
Has he hair that's dark and curly,
Are his eyes black or blue

I think God is red like me,
The Indian boy is heard to say
He wears a crown of feathers,
And turns our nights to day

Each one of us knows that God is there,
In all the colors above
But be sure of this, the one color he is,
Is the beautiful color of love

So when your soul goes to Heaven,
When your life comes to its end

He will be waiting, and his hand to you
Will he extend.

There will be no colors in Heaven,
Everyone will be the same.
You will only be judged by your earthly deeds,
Not your color or your name

So when your time comes,
And you see God in his Heaven above,
Then you will see the only color that counts,
The beautiful color of love.

Arnold (Sparky) Watts

2

ON GIVING

Give what you have.
To some one, it may
be better than
you dare to think.

Henry Wadsworth Longfellow

Golden Shoes for Jesus

Somehow, not only for Christmas
But all the long year through
The joy that you give to others
Is the joy that comes back to you.

John Greenleaf Whittier

It was only four days before Christmas. The spirit of the season had not yet caught up with me, even though cars packed the parking lot of our local discount store. Inside the store, it was worse. Shopping carts and last-minute shoppers jammed the aisles.

Why did I come to town today? I wondered. My feet ached almost as much as my head. My list contained names of several people who claimed they wanted nothing, but I knew their feelings would be hurt if I didn't buy them something.

Buying for someone who had everything and deploring the high cost of items, I considered gift buying anything but fun.

Hurriedly, I filled my shopping cart with last-minute items and proceeded to the long checkout lines. I picked the shortest, but it looked as if it would mean at least a 20-minute wait.

In front of me were two small children—a boy of about five and a slightly younger girl. The boy wore a ragged coat. Enormously large, tattered tennis shoes jutted far out in front of his much-too-short jeans. He clutched several crumpled dollar bills in his grimy hands.

The girl's clothing resembled her brother's. Her head was a matted mass of curly hair. Reminders of an evening meal showed on her small face. She carried a beautiful pair of shiny, gold house slippers. As the Christmas music sounded in the store's stereo system, the small girl hummed along, off-key, but happily.

When we finally approached the checkout register, the girl carefully placed the shoes on the counter. She treated them as though they were a treasure.

The clerk rang up the bill. "That'll be $6.09," she said.

The boy laid his crumpled bills atop the stand while he searched his pockets. He finally came up with $3.12. "I guess we'll have to put them back," he bravely announced. "We'll come back some other time, maybe tomorrow."

With that statement, a soft sob broke from the little girl. "But Jesus would have loved these shoes," she cried.

"Well, we'll go home and work some more. Don't cry. We'll come back," the boy assured her.

Quickly I handed $3.00 to the clerk. These children had waited in line for a long time. And, after all, it was Christmas.

Suddenly a pair of arms came around me and a small voice said, "Thank you, lady."

"What did you mean when you said Jesus would like the shoes?" I asked.

The boy answered, "Our mommy is sick and going to heaven. Daddy said she might go before Christmas to be with Jesus."

The girl spoke. "My Sunday school teacher said the streets up in heaven are shiny gold, just like these shoes. Won't my mommy be beautiful walking on those streets to match these shoes?"

My eyes flooded as I looked into her tear-streaked face. "Yes," I answered, "I'm sure she will."

Silently, I thanked God for using these children to remind me of the true spirit of giving.

Helga Schmidt
Submitted by Kelly Kaman

An Exchange of Gifts

Those who bring sunshine to the lives of others cannot keep it from themselves.

Sir James Matthew Barrie

I grew up believing that Christmas was a time when strange and wonderful things happened, when wise and royal visitors came riding, when at midnight the barnyard animals talked to one another, and in the light of a fabulous star God came down to us as a little child. Christmas to me has always been a time of enchantment, and never more so than the year that my son Marty was eight.

That was the year that my children and I moved into a cozy trailer home in a forested area just outside of Redmond, Washington. As the holiday approached, our spirits were light, not to be dampened even by the winter rains that swept down Puget Sound to douse our home and make our floors muddy.

Throughout that December, Marty had been the most spirited, and busiest, of us all. He was my youngest; a cheerful boy, blond-haired and playful, with a quaint habit of looking up at you and cocking his head like a puppy when you talked to him. Actually, the reason for this was that Marty was deaf in his left ear, but it was a condition that he never complained about.

For weeks, I had been watching Marty. I knew that something was going on with him that he was not telling me about. I saw how eagerly he made his bed, took out the trash, and carefully set the table and helped Rick and Pam prepare dinner before I got home from work. I saw how he silently collected his tiny allowance and tucked it away, spending not a cent of it. I had no idea what all this quiet activity was about, but I suspected that somehow it had something to do with Kenny.

Kenny was Marty's friend, and ever since they had found each other in the springtime, they were seldom apart. If you called to one, you got them both. Their world was in the meadow, a horse pasture broken by a small winding stream, where the boys caught frogs and snakes, where they would search for arrowheads or hidden treasure, or where they would spend an afternoon feeding peanuts to the squirrels.

Times were hard for our little family, and we had to do some scrimping to get by. With my job as a meat wrapper and with a lot of ingenuity around the trailer, we managed to have elegance on a shoestring. But not Kenny's family. They were desperately poor, and his mother was having a real struggle to feed and clothe her two children. They were a good, solid family. But Kenny's mom was a proud woman, very proud, and she had strict rules.

How we worked, as we did each year, to make our home festive for the holiday! Ours was a handcrafted Christmas of gifts hidden away and ornaments strung about the place.

Marty and Kenny would sometimes sit still at the table long enough to help make cornucopias or weave little baskets for the tree. But then, in a flash, one would whisper to the other, and they would be out the door and sliding cautiously under the electric fence into the horse pasture that separated our home from Kenny's.

One night shortly before Christmas, when my hands were deep in Peppernoder dough, shaping tiny nutlike Danish cookies heavily spiced with cinnamon, Marty came to me and said in a tone mixed with pleasure and pride, "Mom, I've bought Kenny a Christmas present. Want to see it?" *So that's what he's been up to,* I said to myself. "It's something he's wanted for a long, long time, Mom."

After carefully wiping his hands on a dish towel, he pulled from his pocket a small box. Lifting the lid, I gazed at the pocket compass that my son had been saving all those allowances to buy. A little compass to point an eight-year-old adventurer through the woods.

"It's a lovely gift, Martin," I said, but even as I spoke, a disturbing thought came to mind. I knew how Kenny's mother felt about their poverty. They could barely afford to exchange gifts among themselves, and giving presents to others was out of the question. I was sure that Kenny's proud mother would not permit her son to receive something he could not return in kind.

Gently, carefully, I talked over the problem with Marty. He understood what I was saying.

"I know, Mom, I know! . . . But what if it was a secret? What if they never found out who gave it?"

I didn't know how to answer him. I just didn't know.

The day before Christmas was rainy and cold and gray. The three kids and I all but fell over one another as we elbowed our way about our little home, putting finishing touches on Christmas secrets and preparing for family and friends who would be dropping by.

Night settled in. The rain continued. I looked out the window over the sink and felt an odd sadness. How mundane the rain seemed for a Christmas Eve! Would and royal men come riding on such a night? I doubted it. It seemed to me that strange and wonderful things happened only on clear nights, nights when one could at least see a star in the heavens.

I turned from the window, and as I checked on the ham and lefse bread warming in the oven, I saw Marty slip out the door. He wore his coat over his pajamas, and he clutched a tiny, colorfully wrapped box in his hand.

Down through the soggy pasture he went, then a quick slide under the electric fence and across the yard to Kenny's house. Up the steps on tiptoe, shoes squishing; open the screen door just a crack; place the gift on the doorstep, then a deep breath, a reach for the doorbell, and a press on it *hard*.

Quickly Marty turned, ran down the steps and across the yard in a wild race to get away unnoticed. Then, suddenly, he banged into the electric fence.

The shock sent him reeling. He lay stunned on the wet ground. His body quivered and he gasped for breath. Then slowly, weakly, confused and frightened, he began the grueling trip back home.

"Marty," we cried as he stumbled through the door, "what happened?" His lower lip quivered, his eyes brimmed.

"I forgot about the fence, and it knocked me down!"

I hugged his muddy little body to me. He was still dazed and there was a red mark beginning to blister on his face from his mouth to his ear. Quickly I treated the blister and, with a warm cup of cocoa soothing him, Marty's bright spirits returned. I tucked him into bed and just before he fell asleep, he looked up at me and said, "Mom, Kenny didn't see me. I'm sure he didn't see me."

That Christmas Eve I went to bed unhappy and puzzled. It seemed such a cruel thing to happen to a little boy while on the purest kind of Christmas mission, doing what the Lord wants us all to do—giving to others—and giving in secret at that. I did not sleep well that night. Somewhere deep inside I think I must have been feeling the disappointment that the night of Christmas had come and it had been just an ordinary, problem-filled night, no mysterious enchantment at all.

But I was wrong.

By morning the rain had stopped and the sun shone. The streak on Marty's face was very red, but I could tell that the burn was not serious. We opened our presents, and soon, not unexpectedly, Kenny was knocking on the door, eager to show Marty his new compass and tell about the mystery of its arrival. It was plain that Kenny didn't suspect Marty at all, and while the two of them talked, Marty just smiled and smiled.

Then I noticed that while the two boys were comparing their Christmases, nodding and gesturing and chattering away, Marty was not cocking his head. When Kenny was talking, Marty seemed to be listening with his deaf ear. Weeks later a report came from the school nurse, verifying what Marty and I already knew. "Marty now has complete hearing in both ears."

The mystery of how Marty regained his hearing, and still has it, remains just that—a mystery. Doctors suspect, of course, that the shock from the electric fence was somehow responsible. Perhaps so. Whatever the reason, I just remain thankful to God for the good exchange of gifts that was made that night.

So you see, strange and wonderful things still happen on the night of our Lord's birth. And one does not have to have a clear night, either, to follow a fabulous star.

Diane Rayner

A Tribute to Hawkins

When my husband called to announce that his new promotion was going to take us away from a lovely, unglaciated pocket of northeast Iowa, my first instinct was the "right" one.

"Congratulations. I'm proud of you," I chirped like a brave little wife in a 1930s movie. My second, more honest instinct, was to wail, "What will we do without Hawkins?"

Any working mother who has ever moved can tell you that the worst chore of moving is not unpacking the jar of bacon drippings that movers have ever-so-delicately wrapped and put in the same box as the silk lamp shades. Nor is it finding a new hairdresser clever enough to camouflage the knobs on the back of her head so she doesn't look like a kingfisher bird.

The worst task by far is searching for the perfect baby-sitter. Any mother worthy of her title approaches it with her stomach queasy from fear and guilt.

When Kate was four years old and Nicholas almost a year, I decided to take them to a baby-sitter a couple of days a week so I could concentrate on getting my career off the ground. I felt a little silly calling a retired drama coach I had just met the week before; after all, I barely knew her, and she had been out of the childrearing scene for decades. But Helen seemed so savvy and well-connected that I just knew she'd give me a good lead.

"I think I might know someone," she mused, indulging in the flair for mystery that must have served her well as a theatrical director, "but I can't tell you who it is until I talk to her."

Helen called back in a few days to tell me that her sister-in-law, Evelyn Hawkins, a retired farm widow who had recently moved into an apartment in town, had experience from rearing scads of kids and grandbabies, smarts, and the patience of Job.

What first struck me on meeting this trim, soft-spoken woman was her extraordinary calmness. Though she seemed a little restrained and serious until I knew her well, I could tell right away that behind her reserve was a great deal of substance.

A wooden cross hanging in her kitchen and a sampler in her upstairs hall gave me clues about her deep faith. The sampler, neatly cross-stitched in green on white, showed a window with a curtain blowing in a gentle breeze. The maxim underneath was, "When God closes a door, he opens a window."

Yet Hawkins was so private and humble that it was months before I learned by accident that the daily "walk" she was returning from when we arrived, however brutal the weather, was really a trip to church.

Though she never told the kids what to call her, she came to be known as Hawkins because Evelyn somehow didn't sound respectful enough to me, and Mrs. Hawkins was too big a mouthful for my little ones to handle. Though the kids are too diplomatic to say so, I am sure that Hawkins' steady style of child rearing was a welcome relief from my own rock-swat-hug-holler-kiss method. The worst of it is, I don't even believe in swatting and hollering.

Though she was an outwardly conservative person who reared her children in a less permissive era than this one, Hawkins was really more of a free spirit than I am. While she was teaching my children, I was learning from her too.

When Kate went through her jealous stage and pretended to be a baby, she wouldn't buy my song and dance about the glories of being a 'big girl.' Later, I learned that Hawkins simply let her drink milk from a baby bottle until she got so tired of the slow flow that she begged for a glass. And when Nick insisted he was a dog one day, he got to eat his Cheerios hunkered down over a plastic bowl set on the floor.

The first time we asked if the kids could spend the night at her house, I warned Hawkins that Nick was going through a stage of waking up frightened, and that she might have to lie with him a few minutes to get him back to sleep. When we arrived in the morning, still a little apprehensive about how it had gone, the kids crowed, "We had a slumber party. We slept in Hawkins' bed!"

Hawkins told us mildly, "Oh well, I figured we might as well start the night all in the same bed." I could just picture the three of them in the upstairs bedroom, Hawkins in her high necked gown with one of my children asleep in the crook of each arm.

Another thing I learned from Hawkins' example was that life is made up of small tasks so we might as well take pleasure in them when we can. Whether it was carefully arranging a circle of gumdrops on a Swedish tea ring my children "helped" her bake or mending the ripped seat of her bachelor brother's pants with careful, even stitches, Hawkins did things right. She went about the small businesses of life so cheerfully that her efforts did not so much demean her as ennoble the tasks. The garment she entered in the county fair came back with a judge's accolade that made her eyes glow—"the finest workmanship."

She took care of my children with the same unhurried grace. She had a way of solemnly inclining her head toward a child who was embroidering a long-winded tale. It put me to shame, because in the same situation, my eyes glaze over; I murmur, "ummm . . .," and I think my own thoughts. Her attitude made me feel that the checks we gave her were secondary to the pleasure she took in filling our need, so much so that the moment of paying her was awkward.

It was little wonder that after two years of taking my children to her, leaving Hawkins was one of the hardest parts of leaving Decorah. I knew I was not likely to find another sitter who embodied the best qualities of Mary Poppins and Captain Kangaroo. Only *her* eyes were dry when she pressed a four-leaf clover charm into the palm of Kate's hand. "Remember," she whispered to my sobbing daughter, "when God closes a door, he opens a window."

Rebecca Christian

The Last Straw

*Let us think about each other and help each
other to show love and do good deeds.*

Heb. 10:24

It was another long, winter afternoon with everyone
stuck in the house. And the four McDonald children were
at it again—bickering, teasing, fighting over their toys. At
times like these, Mother was almost ready to believe that
her children didn't love each other, though she knew that
wasn't really true. All brothers and sisters fight, of course,
but lately her lively little bunch had been particularly
horrible to each other, especially Eric and Kelly, who were
just a year apart. They seemed determined to spend the
whole winter making each other miserable.

"Gimme that. It's mine!"

"Is not, fatso! I had it first!"

Mother sighed as she listened to the latest argument
coming from the living room. With Christmas only a
month away, the McDonald house seemed sadly lacking
in Christmas spirit. This was supposed to be the season of
sharing and love, of warm feelings and happy hearts. A

home needed more than just pretty packages or twinkling lights on the tree to fill it with the Christmas spirit. But how could any mother convince her children that being kind to each other was the most important way to get ready for Christmas?

Mother had only one idea. Years ago her grandmother had told her about an old Christmas custom that helped people discover the real meaning of Christmas. Perhaps it would work for her family. It was worth a try. Mother gathered her four little rascals together and sat them down on the stairs, smallest to tallest—Mike, Randi, Kelly and Eric.

"How would you kids like to start a new Christmas project this year?" she asked. "It's like a game, but it can only be played by people who can keep a secret. Can everyone here do that?"

"I can!" shouted Eric, wildly waving his arm in the air.

"I can keep a secret better than he can," yelled Kelly, jumping up and waving her arm in the air, too. If this was a contest, Kelly wanted to make sure she beat Eric.

"I can do it!" chimed in Randi, not quite sure what was happening but not wanting to be left out.

"Me too, me too, me too," squealed little Mike, bouncing up and down.

"Well then, here's how the game works," Mother explained. "This year we're going to surprise Baby Jesus when he comes on Christmas Eve by making him the softest bed in the world. We're going to build a little crib for him to sleep in right here in our house, and we'll fill it with straw to make it comfortable. But here's the catch: Each piece of straw we put in the manger will represent one kind thing we do for someone between now and Christmas. The more kind things we do, the more straw there will be for the Baby Jesus. The secret part is—we can't tell anyone what good things we're doing and who we're doing them for."

The children looked confused. "How will Baby Jesus know it's his bed?" asked Kelly.

"He'll know," said Mother. "He'll recognize it by the love we've put into the crib, by how soft it is."

"But who will we do the kind things for?" asked Eric.

"It's simple," said Mother. "We'll do them for each other. Once every week between now and Christmas, we'll put all of our names in this hat, mine and Daddy's, too. Then we'll each draw a name and do kind things for that person for a whole week. But here's the hard part. We can't tell anyone whose name we've drawn for that week, and we'll each try to do as many favors as we can for our special person without getting caught. And for every secret good thing we do, we'll put another piece of straw in the crib."

"But what if I pick someone I don't like?" frowned Kelly.

Mother thought about that for a minute. "Maybe you could use extra fat straws for the good things you do for that person, because they might be harder to do. But just think how much faster the fat straws will fill up our crib. Then on Christmas Eve we'll put Baby Jesus in his little bed, and he'll sleep that night on a mattress made of love. I think he'd like that, don't you?

"Now, who will build a little crib for us?" she asked.

Since Eric was the oldest, and the only one of the children allowed to use the tools, he marched off to the basement to give it a try. For the next couple of hours, loud banging and sawing noises came from the basement. Then for a long time there were no noises at all. Finally, Eric climbed back up the stairs with the manger in his arms. "Here it is," he grinned. "The best crib in the world! And I did it all myself."

For once, everyone agreed: the little manger was the best crib in the world. One leg was an inch too short, of course, and the crib rocked a bit. But it had been built with love—and about a hundred bent nails—and it would certainly last a long time.

"Now we need some straw," said Mother, and together they headed out to the car to go searching for some in the nearby fields. Surprisingly, no one fought over who was going to sit in the front seat that day as they drove around the countryside, looking for an empty field. At last they spotted a small, vacant patch of land that had been covered with tall grass in the summer. Now, in mid-December, the grass had dried down to yellow stalks that looked just like real straw.

Mother stopped the car and the kids scrambled out to pick handfuls of the tall grass.

"That's enough!" Mother finally laughed, when she saw that the cardboard box in the trunk was almost overflowing. "Remember, it's only a small crib." So home they went, where they spread the straw carefully on a tray Mother had put on the kitchen table. The empty manger was placed gently on top, and the straw hid its one short leg.

"When can we pick names?" shouted the children.

"As soon as Daddy comes home for dinner," Mother answered.

At the supper table that night, the six names were written on separate pieces of paper, folded up and shuffled around in an old baseball hat. Then the drawing began.

Kelly picked first and immediately started to giggle. Randi reached into the hat next. Daddy glanced at his scrap of paper and smiled quietly behind his hand. Mother picked out a name, but her face never gave away a clue. Next, little Mike reached into the hat, but since he couldn't read yet, Daddy had to whisper in his ear and tell him which name he had picked. Eric was the last to choose, and as he unfolded his piece of paper a frown crossed his face. But he stuffed the name into his pocket and said nothing. The family was ready to begin.

The week that followed was filled with surprises. It seemed the McDonald house had suddenly been invaded by an army of invisible elves, and good things were happening everywhere. Kelly would walk into her room at bedtime and find her little blue nightgown neatly laid out and her bed turned down. Someone cleaned up the sawdust under the workbench without being asked. The jelly blobs disappeared magically from the kitchen counter after lunch one day while Mother was getting the mail. And every morning, while Eric was brushing his teeth, someone crept quietly into his room and made his bed. It wasn't made perfectly, but it was made.

"Where are my shoes?" asked Daddy one morning. No one seemed to know, but before he left for work, they were back in the closet, all shined up.

Mother noticed other changes during that week, too. The children weren't teasing or fighting as much. An argument would start and then suddenly stop for no apparent reason. Even Eric and Kelly seemed to be getting along better. In fact, all the children wore secret smiles and giggled to themselves at times.

By Sunday, everyone was anxious to pick new names again, and this time there was even more laughter and merriment during the picking process, except for Eric. Once again he unfolded his piece of paper, looked at it, and then stuffed it in his pocket without a word. Mother noticed, but said nothing.

The second week of the game brought more amazing events. The garbage was taken out without anyone being asked. Someone even did two of Kelly's hard math problems one night when she left her homework out on the table.

The little pile of straw grew higher and softer. With only two weeks left until Christmas, the children wondered if their homemade bed would be comfortable enough for Baby Jesus.

"Who will be Baby Jesus anyway?" Randi asked on the third Sunday night after they had all picked new names.

"Perhaps we can use one of the dolls," said Mother. "Why don't you and Mike be in charge of picking out the right one?"

The two younger children ran off to gather up their favorite dolls, but everyone else wanted to help pick Baby Jesus, too. Little Mike dragged his Bozo the Clown rag doll from his room and proudly handed it over, sniffling later when everybody laughed. Soon Eric's well-hugged teddy bear, Bruffles, joined the dolls filling up the couch. Barbie and Ken were there, along with Kermit the Frog, stuffed dogs and lambs, and even a cuddly monkey that Grandma and Grandpa had sent Mike one year. But none of them seemed quite right.

Only an old baby doll, who had been loved almost to pieces, looked like a possibility for their Baby Jesus. "Chatty Baby," she had once been called, before she stopped chatting forever after too many baths.

"She looks so funny now," said Randi, and it was true. Once, while playing beauty shop, Kelly had cut her own blonde hair along with Chatty Baby's, giving them both a raggedy crew cut. Kelly's hair had eventually grown back, but Chatty Baby's never had. Now the wisps of blonde hair that stuck out all over the doll's head made her look a little lost and forgotten. But her eyes were still bright blue and she still had a smile on her face, even though her face was smudged here and there by the touch of many chubby little fingers.

"I think she's perfect," said Mother. "Baby Jesus probably didn't have much hair when he was born either, and I bet he'd like to be represented by a doll who's had so many hugs."

So the decision was made, and the children began to make a new outfit for their Baby Jesus—a little leather vest out of scraps and some cloth diapers. Best of all, Baby Jesus fit perfectly into the little crib, but since it wasn't quite time for him to sleep there yet, he was laid carefully on a shelf in the hall closet to wait for Christmas Eve.

Meanwhile, the pile of straw grew and grew. Every day brought new and different surprises as the secret elves stepped up their activity. The McDonald home was finally filled with Christmas spirit. Only Eric had been unusually quiet since the third week of name picking.

The final Sunday night of name picking was also the night before Christmas Eve. As the family sat around the table waiting for the last set of names to be put in the hat, Mother said, "You've all done a wonderful job. There must be hundreds of straws in our crib—maybe a thousand. You should be so pleased with the bed you've made. But remember, there's still one whole day left. We all have time to do a little more to make the bed even softer before tomorrow night. Let's try."

For the last time the hat was passed around the table. Little Mike picked out a name, and Daddy whispered it to him, just as he had done every week. Randi unfolded hers carefully under the table, peeked at it and then hunched up her little shoulders, smiling. Kelly reached into the hat and giggled happily when she saw the name. Mother and Daddy each took their turns, too, and then handed the hat with the last name to Eric. But as he unfolded the small scrap of paper and read it, his face pinched up and he suddenly seemed about to cry. Without a word, he ran from the room.

Everyone immediately jumped up from the table, but Mother stopped them. "No! Stay where you are," she said. "Let me talk to him alone first."

Just as she reached the top of the stairs, Eric's door banged open. He was trying to pull his coat on with one hand while he carried a small suitcase with the other hand.

"I have to leave," he said quietly, through his tears. "If I don't, I'll spoil Christmas for everyone!"

"But why? And where are you going?" asked Mother.

"I can sleep in my snow fort for a couple of days. I'll come home right after Christmas. I promise."

Mother started to say something about freezing and snow and no mittens or boots, but Daddy, who was now standing just behind her, put his hand on her arm and shook his head. The front door closed, and together they watched from the window as the little figure with the sadly slumped shoulders and no hat trudged across the street and sat down on a snowbank near the corner. It was very dark outside, and cold, and a few snow flurries drifted down on the small boy and his suitcase.

"But he'll freeze!" said Mother.

"Give him a few minutes alone," said Dad quietly. "Then you can talk to him."

The huddled figure was already dusted with white when Mother walked across the street 10 minutes later and sat down beside him on the snowbank.

"What is it, Eric? You've been so good these last few weeks, but I know something's been bothering you since we first started the crib. Can you tell me, honey?"

"Aw, Mom, don't you see?" he sniffled. "I tried so hard, but I can't do it anymore, and now I'm going to wreck Christmas for everyone." With that he burst into sobs and threw himself into his mother's arms.

"But I don't understand," Mother said, brushing the tears from his face. "What can't you do? And how could you possibly spoil Christmas for us?"

"Mom," the little boy said through his tears, "you just don't understand. I got Kelly's name *all four weeks*! And I hate Kelly! I can't do one more nice thing for her or I'll die! I tried, Mom. I really did. I sneaked in her room every night and fixed her bed. I even laid out her crummy nightgown. I emptied her wastebasket, and I did some homework for her one night when she was going to the bathroom. Mom,

I even let her use my race car one day, but she smashed it right into the wall like always!

"I tried to be nice to her, Mom. Even when she called me a stupid dummy because the crib leg was short, I didn't hit her. And every week, when we picked new names, I thought it would be over. But tonight, when I got her name again, I knew I couldn't do one more nice thing for her, Mom. I just can't! And tomorrow's Christmas Eve. I'll spoil Christmas for everybody just when we're ready to put Baby Jesus in the crib. Don't you see why I had to leave?"

They sat together quietly for a few minutes, Mother's arm around the small boy's shoulders. Only an occasional sniffle and hiccup broke the silence on the snowbank.

Finally, Mother began to speak softly, "Eric, I'm so proud of you. Every good thing you did should count as double because it was especially hard for you to be nice to Kelly for so long. But you did all those good things anyway, one straw at a time. You gave your love when it wasn't easy to give. Maybe that's what the spirit of Christmas is really all about. If it's too easy to give, maybe we're not really giving much of ourselves after all. The straws you added were probably the most important ones, and you should be proud of yourself.

"Now, how would you like a chance to earn a few easy straws like the rest of us? I still have the name I picked tonight in my pocket, and I haven't looked at it yet. Why don't we switch, just for the last day? It will be our secret."

"That's not cheating?"

"It's not cheating," Mother smiled.

Together they dried the tears, brushed off the snow and walked back to the house.

The next day the whole family was busy cooking and straightening up the house for Christmas Day, wrapping last-minute presents and trying hard not to burst with excitement. But even with all the activity and eagerness, a flurry of new straws piled up in the crib, and by nightfall it was overflowing. At different times while passing by, each member of the family, big and small, would pause and look at the wonderful pile for a moment, then smile before going on. It was almost time for the tiny crib to be used. But was it soft enough? One straw might still make a difference.

For that very reason, just before bedtime, Mother tiptoed quietly to Kelly's room to lay out the little blue nightgown and turn down the bed. But she stopped in the doorway, surprised. Someone had already been there. The nightgown was laid neatly across the bed, and a small red race car rested next to it on the pillow.

The last straw was Eric's after all.

Paula McDonald

The Christmas Scout

If there are poor among you, in one of the towns of the land the Lord your God is giving you, do not be selfish or greedy toward them. But give freely to them, and freely lend them whatever they need.

Deut. 15:7-8

In spite of the fun and laughter, 13-year-old Frank Wilson was not happy.

It was true that he had received all the presents he wanted. And he enjoyed these traditional Christmas Eve reunions of relatives—this year at Aunt Susan's—for the purpose of exchanging gifts and good wishes.

But Frank was not happy because this was his first Christmas without his brother, Steve, who, during the year, had been killed by a reckless driver. Frank missed his brother and the close companionship they had together.

Frank said good-bye to his relatives and explained to his parents that he was leaving a little early to see a friend: from there he could walk home. Since it was cold outside, Frank put on his new plaid jacket. It was his favorite gift.

The other presents he placed on his new sled.

Then Frank headed out, hoping to find the patrol leader of his Boy Scout troop. Frank always felt understood by him. Though rich in wisdom, he lived in the Flats, the section of town where most of the poor lived, and his patrol leader did odd jobs to help support his family. To Frank's disappointment, his friend was not at home.

As Frank hiked down the street toward home, he caught glimpses of trees and decorations in many of the small houses. Then, through one front window, he glimpsed a shabby room with the limp stockings hanging over an empty fireplace. A woman was seated near them weeping.

The stockings reminded him of the way he and his brother had always hung theirs side by side. The next morning, they would be bursting with presents. A sudden thought struck Frank—he had not done his "good turn" for the day.

Before the impulse passed, he knocked on the door.

"Yes?" the sad voice of the woman inquired.

"May I come in?"

"You are very welcome," she said, seeing his sled full of gifts, and assuming he was making a collection, "but I have no food or gifts for you. I have nothing for my own children."

"That's not why I am here," Frank replied. "Please choose whatever presents you'd like for your children from this sled."

"Why, God bless you!" the amazed woman answered gratefully.

She selected some candies, a game, the toy airplane and a puzzle. When she took the new Scout flashlight, Frank almost cried out. Finally, the stockings were full.

"Won't you tell me your name?" she asked, as Frank was leaving.

"Just call me the Christmas Scout," he replied.

The visit left the boy touched, and with an unexpected flicker of joy in his heart. He understood that his sorrow was not the only sorrow in the world. Before he left the Flats, he had given away the remainder of his gifts. The plaid jacket had gone to a shivering boy.

But he trudged homeward, cold and uneasy. Having given his presents away, Frank now could think of no reasonable explanation to offer his parents. He wondered how he could make them understand.

"Where are your presents, son?" asked his father as he entered the house.

"I gave them away."

"The airplane from Aunt Susan? Your coat from Grandma? Your flashlight? We thought you were happy with your gifts."

"I was—very happy," the boy answered lamely.

"But, Frank, how could you be so impulsive?" his mother asked. "How will we explain to the relatives who spent so much time and gave so much love shopping for you?"

His father was firm. "You made your choice, Frank. We cannot afford any more presents."

His brother gone, his family disappointed in him, Frank suddenly felt dreadfully alone. He had not expected a reward for his generosity. For he knew that a good deed always should be its own reward. It would be tarnished otherwise. So he did not want his gifts back, however, he wondered if he would ever again truly recapture joy in his life. He thought he had this evening, but it had been fleeting. Frank thought of his brother and sobbed himself to sleep.

The next morning, he came downstairs to find his parents listening to Christmas music on the radio. Then the announcer spoke:

"Merry Christmas, everybody! The nicest Christmas story we have this morning comes from the Flats. A crippled boy down there has a new sled this morning, another youngster has a fine plaid jacket, and several families report that their children were made happy last night by gifts from a teenage boy who simply referred to himself as the Christmas Scout. No one could identify him, but the children of the Flats claim that the Christmas Scout was a personal representative of old Santa Claus himself."

Frank felt his father's arms go around his shoulders, and he saw his mother smiling through her tears. "Why didn't you tell us? We didn't understand. We are so proud of you, son."

The carols came over the air again filling the room with music.

". . . *Praises sing to God the King, and peace to men on Earth.*"

Samuel D. Bogan

It Really Didn't Matter

The young people at Shively Christian Church, led at the time by Youth Pastor Dave Stone, were fiercely competitive with their neighbor, Shively Baptist, in all things, especially softball. They were also serious about their Christianity, faithfully attending the summer Bible camp led by the youth pastor.

One week, the Bible lesson was about Jesus washing his disciples' feet, from John 13. To make the servanthood lesson stick, Pastor Stone divided the kids into groups and told them to go out and find a practical way to be servants.

"I want you to be Jesus in the city for the next two hours," he said. "If Jesus were here, what would he do? Figure out how he would help people."

Two hours later the kids reconvened in Pastor Stone's living room to report what they had done.

One group had done two hours of yard work for an elderly man. Another group bought ice cream treats and delivered them to several widows in the church. A third group visited a church member in the hospital and gave him a card. Another group went to a nursing home and sang Christmas carols—yes, carols in the middle of

August. One elderly resident remarked that it was the warmest Christmas she could remember.

But when the fifth group stood up and reported what they had done, everyone groaned. This group had made its way to none other than their arch rival, Shively Baptist, where they had asked the pastor if he knew someone who needed help. The pastor sent them to the home of an elderly woman who needed yard work done. There, for two hours, they mowed grass, raked the yard and trimmed hedges.

When they were getting ready to leave, the woman called the group together and thanked them for their hard work. "I don't know how I could get along without you," she told them. "You kids at Shively Baptist are always coming to my rescue."

"Shively Baptist!" interrupted Pastor Stone. "I sure hope you set her straight and told her you were from Shively *Christian* Church."

"Why, no, we didn't," the kids said. "We didn't think it mattered."

Charles W. Colson

Is There a Santa Claus?

6:00 P.M., December 23, 1961. I am writing this en route from New York to Los Angeles by plane. When I get home to Honolulu tomorrow, I must have a Christmas story ready to tell to the neighborhood children. They have asked me to title it, "Is There a Santa Claus?" How can I possibly give an honest answer to skeptical youngsters?

I hope we get to Los Angeles on time. Almost everyone aboard has a connection to make.

8:10 P.M. The pilot has just given us bad news. Los Angeles is fogged in; no aircraft can land. We have to detour to Ontario, California, an emergency field not far from Los Angeles.

3:12 A.M., December 24. With one problem and another, we have just landed in Ontario—six hours behind schedule. Everyone is cold, exhausted, hungry and irritable. All of us have missed our connections. Many will not make it home by Christmas Eve. I am in no mood to make up a story about Santa Claus.

7:15 A.M. I am writing this at the Los Angeles airport. A lot has happened in the last four hours. The airfield at Ontario was bedlam. Scores of Los Angeles-bound planes had to land there. The frantic passengers—over 1,000 of them—had hoped to get word to their families that they would be late. But the telegraph office was closed, and there were endless lines at the telephone booths. No food. No coffee.

The employees at the small terminal were just as frenzied and fatigued as the passengers. Everything went wrong. Baggage was heaped helter-skelter, regardless of destination. No one seemed to know which buses would go where, or at what time. Babies were crying; women were screaming questions; men were grumbling and being sarcastic. The mob pushed and jostled, like a swarm of frightened ants, in the effort to find luggage. It hardly seemed possible that this was the day before Christmas.

Suddenly, amid the nervous commotion, I heard a confident, unhurried voice. It stood out like a great church bell—clear, calm and filled with love.

"Now don't you worry, ma'am," the voice said. "We're going to find your luggage and get you to La Jolla in time. Everything's going to be just fine." This was the first kind, constructive statement I had heard in a long while.

I turned and saw a man who might have stepped right out of "The Night Before Christmas." He was short and stout, with a florid, merry face. On his head was some sort of official cap, the kind that sightseeing guides wear. Tumbling out beneath were cascades of curly white hair. He wore hunting boots, as if, perhaps, he had just arrived after a snowy trip behind a team of reindeer. Pulled snugly over his barrel chest and fat tummy was a red sweatshirt.

The man stood next to a homemade pushcart, composed of an enormous packing box resting on four bicycle wheels. It contained urns of steaming coffee and piles of miscellaneous cardboard cartons.

"Here you are, ma'am," said the unusual man with the cheerful voice. "Have some hot coffee while we look for your luggage."

Pushing the cart before him, pausing only long enough to hand coffee to others, or to say a cheerful "Merry Christmas to you, brother!" or to promise that he would be back to help, he searched among the sprawling piles of luggage. Finally, he found the woman's possessions. Placing them on the pushcart, he said to her, "You just follow me. We'll put you on the bus to La Jolla."

After getting her settled, Kris Kringle (that's what I had started calling him) returned to the terminal. I found myself tagging along and helping him with the coffee. I knew that my bus wouldn't leave for about an hour.

Kris Kringle cut a swath of light through the dismal field. There was something about him that made everyone smile. Dispensing coffee, blowing a child's nose, laughing, singing snatches of Christmas songs, he calmed panicky passengers and sped them on their way.

When a woman fainted, it was Kris Kringle who pushed through the helpless group around her. From one of his cartons, he produced smelling salts and a blanket. When the woman was conscious again, he asked three men to carry her to a comfortable settee and told them to use the loudspeaker system to find a doctor.

Who is this funny little man who gets things done, I wondered. I asked him, "What company do you work for?"

"Sonny," he said to me, "see that kid over there in the blue coat? She's lost. Give her this candy bar, and tell her to stay right where she is. If she wanders around, her mother won't ever find her."

I did as ordered, then repeated, "What company do you work for?"

"Shucks, I'm not working for anyone. I'm just having fun. Every December I spend my two weeks' vacation helping travelers. What with this rush season, there are always thousands who need a hand. Hey, look what we have over here."

He had spotted a tearful young mother with a baby. Winking at me, Kris Kringle perked his cap at a jaunty angle and rolled his cart over to them. The woman was sitting on her suitcase, clutching her baby.

"Well, well, sister," he said, "that's a mighty pretty baby you have. What's the trouble?"

Between sobs, the young woman told him that she hadn't seen her husband for over a year. She was to meet him at a hotel in San Diego. He wouldn't know what had delayed her and would worry, and the baby was hungry.

From the pushcart, Kris Kringle took a bottle of warmed milk. "Now don't you worry. Everything will be all right," he said.

As he guided her to the bus for Los Angeles—the one I was to leave on—he wrote down her name and the name of the hotel in San Diego. He promised her that he would get a message to her husband.

"God bless you," she said, climbing aboard and cradling the now sleeping child in her arms. "I hope you have a merry Christmas and receive many wonderful presents."

"Thank you, sister," he said, tipping his cap. "I've already received the greatest gift of all, and you gave it to me. Ho, ho," he went on, seeing something of interest in the crowd, "there's an old fellow in trouble. Good-bye, sister. I'm going over there to give myself another present."

He got off the bus. I got off, too, since the bus wouldn't leave for a few minutes. He turned to me. "Say," he said, "aren't you taking this jalopy to Los Angeles?"

"Yes."

"Okay, you've been a good assistant. Now I want to give you a Christmas present. You sit next to that lady and look after her and the baby. When you get to Los Angeles"—he fished out a piece of paper—"telephone her husband at this hotel in San Diego. Tell him about his family's delay."

He knew what my answer would be because he left without even waiting for a reply. I sat down next to the young mother and took the baby from her. Looking out the window, I saw Kris Kringle in his bulging red sweatshirt disappearing into the crowd.

The bus started. I felt good. I began thinking of home and Christmas. And I knew then how I would answer the question of the children in my neighborhood: "Is there a Santa Claus?"

I had met him.

William J. Lederer

A Gift of the Heart

*You will find, as you look back upon your life,
that the moments that stand out are the
moments when you have done things for others.*

Henry Drummond

New York City, where I live, is impressive at any time, but as Christmas approaches, it is overwhelming. Store windows blaze with lights and color, furs and jewels. Golden angels, 40 feet tall, hover over Fifth Avenue. Wealth, power, opulence—nothing in the world can match this fabulous display. Through the gleaming canyons, people hurry to find last-minute gifts. Money seems to be no problem. If there's a problem, it's that the recipients so often have everything that they need or want that it's hard to find anything suitable, anything that will really say, "I love you."

Last December, as Christ's birthday drew near, a stranger was faced with just that problem. She had come from Switzerland to live in an American home and perfect her English. In return, she was willing to act as secretary, mind the grandchildren, do anything she was asked. She was just a girl in her late teens. Her name was Ursula.

One of the tasks the employers gave Ursula was keeping track of the Christmas presents as they arrived. There were many, and all would require acknowledgment. Ursula kept a faithful record, but with a growing sense of concern. She was grateful to her American friends; she wanted to show her gratitude by giving them a Christmas present. But nothing that she could buy with her small allowance could compare with the gifts she was recording daily. Besides, even without these gifts, it seemed to her that her employers already had everything.

At night from her window, Ursula could see the snowy expanse of Central Park and beyond it the jagged skyline of the city. Far below, traffic hooted and traffic lights blinked red and green. It was so different from the silent majesty of the Alps that at times she had to blink back tears of the homesickness she was careful never to show. It was in the solitude of her little room, a few days before Christmas, that her secret idea came to her. It was almost as if a voice spoke clearly, inside her head. "It's true," said the voice, "that many people in this city have much more than you do. But surely there are many who have far less." Ursula thought long and hard. Finally on her day off, which was Christmas Eve, she went to a large department store. She moved slowly along the crowded aisles, selecting and rejecting things in her mind. At last, she bought something and had it wrapped in gaily colored paper.

She went out into the gray twilight and looked hopelessly around. Finally, she went up to a doorman, resplendent in blue and gold. "Excuse me, please," she said in a hesitant voice. "Can you tell me where to find a poor street?"

"A poor street?" said the puzzled man.

"Yes, a very poor street, the poorest in the city."

The doorman looked doubtful. "Well, you might try Harlem. Or down in the village. Or in the Lower East Side, maybe."

These names meant nothing to Ursula. She thanked the doorman and walked along, threading her way through the stream of shoppers until she came to a tall policeman. "Please," she said, "can you direct me to a very poor street in . . . in Harlem?"

The policeman looked at her sharply and shook his head. "Harlem's no place for you, Miss." And he blew his whistle and sent the traffic swirling past.

Holding her package carefully, Ursula walked on, head bowed against the sharp wind. If a street looked more poor than the one she was on, she took it. But none seemed like the slums she had heard about. Once she stopped a woman. "Please, where do the very poor people live?" But the woman gave her a stare and hurried on.

Darkness came sifting from the sky. Ursula was cold and discouraged and afraid of becoming lost. She came to an intersection and stood forlornly on the corner. What she was trying to do suddenly seemed foolish, impulsive and absurd. Then, through the traffic's roar, she heard the cheerful tinkle of a bell. On the corner opposite, a Salvation Army man was making his traditional Christmas appeal.

At once, Ursula felt better. The Salvation Army was a part of life in Switzerland, too. Surely this man could tell her what she wanted to know. She waited for the light, then crossed over to him. "Can you help me? I'm looking for a baby. I have here a little present for the poorest baby I can find." And she held up the package with the green ribbon and the gaily colored paper.

Dressed in gloves and an overcoat a size too big for him, he seemed a very ordinary man. But behind his steel-rimmed glasses his eyes were kind. He looked at Ursula and stopped ringing his bell. "What sort of present?" he asked.

"A little dress. For a small, poor baby. Do you know of one?"

"Oh, yes," he said. "Of more than one, I'm afraid."

"Is it far away? I could take a taxi, maybe?"

The Salvation Army man wrinkled his forehead. Finally he said, "It's almost six o'clock. My relief will show up then. If you want to wait, and if you can afford the ride, I'll take you to a family in my own neighborhood who needs just about everything."

"And they have a small baby?"

"A very small baby."

"Then," said Ursula joyfully, "I wait."

The substitute bell-ringer came. A cruising taxi slowed. In its welcome warmth, Ursula told her new friend about herself, how she came to be in New York, and what she was trying to do. He listened in silence, and the taxi driver listened, too. When they reached their destination, the driver said, "Take your time, Miss. I'll wait for you."

On the sidewalk, Ursula stared up at the forbidding tenement, dark, decaying, saturated with hopelessness. A gust of wind, iron-cold, stirred the refuse in the street and rattled the trash cans. "They live on the third floor," the Salvation Army man said. "Shall we go up?"

But Ursula shook her head. "They would try to thank me, and this is not from me." She pressed the package into his hand. "Take it up for me, please. Say it's from . . . from someone who has everything."

The taxi bore her swiftly back from dark streets to lighted ones, from misery to abundance. She tried to visualize the Salvation Army man climbing the stairs, the knock, the explanation, the package being opened, the dress on the baby. It was hard to do.

Arriving at the apartment house on Fifth Avenue where she lived, she fumbled in her purse. But the driver flicked the flag up. "No charge, Miss."

"No charge?" echoed Ursula, bewildered.

"Don't worry," the driver said. "I've been paid." He smiled at her and drove away.

Ursula was up early the next day. She set the table with special care. By the time she had finished, the family was awake, and there was all the excitement and laughter of Christmas morning. Soon the living room was a sea of gay discarded wrappings. Ursula thanked everyone for the presents she received. Finally, when there was a lull, she began to explain hesitantly why there seemed to be none from her. She told about going to the department store. She told about the Salvation Army man. She told about the taxi driver. When she finished, there was a long silence. No one seemed to trust themselves to speak. "So you see," said Ursula, "I try to do a kindness in your name. And this is my Christmas present to you."

How do I happen to know all this? I know it because ours was the home where Ursula lived. Ours was the Christmas she shared. We were like many Americans, so richly blessed that to this child from across the sea there seemed to be nothing she could add to the material things we already had. And so she offered something of far greater value: a gift of the heart, an act of kindness carried out in our name.

Strange, isn't it? A shy Swiss girl, alone in a great impersonal city. You would think that nothing she could do would affect anyone. And yet, by trying to give away love, she brought the true spirit of Christmas into our lives, the spirit of selfless giving. That was Ursula's secret—and she shared it with us all.

Norman Vincent Peale

The Cobbler and His Guest

Remember to welcome strangers, because some who have done this have welcomed angels without knowing it.

Heb. 13:2-3

There lived in the city of Marseilles, a hundred years ago, an old shoemaker, loved and honored by all his neighbors, who affectionately called him "Father Martin."

One Christmas he sat alone in his little shop, reading of the visit of the wise men to the infant Jesus, and of the gifts they brought, and he said to himself, "If tomorrow were the first Christmas, and if Jesus were to be born in Marseilles this night, I know what I would give him!" He arose and took from a shelf two little shoes of softest snow-white leather, with bright silver buckles. "I would give him these, my finest work. How pleased his mother would be! But I'm a foolish old man," he thought, smiling. "The Master has no need of my poor gifts."

Replacing the shoes, he blew out the candle and retired to rest. Hardly had he closed his eyes, it seemed, when he heard a voice call his name. "Martin!" Intuitively, he felt aware of the identity of the speaker. "Martin, you have longed to see me. Tomorrow I shall pass by your window. If you see me and bid me enter, I shall be your guest and sit at your table."

He did not sleep that night for joy. Before it was yet dawn, he arose and tidied up his little shop. Fresh sand he spread on the floor, and green boughs of fir he wreathed along the rafters. On the table he placed a loaf of white bread, a jar of honey, a pitcher of milk; and over the fire he hung a hot drink. His simple preparations were complete.

When all was in readiness, he took up his vigil at the window. He was sure he would know the Master. As he watched the driving sleet and rain in the cold, deserted street, he thought of the joy that would be his when he sat down and broke bread with his guest.

Presently, he saw an old street sweeper pass by, blowing upon his thin, gnarled hands to warm them. *Poor fellow! He must be half frozen*, thought Martin. Opening the door, he called out to him, "Come in, my friend, and get warm, and drink something hot." No further urging was needed, and the man gratefully accepted the invitation.

An hour passed, and Martin next saw a poor, miserably clothed woman carrying a baby. She paused, wearily, to rest in the shelter of his doorway. Quickly, he flung open the door. "Come in and get warm while you rest," he said to her. "You are not well?" he asked.

"I am going to the hospital. I hope they will take me and my baby in," she explained. "My husband is at sea, and I am ill, without a soul to whom I can go."

"Poor child!" cried the old man. "You must eat something while you are getting warm. No? Let me give a cup of milk to the little one. Ah! What a bright, pretty little fellow he is! Why, you have no shoes on him!"

"I have no shoes for him," sighed the mother.

"Then he shall have this lovely pair I finished yester-day." And Martin took down the soft little snow-white shoes he had looked at the evening before, and slipped them on the child's feet. They fit perfectly. Shortly, the young mother went her way full of gratitude, and Martin went back to his post at the window.

Hour after hour went by, and many needy souls shared the meager hospitality of the old cobbler, but the expected guest did not appear.

At last, when night had fallen, Father Martin retired to his cot with a heavy heart. "It was only a dream," he sighed. "I did hope and believe, but he has not come."

Suddenly, so it seemed to his weary eyes, the room was flooded with a glorious light; and to the cobbler's aston-ished vision there appeared before him, one by one, the poor street sweeper, the sick mother and her baby, and all the people whom he had aided during the day. Each one smiled at him and said, "Have you not seen me? Did I not sit at your table?" and vanished.

Then softly out of the silence he heard again the gentle voice, repeating the old, familiar words, "Who so shall receive one such little child in my name receiveth me" (Matt. 18:5). "For I was hungered, and ye gave me meat; I was thirsty, and ye gave me drink; I was a stranger, and ye took me in.

". . . Verily I say unto you, inasmuch as ye have done it unto one of the least of these my brethren, ye have done it unto me" (Matt. 25:35-40).

Author Unknown
Submitted by Jacob S. Miller

A Thanksgiving Story

Help carry one another's burdens and in this way you will obey the law of Christ.

Gal. 6:2

It was the day before Thanksgiving—the first one my three children and I would be spending without their father, who had left several months before. Now the two older children were very sick with the flu, and the eldest had just been prescribed bed rest for a week.

It was a cool, gray day outside, and a light rain was falling. I grew wearier as I scurried around, trying to care for each child: thermometers, juice, diapers. And I was fast running out of liquids for the children. But when I checked my purse, all I found was about $2.50—and this was supposed to last me until the end of the month. That's when I heard the phone ring.

It was the secretary from our former church, and she told me that they had been thinking about us and had something to give us from the congregation. I told her that I was going out to pick up some more juice and soup for the children, and I would drop by the church on my way to the market.

I arrived at the church just before lunch. The church secretary met me at the door and handed me a special gift envelope. "We think of you and the kids often," she said, "and you are in our hearts and prayers. We love you." When I opened the envelope, I found two grocery certificates inside. Each was worth $20. I was so touched and moved, I broke down and cried.

"Thank you very much," I said, as we hugged each other. "Please give our love and thanks to the church." Then I drove to a store near our home and purchased some much-needed items for the children.

At the check-out counter I had a little over $14.00 worth of groceries, and I handed the cashier one of the gift certificates. She took it, then turned her back for what seemed like a very long time. I thought something might be wrong. Finally I said, "This gift certificate is a real blessing. Our former church gave it to our family, knowing I'm a single parent trying to make ends meet."

The cashier then turned around, with tears in her loving eyes, and replied, "Honey, that's wonderful! Do you have a turkey?"

"No. It's okay because my children are sick anyway."

She then asked, "Do you have anything else for Thanksgiving dinner?"

Again I replied, "No."

After handing me the change from the certificate, she looked at my face and said, "Honey, I can't tell you exactly why right now, but I want you to go back into the store and buy a turkey, cranberry sauce, pumpkin pie or anything else you need for a Thanksgiving dinner."

I was shocked, and humbled to tears. "Are you sure?" I asked.

"Yes! Get whatever you want. And get some Gatorade for the kids."

I felt awkward as I went back to do more shopping, but

I selected a fresh turkey, a few yams and potatoes, and some juices for the children. Then I wheeled the shopping cart up to the same cashier as before. As I placed my groceries on the counter, she looked at me once more with giant tears in her kind eyes and began to speak.

"Now I can tell you. This morning I prayed that I could help someone today, and you walked through my line." She reached under the counter for her purse and took out a $20 bill. She paid for my groceries and then handed me the change. Once more I was moved to tears.

The sweet cashier then said, "I am a Christian. Here is my phone number if you ever need anything." She then took my head in her hands, kissed my cheek and said, "God bless you, honey."

As I walked to my car, I was overwhelmed by this stranger's love and by the realization that God loves my family too, and shows us his love through this stranger's and my church's kind deeds.

The children were supposed to have spent Thanksgiving with their father that year, but because of the flu they were home with me, for a very special Thanksgiving Day. They were feeling better, and we all ate the goodness of the Lord's bounty—and our community's love. Our hearts were truly filled with thanks.

Andréa Nannette Mejia

A Coincidence?

*Give and it will be given to you; good measure,
pressed down, shaken together, running over,
they will pour into your lap. For whatever measure you deal out to others, it will be dealt to you
in return.*

Luke 6:38 NIV

I was very proud of my daughter Emily. At only nine
years old, she had been carefully saving her allowance
money all year and trying to earn extra money by doing
small jobs around the neighborhood. Emily was determined to save enough to buy a girl's mountain bike, an
item for which she'd been longing, and she'd been faithfully putting her money away since the beginning of the
year.

"How're you doing, honey?" I asked soon after
Thanksgiving. I knew she had hoped to have all the
money she needed by the end of the year.

"I have forty-nine dollars, Daddy," she said. "I'm not
sure if I'm going to make it."

"You've worked so hard," I said encouragingly. "Keep it

up. But you know that you can have your pick from my bicycle collection."

"Thanks, Daddy. But your bikes are so *old*."

I smiled to myself because I knew she was right. As a collector of vintage bicycles, all my girls' bikes were 1950s models—not the kind a kid would choose today.

When the Christmas season arrived, Emily and I went comparison shopping, and she saw several less expensive bikes for which she thought she'd have to settle. As we left one store, she noticed a Salvation Army volunteer ringing his bell by a big kettle. "Can we give them something, Daddy?" she asked.

"Sorry, Em, I'm out of change," I replied.

Emily continued to work hard all through December, and it seemed she might make her goal after all. Then suddenly one day, she came downstairs to the kitchen and made an announcement to her mother.

"Mom," she said hesitantly, "you know all the money I've been saving?"

"Yes, dear," smiled my wife, Diane.

"God told me to give it to the poor people."

Diane knelt down to Emily's level. "That's a very kind thought, sweetheart. But you've been saving all year. Maybe you could give *some* of it."

Emily shook her head vigorously. "God said *all*."

When we saw she was serious, we gave her various suggestions about where she could contribute. But Emily had received specific instructions, and so one cold Sunday morning before Christmas, with little fanfare, she handed her total savings of $58 to a surprised and grateful Salvation Army volunteer.

Moved by Emily's selflessness, I suddenly noticed that a local car dealer was collecting used bicycles to refurbish and give to poor children for Christmas. And I realized that if my nine-year-old daughter could give away all her money, I could certainly give up one bike from my collection.

As I picked up a shiny but old-fashioned kid's bike from the line in the garage, it seemed as if a second bicycle in the line took on a glow. Should I give a *second* bike? No, certainly the one would be enough.

But as I got to my car, I couldn't shake the feeling that I should donate that second bike as well. And if Emily could follow heavenly instructions, I decided I could, too. I turned back and loaded the second bike into the trunk, then took off for the dealership.

When I delivered the bikes, the car dealer thanked me and said, "You're making two kids very happy, Mr. Koper. And here are your tickets."

"Tickets?" I asked.

"Yes. For each bike donated, we're giving away one chance to win a brand new men's 21-speed mountain bike from a local bike shop. So here are your tickets for two chances."

Why wasn't I surprised when that second ticket won the bike? "I can't believe you won!" laughed Diane, delighted.

"I didn't," I said. "It's pretty clear that Emily did."

And why wasn't I surprised when the bike dealer happily substituted a gorgeous new girl's mountain bike for the man's bike advertised?

Coincidence? Maybe. I like to think it was God's way of rewarding a little girl for a sacrifice beyond her years— while giving her dad a lesson in charity and the power of the Lord.

Ed Koper

3

ON PARENTS AND PARENTING

These commandments that I give you today are to be upon your hearts. Impress them on your children. Talk about them when you sit at home and when you walk along the road, when you lie down and when you get up.

Deut. 6:6, 7 NIV

The Gift of a Mommy

*Train a child in the way he should go,
and when he is old he will not turn from it.*

Prov. 22:6 NIV

I have found nursing patients with cancer to be a challenging and rewarding occupation. It has certainly been a good distraction from my own familiar challenge of parenting two teens. Whenever I start thinking that dealing with drivers' licenses, curfews, grades and peer pressure are overwhelming, I remember what Rebekah faced, the courage she showed, and suddenly my problems don't seem so difficult after all.

I remember the day she was admitted to the ward. As I reviewed her admission papers, I was surprised to see that she was 32 and being admitted for chemotherapy to treat breast cancer that had been diagnosed two weeks earlier. I entered the room and introduced myself. Rebekah, her eyes sparkling with love and her ponytail bouncing, introduced me to her husband, Warren, and her daughters, Ruthie, age six, and Hannah, age four. Cradled in her crossed legs wiggled her third daughter, Molly, age two.

While I filled out forms, Rebekah directed the unpacking of her suitcase—a comforter made by her grandmother, a poster of cheer from her church circle and a family portrait for her bedside table, along with her worn Bible. Warren gathered the girls to go to the airport to pick up Grandmother.

"I need to place a needle in your arm to give you the chemotherapy," I explained.

"I'll do anything to get well for my husband and girls. I can handle throwing up, losing my hair and being tired, but I'm absolutely terrified of needles." Rebekah's voice shook and her eyes brimmed with tears.

"You can cry, but please don't move. On the count of three . . ."

"The Lord is my shepherd, I shall not want." Rebekah said loudly as the needle slid smoothly into the vein. With the successful completion of the intravenous, Rebekah asked, "What is your favorite Bible verse?"

"John 11:35," I answered. "Jesus wept."

"Oh! That's a sad verse," she replied, a bit somberly.

"It brings me comfort, knowing that Jesus is sad when bad things happen to his people. It demonstrates to me a human side of him that I need to know when I care for sick people. I know he can and will heal the sick, but returning to health can entail sad times, so I know he is there to support me in the sad times so that I can support patients."

"I'll have to give that some thought," replied Rebekah.

For the next 18 months, I saw Rebekah on a regular basis to receive chemotherapy and radiation. A chest X ray showed the cancer had spread and there were no further medical weapons to use against the cancer. *How could I support her in this new challenge?*

I entered Rebekah's room and found it cluttered with paper, tapes and a tape recorder. "Nan, I'm making tapes for my daughters, to know what I feel, think and advise on important occasions. I don't want them to forget me. Do you have any suggestions?"

I looked over her list—first day of school, becoming sweet 16, first date, first kiss, confirmation, etc. She let me listen to the tapes, which were moving and filled with motherly advice, encouragement and love. Rebekah taped each day from her notes as she grew weaker and weaker.

Rebekah explained to her young daughters that she was making special tapes that their dad would keep for them to listen to later. She explained that she was going to live with God and help him get a home ready for them when they were very old.

We all knew the end was approaching. I was surprised when I got a frantic phone call at home from a nurse who said that Rebekah was pleading—begging that I come with a blank tape. Making a mental checklist of all the tapes she had made, I could not imagine what topic could have possibly been forgotten.

Entering Rebekah's room, I noticed she was having severe shortness of breath and was very anxious, gasping, "Nan, do you have the tape?"

"Take a deep breath. Of course I have the tape," I replied.

As I set up the tape recorder, she explained, "This is my most important tape." I held the microphone close to her mouth and she began, "Ruthie, Hannah and Molly, some day your daddy will bring a new mommy home. I want you to make her feel very special, and how proud you will make me feel if you are kind, patient and encouraging to her as she learns to take care of each of you. Help her set the table. Please bring her dandelions to put in the special vase—most important, hug her often. Please do not be sad for long. 'Jesus cried.' He knows how sad you are and he knows you will be happy again. I love you so much, Hannah, Ruthie and Molly. Big hugs, your first mommy."

I turned off the tape player. "Thank you. I can sleep now."

I adjusted the pillow under her head and rolled a pillow to her back and exited quietly.

Rebekah died two days later.

I mailed the tape to their dad four years later when Warren and the girls prepared to welcome their new wife and mommy.

Nan Pinkston

In His Mother's Footsteps

It was a busy day in our Costa Mesa, California, home. But then, with 10 children and one on the way, every day was a bit hectic. On this particular day, however, I was having trouble doing even routine chores—all because of one little boy.

Len, who was three at the time, was on my heels no matter where I went. Whenever I stopped to do something and turned back around, I would trip over him. Several times, I patiently suggested fun activities to keep him occupied. "Wouldn't you like to play on the swing set?" l asked again.

But he simply smiled an innocent smile and said, "Oh, that's all right, Mommy. I'd rather be in here with you." Then he continued to bounce happily along behind me.

After stepping on his toes for the fifth time, I began to lose my patience and insisted that he go outside and play with the other children. When I asked him why he was acting this way, he looked up at me with sweet green eyes and said, "Well, Mommy, in Primary my teacher told me to walk in Jesus' footsteps. But I can't see him, so I'm walking in yours."

I gathered Len in my arms and held him close. Tears of love and humility spilled over from the prayer that grew in my heart—a prayer of thanks for the simple, yet beautiful perspective of a three-year-old boy.

Davida Dalton
As told to JoEllen Johnson

"My Sunday School teacher said I should follow Jesus, but I'm not allowed to leave the yard."

My Mother's Hands

This world has many wonders,
God's many vistas grand;
But none can ever rival
The beauty of Mother's hands.

Wilma Heffelfinger

A few years ago, when my mother was visiting, she asked me to go shopping with her because she needed a new dress. I don't normally like to go shopping with other people, and I'm not a patient person, but we set off for the mall together nonetheless.

We visited nearly every store that carried ladies' dresses, and my mother tried on dress after dress, rejecting them all. As the day wore on, I grew weary and my mother grew frustrated.

Finally, at our last stop, my mother tried on a lovely blue three-piece dress. The blouse had a bow at the neckline, and as I stood in the dressing room with her, I watched as she tried, with much difficulty, to tie the bow. Her hands were so badly crippled from arthritis that she couldn't do it. Immediately, my impatience gave way to an overwhelming wave of compassion for her. I turned away to try and hide the tears that welled up involuntarily. Regaining my composure, I turned back to tie the bow for her. The dress was beautiful, and she bought it. Our shopping trip was over, but the event was etched indelibly in my memory.

For the rest of the day, my mind kept returning to that moment in the dressing room and to the vision of my mother's hands trying to tie that bow. Those loving hands that had fed me, bathed me, dressed me, caressed and comforted me, and, most of all, prayed for me, were now touching me in a most remarkable manner.

Later in the evening, I went to my mother's room, took her hands in mine, kissed them and, much to her surprise, told her that to me they were the most beautiful hands in the world.

I'm so grateful that God let me see with new eyes what a precious, priceless gift a loving, self-sacrificing mother is. I can only pray that some day my hands, and my heart, will have earned such a beauty of their own.

Bev Hulsizer

Hands

Thank you Lord for dirty hands
That touch my stove and fridge;
For sticky little fingers that
Try to build a bridge.

For careless hands that go astray
In search of something new;
For hands to hold and show the way
As mothers often do.

For precious little hands in which
Great faith so abounds;
For silly little hands that reach
To touch a mother's frown.

And thank you for your guiding hand
That leads me to the light;
That lifts me when I stumble
And points me to the right.

As little hands reach out to me
To show them what to do,
I'm steadied, reassured and loved
As I reach up to you.

Judith Peitsch

Out of a Job

If you don't have enough time for your family, you can be 100 percent certain you are not following God's will for your life.

Patrick M. Morley

I felt a small tug at my shirtsleeve.

"Dadd-eee!" The exasperated tone in my son's voice told me it was probably his third or fourth attempt to get attention. Seated at the dining room table of our home in Bellrose Village, Long Island, I'd been absorbed in theater trade papers, desperately searching for an acting job. It was summer, 1963, and I hadn't worked for three months.

"What is it?" I asked irritably.

"Daddy," he said, hopefully, "let's go play catch, okay?"

Nels was eight, blond, blue-eyed, the eldest of our three sons. Suddenly, from out of nowhere, his brothers appeared—surrounding me like a band of Indians.

"Yeah, Daddy," said seven-year-old Jimmy, "let's go out and play!"

"Come on, Daddy," piped six-year-old Vincent. "Please!"

"Daddy's busy," I heard my wife, Pat, say, shepherding the kids toward the kitchen.

I returned to the papers, but couldn't concentrate. My work had always meant everything to me. *Everything.* Besides, my idea of being a good husband and father was based upon being a good provider. I felt like a failure.

I stood up and walked over to the living-room window. Outside, the setting sun cast long shadows over the neat green lawns and white frame houses. With sadness, I recalled how happy Pat and I had been when we moved here as a young couple six years ago. When I met Pat, she had her own successful career as a professional dancer; she'd given it all up to marry me and raise our family.

Back then I was still riding high on the wave of success following my long-running role as Nels on the popular *I Remember Mama* TV series, sure I'd go on to be a star. After all, I'd been acting since childhood.

I still recall vividly my first audition. I was seven years old. My grandmother accompanied me to the neighborhood theater in Queens, where MGM Studios was sponsoring a child personality contest. Grandma Van Patten had lived with us for as long as I could remember. I guess at that time she was just about my best friend. Now she remained by my side until I was called before the judges to recite my poem. "You can do it," she whispered, squeezing my shoulder reassuringly.

When I won the contest, which resulted in a four-month contract, Grandma was the one who moved with me to Hollywood. I was 15 when she died. By then, I'd acted in numerous Broadway shows and was working and studying under Alfred Lunt and Lynn Fontaine. I was always glad that Grandma had lived to see my success. *But,* I thought ruefully, *good thing she isn't around to see me now . . .*

In recent years, I'd found myself having to accept

smaller and smaller parts. There was no good explanation why, and I didn't know what to do about it. Not even in church could I find comfort or guidance. My own prayers seemed flat and vague. As I grew increasingly irritable and impatient, my behavior was taking its toll on my family—especially my sons.

I felt the gentle touch of my wife's hand on my shoulder. "Dick," she said softly, "don't worry."

I gave her the same annoyed look I had earlier given my son. But Pat's concerned expression remained unchanged. "Honey," she said, "I think maybe we should pray about this."

"Pray? Don't you think I do?"

"I mean," she said quietly, "let's pray together. Let's pray specifically. You know you've always said you've never prayed without receiving an answer."

Pat was right. I did have faith in a personal God, and strong belief in the power of prayer. But this problem of a declining career and no money coming in was so big—I didn't know how to pray about it.

Pat seemed to sense my thoughts.

"God knows what's best for us," she said. "Let's simply ask him to get us through this summer according to his will." She paused. "Okay?"

"Yes," I said dully. "Okay."

Holding hands, we stood by the window and prayed.

I didn't feel any better.

A few more weeks passed. Nothing changed. Pat asked if I would mind if she tried auditioning for some local dance productions. I wasn't crazy about the idea. But, reluctantly, I agreed. We needed the money.

One muggy morning, I was seated at the dining room table, scanning the trade papers, when Pat rushed in, breathless and smiling. She had just auditioned for a summer production of *Hit the Deck*, at Jones Beach.

"Guess what!" she gasped. "I got the job! They want me in the chorus! And the pay's not bad!"

Instead of being pleased, I felt my stomach tighten into a knot.

"That's great," I said tersely. "That's real nice, Pat."

She came over and hugged me. "Rehearsals begin tomorrow," she said. "I'll be gone a lot during the days. You'll be all right taking care of the kids, won't you?"

"Yeah," I said. "Fine."

By this time, the three boys had found places around the table and were listening with rapt attention.

"Don't you see?" Pat continued. "This is the answer to our prayer."

"Yeah," I said, "right." It was an answer, all right, but it sure wasn't the one I'd been hoping for.

When Pat was working, I didn't really mind taking care of the kids. That is, I didn't mind the duties involved: fixing meals, doing dishes, enforcing naps and bedroom clean-ups.

What bothered me was the way God had chosen to answer our prayers. True, thanks to Pat's income, we were "getting through the summer." But what long-term good could ever come from this situation? It sure wasn't helping my career.

One hot afternoon as I was putting away the last of the lunch dishes, Jimmy entered the kitchen.

"Daddy . . .?"

I stiffened, feeling a request coming on. I was in no mood for requests.

"Daddy, can we go to Greenwood?"

Greenwood was Brooklyn's Greenwood Cemetery, where my grandmother was buried. The kids loved visiting Greenwood; with six square miles of wooded grounds, four lakes, lots of wildlife and great shady trees to climb, it was more like a park. Only 20 minutes away, it was, for our family, a place of good times and happy memories. *Why not?* I thought. *We haven't been to Greenwood in ages.* "That's not a bad idea," I said. "Get your brothers, and let's go."

Once at Greenwood, we walked the familiar hilly path to Great-grandma Van Patten's grave. We talked a little about what a wise, loving lady Great-grandma had been, about how happy she must be up in Heaven and watching us down here on earth. As we talked, I felt myself relaxing, forgetting the tensions of unemployment.

Then we sat cross-legged on the soft green grass and decided what game we'd play. "How about looking for the oldest marker?" I suggested.

"Yeah!" the boys agreed. The game was a family favorite.

"Remember the rules?" I asked.

Big brother Nels was quick to remind us. "Ten minutes to search; report back here when we hear Daddy whistle; then we see who wins."

"That's right," I said, and we set boundaries for our area of play.

"Ready?" I asked. Three heads nodded. "On your mark —Get set—Go!"

A mad scramble, and we were off running and stopping, peering and bobbing, as we hunted for epitaphs of long ago. Caught up in the game, I felt like a kid myself. The sun was warm and friendly on my back. The breeze rustled the leaves of the trees in soothing whispers. Before I knew it, I was daydreaming about my own childhood— and about Grandma Van Patten. She was always there . . . her steady blue eyes shining, her voice encouraging, her gentle touch conveying her trust and love for a little boy.

I found a tall, leafy tree and leaned against its massive trunk. In the distance, I heard the whoops and hollers of my kids having a good time.

"1890! Here's one from 1890!"

"Aw, that's nothing. I found one from 1865!"

I shut my eyes, allowing my thoughts to drift . . .

Why, I wondered, *had Grandma spent so many hours with me? Surely she must have had better things to do. But she'd always been so selfless, so generous with her time—as though being with me was genuinely important to her. Our times together had meant so much to me. I'd been so self-absorbed lately—so wrapped up in worry about my career. Perhaps—I felt a twinge of guilt at the idea—perhaps there was more to being a good father than simply being a good provider. Could it be that God was trying to tell me that my sons might need and benefit from the same kind of love and attention that Grandma had given me?*

"Daddy!"

I opened my eyes to see my three sons standing over me with puzzled expressions.

"Daddy, we've been waiting for your whistle!"

"Daddy, it's been over 10 minutes!"

"Daddy," said Vincent, accusingly, "you've been sleeping!"

"Come on, you guys," I said gruffly, "I was just resting. Now, who found the oldest marker?"

But in the minutes that had passed, something had happened to me. Surrounded by my happily chattering boys, I felt my heart melting. How precious my sons were . . . how short was our time together . . . how much I loved them! For the first time, I fully appreciated that, next to God, *my family* had to be the most important thing in my life—even more important than my career. And with that realization, a great imbalance was corrected in my heart. The weight of worry about getting work had lifted; God, I knew, would take care of that in his own time.

I was also beginning to understand a little better how God works. By keeping me home for the summer, he had shown me how to appreciate and love my family in a new way that otherwise would have been impossible. This was a lesson worth more than all the jobs in the world. It was the kind of lesson—I smiled to myself—that Grandma Van Patten would be pleased to know I'd learned.

After that sunny afternoon in Greenwood, I considered each day an opportunity to grow closer to my family. My sons and I did everything together. Before summer's end, neighborhood kids were coming to the door and asking if Mr. Van Patten could come out to play. The rock-solid foundation of love and trust that was established proved to be invaluable later. In 1970, we moved to Hollywood, where the stresses and strains of show-biz careers have been known to destroy the strongest ties.

Today, we remain as close as ever. Nels still lives at home with Pat and me. Jimmy and Vincent live across the street. Nearly every morning we still manage to get together for breakfast. On Sundays when everyone's in town, we enjoy going to church together.

Thousands of years ago it was written, "And he will turn the hearts of fathers to their children and the hearts of children to their fathers . . ." (Mal. 4:6 RSV). I'm convinced that even in this rapidly changing world, the family *can* work—that it remains God's will for his children. It's up to us to live in accordance with the plan.

Dick Van Patten

THE FAMILY CIRCUS® By Bil Keane

Anytime you're ready, Daddy, I'll be sitting outside growing older.

Reprinted with permission from Bil Keane.

Father Forgets

We never realize ourselves so vividly as when we are in the full glow of love for others.

Source Unknown

Listen, son. I am saying this as you lie asleep, one little paw crumpled under your cheek and the blond curls sticky wet on your damp forehead. I have stolen into your room alone. Just a few minutes ago, as I sat reading my paper in the library, a stifling wave of remorse swept over me. Guiltily, I came to your bedside.

These are the things I was thinking, son. I had been cross to you. I scolded you as you were dressing for school because you gave your face merely a dab with a towel. I took you to task for not cleaning your shoes. I called out angrily when you threw some of your things on the floor.

At breakfast, I found fault, too. You spilled things. You gulped down your food. You put your elbows on the table. You spread butter too thick on your bread. And as you started off to play and I made for my train, you turned and waved a hand and called, "Good-bye, Daddy!" and I frowned and said in reply, "Hold your shoulders back!"

Then it began all over again in the late afternoon. As I came up the road, I spied you, down on your knees playing marbles. There were holes in your socks. I humiliated you before your friends by marching you ahead of me to the house. Socks were expensive—and if you had to buy them, you would be more careful! Imagine that, son, from a father!

Do you remember, later, when I was reading in the library, how you came in, timidly, with a sort of hurt look in your eyes? When I glanced up over my paper, impatient at the interruption, you hesitated at the door. "What is it you want?" I snapped.

You said nothing, but ran across in one tempestuous plunge, and threw your arms around my neck and kissed me, and your small arms tightened with affection that God had set blooming in your heart and that even neglect could not wither. And then you were gone, pattering up the stairs.

Well, son, it was shortly afterwards that my paper slipped from my hands and a terrible sickening fear came over me. What has habit been doing to me? The habit of finding fault, of reprimanding—this was my reward to you for being a boy. It was not that I did not love you; it was that I expected too much of you. I was measuring you by the yardstick of my years.

And there was so much that was good and fine and true in your character. The little heart of you was as big as the dawn itself over the wide hills. This was shown by your spontaneous impulse to rush in and kiss me goodnight. Nothing else matters tonight, son. I have come to your bedside in the darkness, and I have knelt here, ashamed!

It is a feeble moment; I know you would not understand these things if I told them to you during your waking hours. But tomorrow, I will be a real daddy! I will chum with you and suffer when you suffer, and laugh when you laugh. I will bite my tongue when impatient words come. I will keep saying as if it were a ritual: "He is a little boy—let him be a little boy!"

I am afraid I have visualized you as a man. Yet as I see you now, son, crumpled and weary in your bed, I see that you are still a baby. Yesterday you were in your mother's arms, your head on her shoulder. I have asked too much of you, yet given too little of myself. Promise me, as I teach you to have the manners of a man, that you will remind me how to have the loving spirit of a child.

W. Livingston Larned

The Two Sides of Love

Trust in the Lord, with all your heart.
Never rely on what you think you know.
Remember the Lord in everything you do,
and He will show you the way.

Prov. 3:5,6

Darrell stood outside the local pizza parlor, hesitating before he opened the door. He shook his head as if to clear away his last-minute doubts about this meeting. Finally, with a sigh, he forced aside his fear, pushed open the door, and walked into his son's favorite restaurant.

He dreaded this meeting so much that it took all his emotional strength just to walk inside instead of turning away. Little did he know that within a few hours, he would experience one of the most positive events of his life.

Darrell had come to meet his 17-year-old son, Charles. Though Darrell loved Charles deeply, he also knew that of his two boys, Charles was the most different from him.

With his older son, Larry, communication was never a struggle. They acted and thought so much alike that they didn't need to talk much. They just did things together, like hunting or working on their cars. Darrell had always treated Larry as he did the men at his construction sites— rough. And Larry had always responded well to—even thrived on—that kind of treatment.

But Charles was a different case. Darrell could tell early on that Charles was much more sensitive than Larry. Each time Darrell blasted this son to motivate him like his older brother, Darrell could hear an alarm going off deep inside himself.

Darrell had received major doses of discipline and distance in his life—the hard side of love—but only a scant spoonful of warmth and acceptance—love's soft side. And what little he had been given, he had also measured out to his sons.

It's my job to put clothes on their backs and food on the table; it's their mother's job to make them feel loved, he told himself over and over. But he couldn't quite convince himself that that was all there was to being a father. Darrell knew how deeply he had been hurt by his own dad. And he had seen that same hurt in Charles's eyes a hundred times.

Darrell knew what a major part of the problem was. Charles had expected—almost demanded—a close relationship with him over the years. It wasn't enough that they go hunting together. Charles wanted to talk while they were on the trip—even while they were hunting!

Only recently had Darrell realized that the sole reason he and Charles were getting along at the moment was that his son had quit talking to him—altogether! Just as Darrell had done as a teenager with his own tough father, Charles had withdrawn to a safe distance and was doing his best to stay out of his dad's way.

Like many of us, Darrell had been on the run from close relationships. For years, his wife and son had been pursuing him. And for as many years, he'd been running away from them, trying to keep a "comfortable" distance between them.

Then one day Darrell got a clear look at himself during a men's retreat at his church and the running stopped.

That day at the retreat, he came face to face with the fact that there are two sides of love. Like many men, he had become an expert on its hard side. He could hand out the spankings, but not reach out to hug his son. In a heartbeat he could call down a mistake Charles made, but words of encouragement came up only on a holiday or birthday—if then.

At that men's retreat, Darrell learned that as important as a mother's love is, children need more. They desperately need their father's wholehearted love as well.

Darrell was a strong man, both emotionally and physically. Yet as tough as he fancied himself, one question the speaker asked pierced through to his heart: "When was the last time you put your arms around your son and told him face to face that you love him?"

Darrell couldn't think of a "last time." In fact, he couldn't think of a first time.

He listened as the speaker told him that genuine love has two sides, not just one. Instantly he realized he had been loving Charles only halfheartedly and that his son needed both sides of love *from the same person*.

What Charles needed most in a father was a real man who could show him how to love a wife and family wholeheartedly, not an insecure man who had to hand off all the warm and loving actions to his wife. Darrell had spent years hard-siding his son to gain his respect; what he had gained instead was his fear and resentment. And it was this realization that caused Darrell to talk his son into meeting him at the local pizza restaurant after football practice one afternoon.

"Hi, Dad," Charles said, shaking hands with his father, who had just walked in. Charles was six foot two and was used to looking down when he greeted people. But he was looking up to meet his dad's eyes. And although Darrell had turned 51 that same month, he had none of the middle-age spread that most men his age carry. Instead, he still possessed the athletic build that had made him a star on his high school football team.

"Charles," Darrell said, adjusting his glasses and looking down slightly as he spoke, "I've been doing a lot of thinking lately. It's been hitting me hard that this is your last summer at home. You'll be leaving for college soon. And along with the bags of clothing you'll be packing, you'll also be taking emotional bags that, for good or bad, *I've* helped you pack over the years."

Charles was normally the family comedian, but this time, instead of trying to "lighten up" the conversation, he sat quietly. It wasn't like his father to talk about their relationship. In fact, it wasn't like him to talk about *anything* serious. That's why he was all ears as he listened to his father.

"Son, I'd like to ask you to do something. Think back as far as you can—back to three years old even—and remember every time I've hurt your feelings and never made things right; every time I've made you feel unloved or inadequate by something I've said or done.

"I know we're different people. I can see now that I was always pretty hard on you. Actually, I was way too tough on you most of the time. I've tried to push you into being the person I thought you should be. Now I realize I've spent very little time listening to who you really want to become.

"Feel free to share with me anything I've done that's hurt you, and all I'm going to do is listen. Then I'd like for us to talk about it, and I want to ask your forgiveness for each thing you can think of. You don't need to be packing any extra, negative baggage that I may have given you.

You've got enough ahead of you over the next four years in college without that."

"I realize there's been a lot of water under the bridge— a lot of wasted years." Taking off his glasses and wiping tears from his eyes, he sighed, then looked straight at Charles. "We may be here all night," he continued, "and I'm ready for that. But first, you need to know how much I love you and how proud I am of you."

Charles had seen the words "I love you" written on birthday and Christmas cards in his father's handwriting, but this was the first time he had heard them from his father's lips. He'd learned to expect his father's hardness. Now that Dad had added softness to his love, Charles didn't know what to say.

"Dad," he stammered, "don't worry about the past. I know you love me." But at his father's insistence, he put his memory on "rewind" and let his thoughts fly back across the pictures he'd accumulated from 17 years of being with his dad.

Slowly, as Charles grew more confident that the conversational waters really were safe, he unloaded years of hurt right at the table. There were the seasons he spent becoming an outstanding football player to please his father, when all the time he would rather have been playing soccer.

There was the subtle resentment he had always felt that no matter how hard he tried, he could never quite live up to his older brother's accomplishments. And there were the many harsh comments his father had made to motivate him but that had actually been discouraging and hurtful.

As he recounted to his father each experience, large or small, Charles could see a genuine softness and sorrow in his dad's eyes. What's more, he heard words of remorse and healing for even the smallest thing that had left a rough edge on a memory.

Nearly three hours later, the fruitful conversation finally came to an end. As Darrell reached for the check, he said, "I know this was quick notice for you to have to think back on 17 years. So just remember, my door is always open if there's anything else I need to ask your forgiveness for."

Dinner was over, but a new relationship was just beginning for them. After 17 years of being strangers living under the same roof, they were finally on their way to finding each other.

Not long ago, television news cameras captured thousands of people cheering as the Berlin Wall came down after dividing the city for more than 25 years. And that night in the restaurant, we can just imagine that angels stood all around and cheered as the first hole in an emotional wall between a father and son was blown open.

It had been a moving night and an important one for both of them. But as they stood up, Charles did something that shocked his father.

Several people looked up from tables nearby as a big, strapping football player reached out and gave his equally strong father a warm bear hug for the first time in years. With tears in their eyes, those two strong men stood there holding each other, oblivious to the stares.

Gary Smalley and John Trent

Don't Let It End This Way

Forgiveness is the final form of love.

Reinhold Niebuhr

The hospital was unusually quiet that bleak January evening, quiet and still, like the air before a storm. I stood in the nurses' station on the seventh floor and glanced at the clock. It was 9:00 P.M.

I threw a stethoscope around my neck and headed for room 712, last room of the hall. Room 712 had a new patient, Mr. Williams. A man all alone. A man strangely silent about his family.

As I entered the room, Mr. Williams looked up eagerly, but dropped his eyes when he saw it was only his nurse. I pressed the stethoscope over his chest and listened. Strong, slow, even beating. Just what I wanted to hear. There seemed little indication he had suffered a slight heart attack a few hours earlier.

He looked up from his starched white bed. "Nurse, would you . . ." He hesitated, tears filling his eyes. Once before he had started to ask me a question, but had changed his mind.

I touched his hand, waiting.

He brushed away a tear. "Would you call my daughter? Tell her I've had a heart attack. A slight one. You see, I live alone and she is the only family I have." His respiration suddenly sped up.

I turned his nasal oxygen up to eight liters a minute. "Of course, I'll call her," I said, studying his face.

He gripped the sheets and pulled himself forward, his face tense with urgency. "Will you call her right away—as soon as you can?" He was breathing fast—too fast.

"I'll call her first thing," I said, patting his shoulder. "Now you get some rest."

I flipped off the light. He closed his eyes, such young blue eyes in his 50-year-old face.

Room 712 was dark except for a faint night-light under the sink. Oxygen gurgled in the green tubes above his bed. Reluctant to leave, I moved through the shadowy silence to the window. The panes were cold. Below, a foggy mist curled through the hospital parking lot. Above, snow clouds quilted the night sky. I shivered.

"Nurse," he called. "Could you get me a pencil and paper?"

I dug a scrap of yellow paper and a pen from my pocket and set it on the bedside table.

"Thank you," he said.

I smiled at him and left.

I walked back to the nurses' station and sat in a squeaky swivel chair by the phone. Mr. Williams' daughter was listed on his chart as the next of kin. I got her number from information and dialed. Her soft voice answered.

"Janie, this is Sue Kidd, a registered nurse at the hospital. I'm calling about your father. He was admitted today with a slight heart attack and . . ."

"No!" she screamed into the phone, startling me. "He's not dying is he?" It was more a painful plea than a question.

"His condition is stable at the moment," I said, trying hard to sound convincing.

Silence. I bit my lip.

"You must not let him die!" she said. Her voice was so utterly compelling that my hand trembled on the phone.

"He is getting the very best care."

"But you don't understand," she pleaded. "My daddy and I haven't spoken in almost a year. We had a terrible argument on my twenty-first birthday, over my boyfriend. I ran out of the house. I . . . I haven't been back. All these months I've wanted to go to him for forgiveness. The last thing I said to him was, 'I hate you.'"

Her voice cracked and I heard her heave great agonizing sobs. I sat, listening, tears burning my eyes. A father and a daughter, so lost to each other! Then I was thinking of my own father, many miles away. It had been so long since I had said I love you.

As Janie struggled to control her tears, I breathed a prayer. "Please God, let this daughter find forgiveness."

"I'm coming, now! I'll be there in 30 minutes," she said. *Click.* She had hung up.

I tried to busy myself with a stack of charts on the desk. I couldn't concentrate. Room 712. I knew I had to get back to 712. I hurried down the hall nearly in a run. I opened the door.

Mr. Williams lay unmoving. I reached for his pulse. There was none.

"Code 99. Room 712. Code 99. Stat." The alert was shooting through the hospital within seconds after I called the switchboard through the intercom by the bed.

Mr. Williams had had a cardiac arrest.

With lightning speed I leveled the bed and bent over his mouth, breathing air into his lungs. I positioned my head over his chest and compressed. One, two, three. I tried to count. At 15, I moved back to his mouth and breathed as deeply as I could. Where was help? Again I compressed and breathed. Compressed and breathed. He could not die!

"Oh, God," I prayed. "His daughter is coming. Don't let it end this way."

The door burst open. Doctors and nurses poured into the room, pushing emergency equipment. A doctor took over the manual compression of the heart. A tube was inserted through his mouth as an airway. Nurses plunged syringes of medicine into the intravenous tubing.

I connected the heart monitor. Nothing. Not a beat. My own heart pounded. "God, don't let it end like this. Not in bitterness and hatred. His daughter is coming. Let her find peace."

"Stand back," cried a doctor. I handed him the paddles for the electrical shock to the heart. He placed them on Mr. William's chest.

Over and over we tried. But nothing. No response. Mr. Williams was dead.

A nurse unplugged the oxygen. The gurgling stopped. One by one they left, grim and silent.

How could this happen? How? I stood by his bed, stunned. A cold wind rattled the window, pelting the panes with snow. Outside—everywhere—seemed a bed of blackness, cold and dark. How could I face his daughter?

When I left the room, I saw her against the wall by a water fountain. A doctor, who had been in 712 only moments before, stood at her side, talking to her, gripping her elbow. Then he moved on, leaving her slumped against the wall.

Such pathetic hurt reflected from her face. Such wounded eyes. She knew. The doctor had told her her father was gone.

I took her hand and led her into the nurses' lounge. We sat on little green stools, neither saying a word. She stared straight ahead at a pharmaceutical calendar, glass-faced, almost breakable-looking. "Janie, I'm so, so sorry," I said. It was pitifully inadequate.

"I never hated him, you know. I loved him," she said.

God, please help her, I prayed.

Suddenly she whirled toward me. "I want to see him." My first thought was, *Why put yourself through more pain? Seeing him will only make it worse.* But I got up and wrapped my arm around her. We walked slowly down the corridor to 712. Outside the door I squeezed her hand, wishing she would change her mind about going inside. She pushed open the door.

We moved to the bed, huddled together, taking small steps in unison. Janie leaned over the bed and buried her face in the sheets.

I tried not to look at her, at this sad, sad good-bye. I backed against the bedside table. My hand fell upon a scrap of yellow paper. I picked it up. I read.

My dearest Janie, I forgive you. I pray you will also forgive me. I know that you love me. I love you, too. Daddy.

The note was shaking in my hands as I thrust it toward Janie. She read it once. Then twice. Her tormented face grew radiant. Peace began to glisten in her eyes. She hugged the scrap of paper to her breast.

"Thank you, God," I whispered, looking up at the window. A few crystal stars blinked through the blackness. A snowflake hit the window and melted away, gone forever.

Life seemed as fragile as a snowflake on the window. But thank you, God, that relationships, sometimes as fragile as a snowflake, can be mended together again. But there is not a moment to spare.

I crept from the room and hurried to the phone. I would call my own father. I would say, "I love you."

Sue Kidd

The Halfhearted Gift— A Dog for David

A house is built of logs and stone, of tiles and posts and piers;
A home is built of loving deeds that stand a thousand years.

Author Unknown

"What have I gone and done?" I nervously asked myself as I peeked through the window at the fawn-colored puppy I'd bought that morning. She yipped and pawed while chewing the rope that bound her to the leg of the picnic table.

For three years I'd resisted my nine-year-old son David's pleas for a dog. The peace, beauty and order I enjoyed wouldn't mix with puppy problems. But while dusting one day, I found 30 notes. Each one read, "Dear Mom, I want a dog."

I don't want him growing up feeling deprived, the motherly part of my heart prodded. *But I don't want a dog*, my meticulous self protested.

Even so, I halfheartedly scanned the "Pets for Sale" column in the local paper. The only dogs listed were mixed breed collie/shepherds. Now, one of them serenaded the neighbors from my back yard. I tensed up expecting complaints.

For David and Tippy, named for the white tip on the end of her tail, it was instant bonding and hours of "chase the stick" and "sit, girl, heel, girl. That's a good girl." But while David attended school, the spirited puppy became bored into mischief.

It fell on me to rescue the socks, slippers and the mailman. When I tied a garden-digging Tippy to a tree, her whines got on my nerves. And I hated cleaning up after her "mistakes." "I'm going to get rid of that dog," I'd threaten.

"Just leave the messes 'til I get home," David offered anxiously, whisking Tippy outside for her obedience lesson. But the worst was yet to come.

One morning, when Tippy was seven months old, ominous snarls and growls from outside sent me running to the door. Tippy danced in circles begging to go out. As I gingerly opened the door a crack, a determined German shepherd tried to squeeze in.

"Oh, no!" I wailed, thrusting the door in his muzzle. "Tippy's in heat! This is the last straw!" So I thought.

For the next 10 days, our yard became a battleground. From behind my curtains I watched, terrified, as seven dogs at once bit, clawed and wrestled for the love of Tippy. We'd wait for a chance to sneak Tippy out the back door for a quick run. One morning she gave an extra hard tug. I stood holding a limp leash as Tippy dashed for the woods with a collie—and all the dogs from the front yard in pursuit.

Nine weeks later, to no one's surprise, Tippy presented us with a litter of pups. David was ecstatic. After counting nine noisily nursing puppies, I turned away to nurse a threatening migraine. All I could think about was Tippy's rambunctious puppyhood about to be repeated nine times—at once!

First, dogs outside. Now, dogs inside. Peace, beauty and order seemed farther away than ever.

When the puppies were five weeks old, Tippy ran a high fever and wouldn't eat. "She has mastitis," the veterinarian told us. "Her life is in danger. She cannot nurse her pups. Since she'll try to as long as they're with her, you'll have to give them away immediately."

The sudden separation sent Tippy into a frenzy. She raced from room to room, crying, scratching, sniffing. Unable to find her babies, she cuddled a fur-topped boot and tenderly lapped it.

Then she dragged home the carcasses of rabbits and squirrels, sitting guard over them in the yard. If anyone came near, she bared her teeth and growled.

When her threats marooned friends in their car in our driveway, I'd had it. Dangerous dogs, dead animals, now dear friends afraid to come to our door. This dog dominated my life. Tippy would have to go. I'd given it a fair try. David would have to understand.

The next morning I boosted Tippy into the station wagon and headed for the animal adoption center. Driving along, I glanced at Tippy through the rear view mirror. Unexpected tears trickled down my cheeks. *This is the right thing to do*, I told myself—I didn't want to think otherwise.

At the adoption center an attendant led Tippy to a cage in the showroom. Tippy cowered down in a corner, her head on a paw. Taped to the cage, a note explained her bizarre behavior. I lingered, hoping that someone braver than I would adopt Tippy while I was still there. Then I could tell David that Tippy definitely had a new home.

Almost immediately, a young couple asked for her. I stepped forward, telling the pair that I had brought Tippy in. The man, Mr. Bradley,[1] suggested that we exchange phone numbers—"just in case we have a question."

Returning home, I found David huddled on his bed, staring at a picture of Tippy. "She has a new home, Dave," I told him. "Now she'll have a chance to forget her puppies and get well. Aren't you glad for her?"

He wasn't glad. He couldn't eat. He couldn't sleep. He moped around in his room where even a ball game couldn't entice him out.

A quiet sadness settled over our house. *Where,* I wondered, *was the peace, beauty and order being dogless was supposed to bring?*

A neat and orderly house didn't seem so important anymore.

A happy one did—with laughter and running and, yes, joyful barks.

"Dear Lord," I prayed, "What have I done? Would it be fair to the Bradleys to ask for Tippy back? If they said yes, could I handle it? Please show me what to do."

When David continued to mourn the next day I felt compelled to go to the telephone. "Our son is depressed, or I'd never ask," I told Mr. Bradley. "Would you consider letting us buy Tippy back?"

"I'm sorry to hear about David," Mr. Bradley began. "Tell him that Tippy is doing just fine. There's none of the strange behavior you'd mentioned. Guess it worked to transfer her to another place. Our girls are crazy about her. I'm sure that David will be fine in a few days."

Several nights later I tried to read the newspaper but I couldn't concentrate. I knew that David was curled up as usual on his bed, hugging his picture of Tippy. I wanted

---

[1] Names have been changed to ensure privacy.

to comfort him, but how? After all, I was the one who had given away his beloved dog. I was beginning to see that unless a gift is given from the whole heart, "no leash attached," it isn't a gift at all but a burden to both the giver and receiver.

I sat on the edge of David's bed. He turned toward me and I saw that his eyes were red and swollen.

"Mom, do the Bradleys live on a busy street? Do they keep Tippy tied? Do they know how much to feed her? And . . ." a flood of tears.

Reaching for David's hand I said, "You're really concerned about Tippy, aren't you? Why don't we talk to God about her?"

David bolted upright. "Yeah! I'll pray that Tippy will come home!"

"Dave, I want you to know that I'm willing to have Tippy back. I see how much you love her. But the Bradleys love her, too, and they say she's fine over there. You want what's best for Tippy, right?"

David nodded.

"Let's not tell God what to do," I suggested. "Let's just ask him to make everything turn out right for everybody—Tippy, the Bradleys and us."

David bowed his head. "Dear Jesus, please make Tippy feel better and keep her safe, and make everybody happy no matter who gets to keep her—even if it's not us. Amen."

Then, with a deep sigh and the hint of a smile, David flopped down on his pillow and fell asleep. I marveled at how quickly peace touched his heart when he prayed.

As I spread a blanket over him, I noticed a warm feeling in my heart, too. It was as though my divided heart came together in one overwhelming desire. I'd been willing to have Tippy back, now I wanted her! It seemed that the moment David became willing to give up his dog for her sake, I wanted her back for his. I wondered whether God was preparing us for Tippy to stay, or to return. I would soon know.

The next afternoon, Mr. Bradley called. "I've been thinking about David and wondering if you still want Tippy back?"

"Oh, yes!" I almost shouted. "Yes, yes!" I knew that because of the change in my heart, Tippy could do *nothing* to make me change my mind now.

An hour later Tippy bounded in the front door. Like a nail drawn to a magnet, she zoomed straight for David. What a blending of flesh and fur, arms and paws, legs and a tail! David kept saying, "Oh, Tippy, oh, Tippy," and Tippy kept yipping and lapping David's face. Then all of us were hugging and crying as Tippy gave us loving laps.

Did peace, beauty and order return to our household? No, not exactly, but love and laughter did. And I can say with my whole heart, I'm glad!

Priscilla Larson

PEANUTS® by Charles M. Schulz

PEANUTS reprinted with permission from United Feature Syndicate, Inc.

Andy's Dream

I once wished I could erase the image from my memory: my firstborn child, the boy I loved with all my heart, glaring at me as I turned to walk away and leave him in a juvenile treatment center.

"I hate you!" he screamed, and his rage pierced me like a knife. "I never want to see you again!"

How had things gone so terribly wrong? I agonized.

And yet that image is now a reminder of how far my son has come—and of the love that helped him when his family's could not.

Andy had always been a little mischievous, so his stepdad, Dan, and I didn't worry too much when teachers complained that he disrupted the class.

"All he needs is a little discipline—and a lot of love," we told each other. We'd take him fishing when he'd been good and ground him when he hadn't, but his behavior only got worse. He'd fight with kids at school and fly into rages at home. Nothing we did—pleading, taking away privileges—had any impact on him.

In the fourth grade, Andy was diagnosed with learning disabilities and put in a special class. He'll get the attention he needs, I told myself. Each day when I returned from my job as a corrections officer at a prison, I'd ask him, "How was school?"

"Fine," he'd tell me.

So I was shocked when his school called to say he had been absent for four weeks! "But *why*, Andy?" I entreated him.

"I just hate it, that's all," he said.

I now realize that his learning disabilities must have made him feel dumb and angry at himself, so he tried to stop caring. By age 13, Andy was hanging out with a wild crowd, smoking and fighting. Again, we tried punishment, lectures—even therapy—but nothing helped. My other sons, Justin, 10, and Joshua, two, were well-behaved. I couldn't help but remember the good counsel I'd gotten as a child: from my parents, from my loving Bible-trusting grandparents. I'd tried so hard to pass along the same values. *What was I doing wrong with Andy?* I agonized. "Lord, help me!" I whispered.

One night, Andy was arrested for breaking into a home—just for kicks. "What is the *matter* with you?" I screamed. At work I'd look into the hard eyes of prisoners and think, *If Andy keeps up like this, he'll end up here.*

But it was a call from Andy's guidance counselor that finally pushed me to take action. When she'd asked him why he hadn't done his homework, he'd shrugged and said, "I don't know. I think I'll just shoot myself."

Chills raced down my spine. This has to stop *now*, I vowed. I phoned a juvenile center I'd heard about called Green Leaf. *Maybe they can help*, I thought.

After Andy's first week in treatment, his counselor called. Andy was breaking every rule. When I cried in frustration, Dan reassured me, "He'll get better." But each week, the news was the same: Andy was hostile. Andy kicked in a wall. Andy hated life.

Then one day, his counselor told me Andy had begun opening up in therapy. *It's a start*, I told myself, feeling a rush of hope. The next week, Andy called and when I heard his voice, I gasped. Miraculously, his anger was gone—and in its place was an unfamiliar lilt.

"Hey, Mom!" he said cheerfully. "I miss you. How are you?"

Each week brought even better reports. Andy was doing well in class and speaking with respect. "His progress is incredible," his counselor told me. Four months after Andy entered the program, he came home for good, and I saw in his eyes something I hadn't seen for years: joy. Now the son who had left in fury was offering to baby-sit for Joshua and do chores. Soon he returned to school—in a regular class!

I felt grateful to Green Leaf, assuming they'd worked magic. And in many ways, they had. But a year later, I found out Andy had had extra help. One night, the family was sitting around our fireplace when Andy said, "Mom, there's something I never told you."

He shared a dream he'd had about two months after arriving at Green Leaf. He was walking down a dirt road and came to an old house where an elderly woman sat on the porch, reading her Bible. "She was short and stout," he said, "with white hair in a bun and beautiful blue eyes. She was wearing a white fringed shawl with some kind of diamond pattern."

He didn't notice the tears in my eyes as he went on. "I told her I was thirsty and asked for a drink of water," he said. "She looked at me and said, 'Andy, you are going the wrong way.'

"I asked again, and she said, 'Andy, I'm your great-grandmother. And you have got to change your ways.'"

"I can't explain it, Mom," Andy said. "But the next day, I felt very different—less angry. The dream stayed with me for a long time."

I was sobbing, "Oh Andy, she *was* your great grandmother!"

As the children listened, dumbstruck, I told them how I used to sit with my grandmother on her porch as she read her Bible. She looked exactly as Andy had described. She died a month before Andy was born, and in her will she left me her favorite fringed shawl with a diamond pattern.

Though I'd spoken a little to Andy about Granny, he'd never seen a picture of her past age 30, and the shawl had been tucked away since she'd passed on.

"She must have been sent to help me!" Andy cried.

I smiled and nodded. That night as I checked on my sleeping children, I whispered, "Thank you, God—and *thank you*, Granny."

Today, Andy is 20, and a constant source of pride. He's in the National Guard's 269th Company and says that one day he'd like to have a family of his own.

"You can do whatever you want," I tell him. "After all, someone special is looking out for you."

Anne Bembry
Excerpted from *Woman's World Magazine*

Safety Blanket

When I was fresh out of the seminary, my wife, Kathy, and I moved with our two-year-old son, Nate, to a small native village in Alaska. The small three- and four-passenger planes we took on our connecting flights so terrified our little boy that he took his favorite blanket and covered his head until we set down on the small dirt landing strips. Later, during the long adjustment months that followed, when we were learning how to live in a new place among new people of a different culture, my son carried his security blanket everywhere, and it soon became soft and well-worn. He couldn't fall asleep until he had his blanket and could snuggle into its warmth.

The second year that we were in the village, I had a chance to guest speak at a mission conference in Seattle. While I was packing for the trip, my son followed me around the room, asking where I was going, and how long would I be gone, and why did I have to speak to those people, and was anyone going with me? Fine-tuning my speech in my mind, I was a little distracted and concerned about catching the small plane out of the village on time. My son seemed most worried about my having to fly out in bad weather on one of those small planes he feared so much. I reassured him that I would be fine, and I asked him to take care of his mom until I came back. With a hug at the door, I was off to the village landing strip and on to my speaking engagement.

When I got to the hotel in Seattle, I didn't have time to unpack until later that evening, and I was horrified when I opened my luggage and found my son's security blanket inside. I pictured my wife trying desperately to find the lost blanket as she prepared our son for bed. I immediately rushed to the phone to call Kathy and tell her that the blanket was in my luggage, so she could reassure our frantic son.

Kathy picked up the phone and barely had time to answer when I began to explain that the blanket was in my luggage and I had no idea how it had accidentally been packed. I was in the midst of my apology when Kathy calmed me down with the news that she already knew where the blanket was.

She told me that she had picked Nate up and held him by the window to let him watch me drive away from the house. She had suggested that they pray for "Daddy to have a safe trip." Knowing that our son would be most afraid of the small plane ride to the major airport, she prayed, "Dear Lord, please help Daddy feel safe on the little plane." When the prayer was over, our son Nate spoke up and comforted his mom. "Don't worry, Mom, I gave Daddy my blanket to keep him safe."

Reverend Dr. Bruce Humphrey

My Father

Two are better than one, because together they can work more effectively. If one of them falls down, the other can help him up, but if someone is alone and falls, it's just too bad, because there is no one to help him.

Eccles. 4:9,10

Ever since I can remember, my father would come into our bedroom bright and early every morning, turn on the overhead ceiling light, pull the covers off my brother's and my beds, and say in a very loud and distinctive voice, "You still in bed? Half the day is gone!" It was 7:00 A.M. But if you slept after that, you were just plain lazy, and he wouldn't hear of it—not with *his* sons!

My father worked 30 years in a factory and never missed a day of work until he was diagnosed with cancer and forced to retire. He was a jack-of-all-trades: carpenter, electrician, plumber, mechanic, bricklayer—there was nothing he couldn't do. And he never made a mistake; he would just say, "That's the way I wanted it!"

My father's dream was to build his own home for his

family, but we were always just a little too poor. And our "new" car was always someone else's, though it was new to us. Dad and Mom put my brother and me through college and graduate school, bought and paid for two homes, and always had food on the table, clothes on our backs and the cleanest house in town. But my father never got to build his own home, as he had always dreamed of doing.

When I was 35 years old and the father of two daughters, my wife and I decided to build our own home. This was going to be a true milestone in our family's history! I was a college graduate with a master's degree, and now I was building my own home. It didn't get any better than that for an Italian family who "came over on the boat" in the early 1900s.

My wife and I finalized blueprints for our house and hired a contractor. I'll never forget the day I went to my father's home to share the news. I was so proud that I thought I would burst. And I believed my dad would be just as proud and happy for me. Well, that's not exactly what happened.

My father was now 65 years old and had just beaten cancer for the second time. He looked up at me from the kitchen table and said, "Boy, I strongly think you shouldn't do this." Talk about taking the wind out of my sails—this wasn't the way it was supposed to go. I was going to build the home he had always wanted to build, and he should have been excited for me.

I just stood there, stunned, and asked him why he thought that. Dad said very emphatically, "You don't have enough money or skill to build a house, and I'm too old now." Of course I disagreed, and I said I was going to do it anyway, with or without his blessing. Big talk from a guy who couldn't even drive a nail.

Dad said I didn't have enough experience and that building the home was only half the job. There were a million other things to finish that I hadn't even considered. He said it would take us 10 years to completely finish the home we wanted to build. My mother, on the other hand, told us to do what we wanted and wished us good luck.

We began with getting a loan from the bank and lining up all the contractors and subcontractors. It didn't take long for me to have to eat crow. I came up $3,000 short for securing my loan and we hadn't even started in. So with my hat in hand, I went to the "old man" and very humbly asked if I could borrow $3,000. I assured my father I would pay him back on his terms any way he wanted it. Dad was sitting at the kitchen table with my mother, having a cup of coffee. He said to my mother, who is the financier of the family, "Write the boy a check for $5,000." I thought he misunderstood me, so I repeated myself. He said he had heard me, and that I was the one who didn't understand. Dad said he had already anticipated I'd come up short, and he and my mother had decided to give me $5,000 as a gift to get us started.

Tears were now flowing down my face. I saw an old man who had never missed a day's work in 30 years giving his hard-earned money away to a son with big ideas and little money to back them up. My mother just got out the checkbook and wrote me a check as my father requested.

But our problems had just begun. The contractor started building in February. My wife and I are both school teachers, and neither of us could be there in the daytime to supervise the job. So I did what I always did: I went and got the "old man" and told him to run the show! Now *he* got tears in *his* eyes, and I had my own foreman— good for me, bad for all the contractors and workers. If it wasn't perfect, he would make them start over and do it again. He was their worst nightmare, and when they threatened to quit, I just reminded them who was writing the checks, and that the "old man" was calling the shots, period. Everyone began to work hard, fast—and politely—until the last check was written.

But my problems still weren't over. One day the money was gone, and so were the workers—and my house was only three-fourths finished. The night after the last worker left, I went to bed in my new and unfinished home. The children had been in bed for hours, and my wife had fallen asleep earlier from exhaustion. I was lying awake, staring at the ceiling and thinking, *What in the world am I going to do now—no money and no skill!* I didn't sleep all night. At 7:00 A.M. sharp the next day, I heard a car coming down the gravel road of my dead-end street and saw headlights shining through my bedroom window. I jumped out of bed like a little kid on Christmas morning, ran down three flights of steps with my pajama bottoms on and threw open the basement door. There was my dad, bigger than life, with his ball cap on, and all the tools, shovels and picks he could fit into his brand new car—and it finally was his own new car. As I stood there barefoot in my pajama bottoms, he just looked at me and said, "Hey, boy, you still in bed? Half the day is gone, and we've got a lot of work to do!"

With a lump in my throat and tears in my eyes, I just stood there, speechless. I was never so glad or so relieved to see the "old man." Now I knew everything was going to be okay. And why shouldn't it be? Dad had always been there when I needed him!

Five years later, my new home is completely finished inside and out, all three floors and the landscaping. And my dad never missed a day's work at my house in five years. The "old man" is the most hard-headed, hard-nosed and loving man I've ever met. I hope he lives forever, but if he doesn't, I know where to find him. He'll be fixing the golden gates in Heaven.

Tom Suriano

The Bible

Dear Abby:

A young man from a famous family was about to graduate from high school. It was the custom in that affluent neighborhood for the parents to give the graduate an automobile. Bill and his father had spent months looking at cars, and the week before graduation they found the perfect car. Bill was certain that the car would be his on graduation night.

Imagine his disappointment when, on the eve of his graduation, Bill's father handed him a gift-wrapped Bible! Bill was so angry, he threw the Bible down and stormed out of the house. He and his father never saw each other again. It was the news of his father's death that brought Bill home again.

As he sat one night, going through his father's possessions that he was to inherit, he came across the Bible his father had given him. He brushed away the dust and opened it to find a cashier's check, dated the day of his graduation, in the exact amount of the car they had chosen together.

Beckah Fink

Graduation Car

A high school senior went to his father in January of the year he was to graduate. "Dad," he said, "for graduation, I think I deserve a new car."

His father thought a minute and replied, "Son, I'll get you that new car, but first you must do three things—bring your grades up, read the Bible more and get a haircut."

In May, just before graduation, the son went to his father and asked, "How am I doing? Am I going to get a new car for graduation?"

"Son, you've brought your grade average up from a C to an A. That's great," answered the father. "I've also noticed that you've been studying the Scriptures every morning before school. That's wonderful. But you still haven't had a haircut."

"But, Dad," the son retorted, "while studying the Bible, I've noticed that Moses is always depicted in the illustrations as having long hair. Even Jesus had long hair."

At that, the father replied, "Son, you must remember that Moses and Jesus walked everywhere they went—and so will you, unless you get a haircut!"

Author Unknown
Submitted by Joanne Duncalf

I made the mistake of telling him to get his hair out of his eyes.

Home for the Holidays

Twenty-eight years ago I gave birth to a son. I was 18 and my boyfriend was 22. I was right out of high school, had no job, and my boyfriend was working for minimum wage. At the time, my family was struggling with some personal problems, and I didn't want to burden them with my unexpected pregnancy. Most important, I wanted the baby to be raised in a good home, with two parents who could care for him and give him everything he needed. So I made the difficult decision to have the baby on my own, and then to give him up for adoption.

I decided to stage a little argument with my mother so I would have an excuse to move out. She thought I was just asserting my independence, but I was actually very close to my family and it was hard to leave them. I had an older sister who was married with four children and a younger sister who was 16. I missed them all so much. After I moved out, I talked to my family on the phone, but always managed to avoid seeing them when holidays or get-togethers came around.

On February 24, 1966, I gave birth to a boy. I was never allowed to see him, and I spent three days talking with the chaplain, making sure I was doing the right thing. He convinced me that adoption was best for the baby, and so I gave up my son, praying he would get wonderful, caring parents. I cried from morning to night for weeks after, and I could never get him off my mind and heart. I prayed for him all the time.

In September, 1966, his father and I got married. We had two sons, Robert and Gary. We were truly blessed, but something was missing in our lives and our marriage. In 1971, my husband and I started having marital problems and we separated. After everything we had been through, I was devastated. To top it off, I was pregnant with our third son, Stephen, at the time.

In 1972, I found Jesus Christ as my savior. I persuaded my husband to seek counseling, and he, too, was led to the Lord. We put our marriage back together, and it was stronger than ever. I continued to pray every day for the son that I had never met and asked God to bring him home to us some day, if it was his will.

Eight years ago while hunting, my husband was struck by lightning. He was very close to death, but the Lord saved him and brought him back to the family. Later, he often said, "There is something more I haven't done yet in my life with the Lord."

In April of 1994, my husband and I were talking one morning and he said to me, "You know, Linda, he is just at the age where he will start looking for us." Only a week before I had been thinking just the same thing, and I was amazed my husband had been having the same thoughts. He and I had never talked about our first son. Emotionally, it was just too hard for me. My husband had wanted to look for him a few times, but after we discussed it, we decided it would be unfair to show up after so many years and say, "Here we are."

On May 1, 1994, at 9:30 in the morning, the doorbell

rang. Stephen answered the door, and a young man, accompanied by a young lady, asked to speak to me. I came to the door and there stood a tall, dark and handsome young man who had the family eyes. My heart went to my stomach and I thought, *Could this be my son?* A voice inside me countered immediately, *Don't be stupid. You wanted this for too long.* Instead I asked, "May I help you?"

He said he was here to talk to me about a private matter and I asked, "What?" My husband wasn't home and I was still in my nightgown.

"I would like to talk to you alone outside," he answered, "and I can wait for you to get dressed."

My heart was pounding as I was pulling on clothes, and I went outside to an equally shaken young man. I said, "What is this about?"

He took a very deep breath and said, "Twenty-eight years ago I was adopted."

I started crying, threw my arms around him and couldn't say anything except, "Oh, my God!" about 50 times.

"Are you healthy?" I asked him. "Have you been happy? Did you have good parents?"

I couldn't believe that the day I had prayed for all those years had arrived. I was trembling and could feel the presence of the Lord between us. It was as if he was in the middle of us saying, "Ask and you shall receive."

"I married your father," I then told him, "and we have been married 27 years. You have three brothers."

He asked, "Was that my brother who answered the door?"

"That's your baby brother, Stephen."

I decided we had to tell Stephen the story right away, so I asked him to come outside for a minute. When I told him who the young man was, Stephen just said, "No." He wouldn't believe it.

Then Robert held out his hand and said, "Stephen, I'm Robert, your brother." Then Stephen said he knew immediately. He felt a love for Robert instantly, as if he had known him all his life. We then called the two other boys, and they all came over to the house. Everyone was in shock.

When my husband came home from Sunday school a few hours later, he wondered why all the cars were out front. I went out to meet him and said, "Bob, we have a visitor. Someone we have waited 28 years to meet. Our son!" When Bob walked into the house, Robert stood up and gave him his hand. But Bob grabbed him and hugged him, and began to cry.

Linda Vlcek

4

ON FAITH

A life of faith . . . enables us to see God in everything and it holds the mind in a state of readiness for whatever may be His will.

François Fenelon

All that I have seen readies me to trust the Creator for all I have not seen.

Ralph Waldo Emerson

I don't really think that T-shirt is necessary now that you're up here.

Reprinted with permission from Dan Rosandich.

God Calling

For he will give his angels charge of you, to guard you in all your ways . . .

Ps. 91:11

It had always been Ken Gaub's goal to help those who were hurting. "Some people just need a little boost, and I wanted to influence their lives in a positive way," he says. He became a traveling missionary and with his family, conducted crusades not only throughout America but in many foreign countries. He established a magazine, a radio and television ministry and a youth outreach program.

But sometimes even preachers get drained and discouraged, and they wonder if they should consider another line of work. That was how Ken felt one day in the 1970s as he, his wife, Barbara, and their children drove their two ministry buses down I-75 just south of Dayton, Ohio. *God, am I doing any good, traveling around like this, telling people about you?* he wondered silently. *Is this what you want me to do?*

"Hey, Dad let's get some pizza!" one of Ken's sons suggested. Still lost in thought, Ken turned off at the next exit, Route 741, where one sign after another advertised a wide variety of fast food. *A sign,* Ken mused. *That's what I need, God, a sign.*

Ken's son and daughter-in-law had already maneuvered the second bus into a pizza parlor's parking lot, and they stood waiting as Ken pulled up. The rest of the family bounced down the steps. Ken sat staring into space.

"Coming?" Barbara asked.

"I'm not really hungry," Ken told her. "I'll stay out here and stretch my legs."

Barbara followed the others into the restaurant, and Ken stepped outside, closed the bus doors, and looked around. Noticing a Dairy Queen, he strolled over, bought a soft drink, and ambled back, still pondering. He was exhausted. But were his doldrums a sign of permanent burnout?

A persistent ringing broke Ken's concentration. The jangle was coming from a pay telephone in a booth at the service station right next to the Dairy Queen. As Ken approached the booth, he looked to see if anyone in the station was coming to answer the phone. But the attendant continued his work, seemingly oblivious to the noise.

Why doesn't someone answer it? Ken wondered, growing irritated. *What if it is an emergency?*

The insistent ringing went on. Ten rings. Fifteen. . . .

Curiosity overcame Ken's lethargy. Walking to the booth, he lifted the receiver. "Hello?"

"Long-distance call for Ken Gaub," came the voice of the operator.

Ken was stunned. "You're crazy!" he said. Then, realizing his rudeness, he tried to explain. "This can't be! I was just walking down the road here, and the phone was ringing—"

The operator ignored his ramblings. "Is Ken Gaub there?" she asked. "I have a long-distance phone call for him."

Was this a joke? Automatically, Ken smoothed his hair for the *Candid Camera* crew that must surely appear. But no one came. His family was eating pizza in a randomly selected restaurant just a few yards from where he stood. And no one else knew he was here.

"I have a long-distance call for Ken Gaub, sir," the operator said again, obviously reaching the limits of her patience. "Is he there or isn't he?"

"Operator, I'm Ken Gaub," Ken said, still unable to make sense of it.

"Are you sure?" the operator asked, but just then, Ken heard another woman's voice on the telephone.

"Yes, that's him, Operator!" she said. "Mr. Gaub, I'm Millie from Harrisburg, Pennsylvania. You don't know me, but I'm desperate. Please help me."

"What can I do for you?" Ken asked. The operator hung up.

Millie began to weep, and Ken waited patiently for her to regain control. Finally she explained: "I was about to kill myself, and I started to write a suicide note. Then I began to pray and tell God I really didn't want to do this." Through her desolation, Millie remembered seeing Ken on television. If she could just talk to that nice, kindly minister, the one with the understanding attitude. . . .

"I knew it was impossible because I didn't know how to reach you," Millie went on, calmer now. "So I started to finish the note. And then some numbers came into my mind, and I wrote them down." She began to weep again. Silently Ken prayed for the wisdom to help her.

"I looked at those numbers," Millie continued tearfully, "and I thought—wouldn't it be wonderful if I had a miracle from God, and he has given me Ken's phone number? I can't believe I'm talking to you. Are you in your office in California?"

"I don't have an office in California," Ken explained. "It's in Yakima, Washington."

"Then where are you?" Millie asked, puzzled.

Ken was even more bewildered. "Millie, don't you know? You made the call."

"But I don't know what area this is." Millie had dialed the long-distance operator and given the numbers to her, making it a person-to-person call. And somehow she had found Ken in a parking lot in Dayton, Ohio.

Ken gently counseled the woman. Soon she met the one who would lead her out of her situation into a new life. Then he hung up the phone, still dazed. Would his family believe this incredible story? Perhaps he shouldn't tell anyone about it.

But he had prayed for an answer, and he had received just what he needed—a renewed sense of purpose, a glimpse of the value of his work, an electrifying awareness of God's concern for each of his children—all in an encounter that could only have been arranged by his heavenly Father.

Ken's heart overflowed with joy. "Barb," he exclaimed as his wife climbed back into the bus, "you won't believe this! God knows where I am!"

Joan Wester Anderson
Submitted by Nancy Leahy

Reprinted with permission from Johnny Hart and Creators Syndicate, Inc.

Invisible Guardians

Yea, though I walk through the valley of the shadow of death, I will fear no evil, for Thou art with me.

Ps. 23:4

In 1980, 25-year-old Dave Carr of Bangor, Maine, started to feel one of those inner urges that defy logic and reason. He had a strong impulse to open a gathering place for the homeless or people down on their luck. "I thought of providing them with a soft drink or coffee and something to eat, along with a hug and some words of encouragement," Dave says. "Most important, I wanted them to learn about the Bible, and hopefully to accept Jesus into their hearts."

This "heavenly nudge" grew stronger over the next several years. But Dave argued with it. How could *he* open such a place? True, he had always lived a life of service and had helped on similar projects through the church. But he was a truck driver, not a minister or psychologist, and he had a young family to support, with nothing left over for rent on a drop-in center. The whole idea was impossible.

But Dave continued to think about it. Street people led hard lives, he knew; not only were they hungry and often cold in Maine's hard climate, they were vulnerable to threats from those stronger than they. Recently a man had been murdered in the middle of the night and thrown over the bridge into the Penobscot River. The police had not found his attackers. And without some kind of safe oasis, Dave thought, such a thing was sure to happen again.

Finally Dave drove to downtown Bangor about 10:00 one September evening. It wouldn't hurt to at least *look* at possible sites. "I need nighttime hours to think quietly, and I thought it would be easier to check out storefronts without being distracted by traffic," he says. He parked and walked through the neighborhoods, looking at abandoned buildings. Some possibilities, but nothing definite.

At 1:00 A.M. Dave was ready to call it quits. But he hadn't investigated Brewer yet, the city that lies across the Penobscot River from Bangor. He would look at a few sites there, then head home.

The street was deserted as Dave started walking up the bridge. Then a car approached from Brewer. As its headlights caught him, the car slowed. Uneasily Dave realized that there were three men inside. Despite the cool night air, their windows were rolled down. "Let's throw him over!" Dave heard one of them say. The car stopped, its doors opened, and all three jumped out and came toward him.

Horrified, Dave suddenly recalled the murder of the street person. It had been on this bridge! Had these men done it? He would be no match for them, he knew his only option was to pray that he survived the icy water. But as he looked down, he realized that the tide had gone out, and only rocks and dirt were directly below him. "God, help me," Dave murmured.

Immediately he felt a presence near him, something

unseen but definitely *there.* A warm safe feeling flooded him. His fear vanished, and he knew, without knowing quite how he knew, that he was not alone.

Now the men were almost upon Dave. All three were large, muscular—and leering. "Get him!" one shouted. Suddenly they stopped. "They all stared at me, then looked to the right and left of me," Dave says. "They seemed terrified. One said, 'Oh, my God!' They turned and began shoving one another to get back to the car. And when they sped away—it sounded like they tore the transmission right out—I could still hear them cursing and yelling, 'Run, run!'"

Dave stood for a moment on the deserted bridge, basking in the warmth that still surrounded him. What was it? What had the men seen? Whatever it was, it had shielded him from certain death. "Thank you, God," he whispered.

He felt exalted, so buoyant that he decided to go on to Brewer and finish his search. As he crossed the rest of the bridge, Danny, a friend of his, drove by, honked at him, and kept going, unmindful of Dave's narrow escape. Dave waved, still surrounded by peace.

A while later, Dave came across some derelicts standing on a Brewer street corner. But as he approached, they all fell back.

One put his hands over his eyes. "You're shining!" he whispered. "It hurts to look!"

"I can feel the Holy Spirit all around you!" said another, as he inched away.

Dave was awed. It was *heaven's* glow surrounding him, it had to be! But he wasn't absolutely positive until the next day, when he ran into Danny again.

"Sorry I didn't stop for you last night on the bridge," Danny said, "But I had passengers and I never could have fit all of you in my car, too."

"All of us?" Dave asked, puzzled.

"Those three huge guys walking with you," Danny explained. "They were the biggest people I had ever seen. One must have been at least seven feet tall!"

Dave never resisted a heavenly nudge again. He opened and funded a Bangor coffeehouse in 1986, which is still running today under a friend's management. At least 100 people are fed every night, with coffee, hugs— and the word of the Lord.

Joan Wester Anderson

"That was fast."

A Reason to Heal

I hope that someday soon you'll come to the tea my husband, Dave, and I serve in the Victorian-style house we built near the Cajon Pass in Southern California.

When you arrive, you will be welcome to browse. Surely someone will notice the unusual frame around the photo of a handsome young man with twinkling eyes, black hair and a dashing mustache. The young man is my only child, Bill. The frame is a Victorian-era mourning frame. The crosses carved into the wood are appropriate because of Bill's faith; the anchors because he was in the Navy. Bill died five years ago during Operation Desert Storm, when he was 28 years old.

Bill and I were not only son and mother, we were best friends. Perhaps because his father left us early on, we relied on each other a lot. We also had fun. Bill had a sharp sense of humor, and I loved his jokes. Sometimes he made me burst out laughing with just a look. He was also protective of me. When I had trouble getting out of a snowy driveway while we were living in Michigan, my little boy looked at me seriously and vowed, "When I grow up, Mom, I'll get you snow tires."

Snow tires weren't necessary when we moved to California, where I met and married a wonderful widower, Dave Kincaid. Bill loved him, and the three of us became a team. Life was suddenly the way I had always dreamed it could be.

My son had a brilliant mind and enjoyed working with electronics. The Navy provided him with the perfect career. Although what he was doing was often top secret and he could tell us little, he seemed to enjoy his work. He was based in San Diego, two hours away, and many times the phone rang at our home in Apple Valley, with Bill saying, "Mom, it's me. I'm coming home on leave, and bringing a buddy!" That same afternoon, he would stick his head into my vintage-clothing store. "Hi Mom. This is my friend Joe. We'll see you at home for supper!"

In the summer of 1990, he re-enlisted. The Persian Gulf conflict was heating up. Bill spent the week before he left finishing all the projects he had started around the house. For some reason, he made sure his papers were in order, and said a special good-bye to his girlfriend.

At midnight on the eve of his leaving, I found him still working on a new electric-eye light over the garage. "Bill, don't worry about it," I said. "You'll be back in no time." But he insisted on installing it for me.

He called every Sunday, and things always sounded fine. So I thought nothing was strange that August Friday when I looked through the picture window as a van pulled up in front of the house. *A repairman, probably,* I thought.

The van doors opened and several men got out, Navy men: an officer, a chaplain and an enlisted man in his dress whites—there's only one reason that a configuration of Navy personnel comes to your house.

I panicked. I started pacing up and down the hallway, shouting, "Oh, no! No, no!" Dave wasn't home; I felt so alone.

The doorbell rang. Still I paced, somehow thinking that if I didn't answer, it wouldn't be true.

When I heard the knocks, I knew I had to go. I opened the door and said to the solemn-faced officer, "Don't you tell me what you're going to tell me!"

"I'm sorry, ma'am," he replied, "I have to."

Bill was dead. My only son was gone.

As an officer was telling me what details he could, a strange thing happened. I felt a warm pressure, like someone laying a hand on my shoulder. And from behind me, I heard the words, "He's all right". An unexpected calm descended and carried me through the next few days and the funeral.

There comes a time after a personal tragedy that's especially hard: After all the fuss, everyone else's life goes back to normal, yet yours remains shattered. The devastating news of my son's death kept coming back to me in different ways, each one as if I were hearing it for the first time. As brilliant as Bill was, he had an absent-minded habit of losing his sunglasses. When the Navy returned his personal effects—a shiny new pair of sunglasses on top—I wanted to scream. Now I had Bill's sunglasses, but I didn't have Bill.

I closed my store in Apple Valley. I put my antiques and clothing collection into storage. Time stretched on unbearably. Even my husband could not comfort me. Nothing mattered anymore.

One day I decided to take a drive, just to get out. "Use the Nissan," Dave said. "I had new tires put on." I got in the car and took off alone.

As I drove, I turned to God in anguish, "Why?" I asked. "What plan of yours is so important that you had to take my only child?" I wondered if God cared that my heart was broken, my life in ruins. Then, as I approached the Cajon Pass, there was a loud pop. One of the tires had blown.

I managed to steer the car off the road. Traffic was heavy; I was lucky I hadn't caused an accident. I went to a call box and asked the operator to contact my husband. Then I walked back to the car for a long wait. One thought was in my mind: If Bill were here, he would help me. *If Bill were here . . .* I started to cry.

"Excuse me!" I heard a voice say and I wiped away my tears. Across a barbed-wire fence was a wide-open bumpy field. There sat a small car, and in front of it a young man waved at me. He looked a lot like Bill.

"Can I help you?" he asked as he hopped the fence easily. "I didn't want to startle you."

I looked at his car strangely placed in the field. Why hadn't I noticed it before?

"You need help," he said, inspecting the blown tire. "Let me take care of this."

"Where are you from?" I asked.

"Around here."

"I could have sworn I knew everyone." *Especially someone who reminds me so much of Bill,* I thought.

The young man took the lug nuts off the tire and removed it. "I'm going to have to get this patched," he said. "There's a garage over the hill. It won't take long."

He put his sunglasses on the hood next to me. "So you know I'll be back." He winked and hopped across the fence to his car. As he drove into the distance, I wondered how his small car could handle the rough field.

Before long, he was back. "You sure can hop a fence," I said. He flashed a big smile, and as he put on the patched tire, we talked. I wound up telling him about Bill's death, and how hard it was to get through.

"Yeah, I know," he said gently, "It's rough."

The young man finished tightening the nuts, looked up at me, and said with authority, "Remember, your son is fine." Instantly I was bathed with the same sort of peace as the time I had felt the hand on my shoulder and heard the whispered words, "He's all right." I felt as though I had been given a gift.

When Dave arrived, I introduced the two men. They shook hands, then Dave gave me a bear hug. For a split second I buried my face in his neck. We both turned to wave good-bye to the young man.

But, to our amazement we found he wasn't on either side of the fence. There was no car in the field.

Dave and I looked into each other's eyes, both of us trying to take in what had happened. "Bill's okay," I said, breaking our silence. "He's in Heaven, and he's fine."

Neither of us had any doubt who the mysterious young man was. When we returned to the dealership where Dave had bought the tires, the manager shook his head in confusion. "There's no reason this tire should have blown," he said. "I don't get it." We did.

The heavenly reassurance didn't take away the ache of not having Bill here on earth, but the sense of peace, of being loved and cared for, stayed with me. I realized I had to make a conscious decision to get past my grief and go on with life. And I knew which choice God, and Bill, would want me to make.

Shortly thereafter, Dave and I bought property near the Cajon Pass and built our house, along with a workshop for the hats I make, and a small "museum" for the antiques and vintage clothing we can't fit in the house. And I began giving teas, for a dozen or so people at a time. I dress in Victorian clothing, with a neat Gibson girl hairdo, to entertain my guests. It's fun to follow the customs as if we're actually having tea one hundred years ago.

When my guests ask about Bill, I tell my story. I'll never forget one young woman who came with her mother. They made it clear that they had come only to see the antiques; they sat off by themselves. But as I was explaining about the mourning frame, I saw the young woman, Maureen, listening intently. About a month later, a beautiful woman called out to me when I was downtown. "Hello, Mrs. Kincaid!" she said. "Do you remember me?"

"Maureen?" I asked, incredulous.

"I have to thank you," she said, "and explain. Not long before the tea, my fiancée died. I thought I would never accept it. But when I considered what you said—that we have to make a conscious decision—I realized that if you could do it, I could too!"

God had sent his angel not only to show me he cared, but so I could, in turn show others I understood, and cared. That seems to be the angel's message: God loves you. Pass it on.

Barbara Kincaid

Expect a Miracle

For with God nothing shall be impossible.

Luke 1:37

Wherever I go, I carry a small gray stone. It's in my purse all day, tucked under my pillow each night. And on it are painted three simple words: *Expect a miracle.* I did expect one, and against all odds, that's exactly what I was given.

A year ago, when I first had bloating and pains in my pelvis and lower abdomen, I passed it off as side effects from the estrogen I was taking for menopause. But driving home one day, the pains got so wrenching I nearly crashed my car.

This can't be normal! I thought in fear. I'm a nurse, so I raced to my medical books as soon as I got home. Almost as if I were directed, I picked one from the shelf and opened straight to the page on ovarian cancer. A chill raced down my spine as I read the symptoms—bloating, pain, frequent urination . . . I had every one.

"We'll have to run some tests," my doctor said after examining me. "But it could be ovarian cancer."

Driving home, I felt so scared I could barely breathe. And when I walked in the door, my husband, Rich, took one look at me—and hugged me close. "We just need to pray," he told me.

But my test results were terrifying: I had a large tumor, and a blood test that indicated the possible presence of ovarian cancer read 462—normal is 30. *I'm going to die!* I wept.

That night, I forced myself to stay calm as I told our two teenage daughters that I had cancer. But when I saw the fear in their eyes, my heart nearly broke in two. So I wouldn't burden them with my fear, I said I had to run to the store and slipped out to my car, tears coursing down my cheeks.

In my mind, I pictured all the faces I loved: Rich, the girls, our five other children through previous marriages, parents, friends . . .

Oh, God, please don't take my life, I pleaded. *I still have so much to live for.*

"Don't do this alone," my priest told me when I cried to him. "Let others help you." And the next day, all those faces I pictured the night before were in my home, surrounding me with their love.

Their love carried me through my surgery to remove the tumor, along with my fallopian tubes and ovaries. But I was far from out of danger. "You still have only a 15 percent chance of making it," one doctor told me. "Your only hope is chemotherapy."

Half crazed with fear, I began making frantic bargains: if you heal me, God, I'll be a better wife, a better mom, a better person. Just give me a second chance.

I had six chemo treatments, one every three weeks. Sometimes I thought I wouldn't make it through them, they made me so weak and sick. But when I most needed a boost, a friend would show up with dinner or drop by to take the girls out. Folks even organized fund-raisers to help us pay my medical bills!

Buoyed by so much love, I knew I owed it to others—and to myself—to stay optimistic. So I read books on healing and listened to tapes that helped me visualize getting well. *I'm not giving in,* I'd think.

Rich was my strength whenever I felt afraid, praying with me and holding me. My daughters stayed positive, too. Lindsay, 14, and Sarah, 16, refused to believe I would die. "You're going to be all right, Mom," they'd say.

But after my last treatment, I faced a terrifying moment of truth. Doctors were going to take 100 biopsies, one in every place they feared the cancer might have spread.

"To be honest, we don't expect to find you're cancer-free," they warned. And if the chemo hadn't destroyed the cancer cells, my chances for survival were slim.

I could feel terror creeping into every fiber of my being. *I can't give up hope now,* I thought fiercely. So before leaving for the hospital, I opened the drawer where I kept a good-luck symbol a friend had given me, a small, hand-painted rock. *Expect a miracle,* I read, then slipped the stone in my purse.

The stone was still in my purse the next day, when I opened my eyes after surgery to find a pretty woman with dark hair and a white dress leaning over my hospital bed.

She must be a nurse, I thought. But she had no pills in her hand, no blood pressure monitor to hook up. Instead, she looked at me kindly and asked, "Are you the one who's looking for a miracle?"

Confused, I stammered, "Yes." *But how did she know?* I wondered. Then, before the question left my lips, she'd vanished.

The next morning, the woman in white was beside me once again. In her hand was a plaque that read: *Miracles*

Happen Every Day. "Is this what you're looking for?" she asked gently.

Tears sprang to my eyes, but before I could say a word, once again she was gone. As I gazed at the plaque she'd given me, I felt a funny tingly sensation throughout my body . . .

"Dawn," Rich said as I groggily opened my eyes, "the results of the biopsies are in. They were negative—each and every one!"

I'll never know whether the woman was a nurse—or an angel. But it doesn't matter. She came to let me know that hopes are never foolish, prayers never wasted.

Today, I'm 49 and cancer-free. And each time I hug my daughters, share a quiet moment with Rich or just watch autumn leaves scuttle across the sidewalk, I remember again that every new day is a blessing, a new chance to expect a miracle.

Dawn Stobbe
As told to Meg Lundstrom
Woman's World *Magazine*

Perfect Freedom

As one who has served time in prison and has since spent most of my life working in them, I'll never forget the most unusual prison I've ever visited.

Called Humaita Prison, it is in Sao Jose dos Campos in Brazil. Formerly a government prison, it is now operated by Prison Fellowship Brazil as an alternative prison, without armed guards or high-tech security. Instead, it is run on the Christian principles of love of God and respect for men.

Humaita has only two full-time staff; the rest of the work is done by the 730 inmates serving time for everything from murder and assault to robbery and drug-related crimes. Every man is assigned another inmate to whom he is accountable. In addition, each prisoner is assigned a volunteer mentor from the outside who works with him during his term and after his release. Prisoners take classes on character development and are encouraged to participate in educational and religious programs.

When I visited this prison, I found the inmates smiling—particularly the murderer who held the keys, opened the gates and let me in. Wherever I walked, I saw

men at peace. I saw clean living areas. I saw people working industriously. The walls were decorated with motiva-
tional sayings and Scripture.

Humaita has an astonishing record. Its recidivism rate
is 4 percent, compared to 75 percent in the rest of Brazil.
How is that possible?

I saw the answer when my inmate guide escorted me to
the notorious cell once used for solitary punishment.
Today, he told me, it always houses the same inmate. As
we reached the end of the long concrete corridor and he
put the key into the lock, he paused and asked, "Are you
sure you want to go in?"

"Of course," I replied impatiently. "I've been in isolation
cells all over the world." Slowly he swung open the massive door, and I saw the prisoner in that cell: a crucifix,
beautifully carved—Jesus, hanging on the cross.

"He's doing time for the rest of us," my guide said softly.

Charles W. Colson

Tell the World for Me

We love, because God first loved us.

1 John 4:19

Some 14 years ago, I stood watching my university students file into the classroom for the opening session in my "Theology of Faith" class. That was the first day I saw Tommy. He was combing his long flaxen hair, which hung six inches below his shoulders. I know it's what's in your head, not on it, that counts; but at that time I was unprepared for Tommy and wrote him off as strange—very strange.

Tommy turned out to be the atheist in residence in my course. He constantly objected to or smirked at the possibility of an unconditionally loving God. We lived in relative peace for one semester, although at times he was a pain in the back pew. At the end of the course when he turned in his final exam, he asked in a slightly cynical tone, "Do you ever think I'll find God?"

I decided on a little shock therapy. "No!" I said emphatically.

"Oh," he responded. "I thought that was the product you were pushing."

I let him get five steps from the door, then called out, "Tommy! I don't think you'll ever find him, but I am certain that he will find you!" Tommy just shrugged and left. I felt slightly disappointed that he had missed my clever line.

Later I heard that Tom had graduated and I was duly grateful. Then came a sad report: Tommy had terminal cancer. Before I could search him out, he came to me. When he walked into my office, his body was badly wasted, and his long hair had fallen out because of chemotherapy. But his eyes were bright and his voice was firm for the first time in a long time. "Tommy, I've thought about you so often. I hear you are sick," I blurted out.

"Oh yes, very sick. I have cancer. It's a matter of weeks."

"Can you talk about it?"

"Sure, what would you like to know?"

"What's it like to be 24 and know you are dying?"

"Well, it could be worse!"

"Like what?"

"Well, like being 50 and having no values or ideals. Like being 50 and thinking that booze, seducing women and making money are the real biggies in life.

"But what I really came to see you about is something you said to me on the last day of class. I asked if you ever thought I would find God and you said no, which surprised me. Then you said, 'But he will find you.' I thought about that a lot, even though my search was hardly intense at that time. But when the doctors removed a lump from my groin and told me it was malignant, I got serious about locating God. And when the malignancy spread to my vital organs, I really began banging against the doors of heaven. But nothing happened. Well, one day I woke up, and instead of throwing a few more futile appeals to a God who may or may not exist, I just quit. I decided I didn't care about God and the afterlife—or anything else for that matter.

"I decided to spend what time I had left doing something more profitable. I thought about you and something you had said in one of your lectures: 'The essential sadness is to go through life without loving.' But it would be equally sad to leave this world without telling those you love that you have loved them. So I began with the hardest one: my dad.

"He was reading the paper when I approached him. 'Dad, I would like to talk to you.' 'Well, talk,' he replied. 'I mean, it's really important, Dad.' The newspaper came down three slow inches. 'What is it?' he asked. 'Dad, I love you. I just wanted you to know that.'"

Tom smiled at me and said with obvious satisfaction, as though he felt a warm and secret joy flowing inside him, "The newspaper fluttered to the floor. Then my father did two things I couldn't remember him doing before. He cried and he hugged me. And we talked all night even though he had to go to work the next day.

"It was easier with my mom and little brother. They cried with me, too, and we hugged each other and shared things we had been keeping secret for so many years. I was only sorry that I had waited so long. Here I was, in the shadow of death, and I was just beginning to open up to all the people I had actually been close to.

"Then one day I turned around and God was there. He didn't come to me when I pleaded with him. Apparently, God does things his own way at his own hour. The important thing is you were right. He found me even after I stopped looking for him."

"Tommy," I gasped, "I think you're saying something much more universal than you realize. You are saying that the surest way of finding God is not to make him a private possession or an instant consolation in time of need, but rather by opening up to love.

"Tom, could I ask you a favor? Would you come to my 'Theology of Faith' class and tell my students what you just told me?"

Though we scheduled a date, he never made it. Of course, his life was not really ended by his death, it was only changed. He made the great step from faith into vision. He found a life far more beautiful than the eye of man has ever seen or the mind of man has ever imagined.

Before Tom died, we talked one last time. "I'm not going to make it to your class," he said.

"I know, Tom."

"Will you tell them for me? Will you tell . . . the whole world for me?"

"I will, Tom. I will tell them."

John Powell

Thank You, Miss Evridge

Perhaps you've seen her. She may be a member of your church, a soloist in your choir. It's possible she's on the mission field. For 10 years, she had a profound influence on my life. Then she vanished.

If you know her, tell her I said thanks. Thanks. That word seems inadequate for someone who contributed so much to molding my character and shaping my future. But I would like somehow to express my gratitude.

I'd write her a letter or pick up the phone and tell her thank you in a more personal way, if I could. Several years ago, she mailed me her wedding announcement, but I lost it. In so doing, I also lost my only contact with her. I know she has a new name now, but she will always be "Miss Evridge" to me.

Moving up to junior high school was one of the most frightening experiences of my life. I'd heard horror stories about ninth-graders who lurked in the shadows to jump seventh-grade guys and take off their pants. I'd heard that the vice principal toted a paddle that was four feet long, and that the teachers hated kids like me. The stories were right about most of the details, but they were wrong about Miss Evridge.

She cared. None of the other teachers even noticed me, but she did. I was a short, fat, shy kid. In those days I was one of the few kids who didn't have a dad living at home. We were poor, and that poverty reached deep into my heart, making me feel worthless.

In the beginning, I was scared of Miss Evridge.

I had good reasons. She was tall. When she put her hair up in a bun, that must have added another six inches. She seemed like a giant.

She was strict. Talking in class was not allowed, and she'd shoot a chilling stare at anyone who dared speak. She refused to bend in her rule about tardiness.

"If the bottom portion of your anatomy is not in juxtaposition to the fine wood grain on the seat of your chair at the beginning—I repeat, at the beginning—of the ringing of the bell (she paused for dramatic flair), then you will be tardy."

Whew! We didn't even know what juxtaposition meant, but we realized we had to be in our chairs before the bell rang or we were food for the vice principal's paddle.

During the second week of school, I rushed into the classroom just as the tardy bell rang. It wasn't my fault. Some big guys wouldn't let me into my locker to get my book. But Miss Evridge made me get a tardy pass. That convinced me she was the ogre everyone said she was.

Another reason I feared Miss Evridge was her language. No teacher had ever called us urchins before. "I'll hang you little urchins by your ears from the ceiling fan and turn it on high 'til the blood rushes to your feet and your toes pop." That sounded at first like torture, but it didn't take me long to realize that she was a comedian.

My fear turned to fascination. Her classes were fun. She had a game for every part of speech, an activity for every diagram. No other teacher had a wheel to spin for questions and prizes. No other class allowed us to laugh and learn at the same time. She led us in victory over verbs and conquest of conjunctions. We learned to stand valiantly against the dreaded preposition.

Miss Evridge was different in another way. She was a Christian teacher in a public school, and she was not afraid to let us know.

One student, with a defiant look, hurled a question at her: "What do you think of Jews?"

"I love Jews," she replied calmly. "My Savior was a Jew."

Having trusted Jesus just a year before, I was eager to tell her that I was also a Christian.

Stopping by her desk, I whispered, "Jesus is my Savior, too."

"I know," she said matter-of-factly.

"How did you know?"

"I can just tell," she smiled.

Perhaps it was our common faith that bonded our relationship. Miss Evridge loved all of her students, but I sensed that she took a special interest in me. No one had ever shown any interest in the chubby kid who was too shy to say much, but Miss Evridge did.

"Joe, I have a speech contest I want you to enter," she informed me one day. Why in the world would she challenge me to enter a speech contest? I was too timid. But she coaxed me and coached me. She pushed me beyond my limits. I won! The next year I won again. The third year my best friend, Leon, beat me. Miss Evridge consoled me, but she also warned me against pride.

"Pride got Lucifer kicked out of heaven," she counseled. "Joe, God may want to use your gift in speaking someday. Perhaps he will call you to be a preacher, but he cannot use you if pride gets in the way."

"No, thank you. I don't want to be a preacher," I insisted. "I want to be a scientist."

"What kind of scientist?"

"I don't know yet. But my mind is made up. That's what I'm going to be someday."

She smiled. I hated it when she smiled that way because it was as if she knew something I didn't. She encouraged me in my scientific endeavors, but gently reminded me that God might have other ideas.

God, indeed, had other ideas. I've been a pastor for the past 17 years. I also head the church ministries department at a Bible college where I try to prepare other young men for a ministry in preaching. I wish I could tell her that.

I miss her for a lot of reasons. I recall how she made my three years at Daggett Junior High School a wonderful learning experience. When I graduated, she also left the school to work on her doctorate in another city. I thought I would never see her again.

What a surprise one morning when she walked into the grocery store where I worked and convinced my boss to let me off long enough for her to take me to lunch. She probably told him she would flunk him from life if he said no. I don't remember what we ate, but the spiritual food she shared nourished my soul.

She couldn't come to my high school graduation because of her graduate work, but she wrote to congratulate me. The day before I left for Bible college, she took me out again and reminded me that God could really use me if I remained a clean vessel. Three years later, she was there for my wedding.

Then we lost contact. She was to be married. Her new address was on the invitation, but I lost it. How I've regretted that! But I still have a part of her with me—a faded and yellowed piece of paper with a poem from her. It was a note of encouragement when I failed to win the "student service award" at ninth grade graduation:

*If you don't get an award when you really know you
    should,*
*Don't be disappointed, God knows when you are
    "good."*
It isn't always the best man who is honored here below,
*Because people give the awards, and there's so much
    they don't know.*
*So when you fail or think that you have had tremen-
    dous loss,*
*Remember, our Savior was perfect and his reward was
    a cross.*
*And remember, my friend, as you travel through life
    with all its strife and sin,*
*That as long as you please Christ, you're the fellow who
    will win!*

I'd like to see her again before Heaven. I just want her
to know that those years she spent as a junior high school
teacher were not spent in vain. She touched my life and
molded me to be more useful for God's kingdom. So, with
all my heart I have to say, "Thank you, Miss Evridge,
wherever you are."

Joseph E. Falkner

Recollection of a Gravel-Clutcher

*So you have sorrow now; but I will see you
again, and your hearts will rejoice, and no one
will take your joy from you.*

John 16:22

I don't think much about the World War II now, even
though this year marks the passage of over 50 years since
it ended. I'm just comforted to know I had some wee small
part in its outcome.

Sometimes events of the past are either reduced to
insignificance by people born after them, or enlarged
beyond recognition by nostalgic reminiscences. Still,
every once in a while, I can hear again that cry in the
woods high on a ridge overlooking the town of
Hitchenback in the Ruhr Valley . . .

Our unit had marched all day and was looking forward
to some rest when the order came down: we would soon
take part in our first large-scale night attack. We were to
wait in the woods above the village while our artillery and
air support dropped high explosives on the targeted
town. Then we were to attack and take over the town.

Toward evening, we took our places. At first, the whining sound of shells passing overhead was largely ignored. But gradually the shells came closer to the tops of the pine trees where we waited, until there was only a split second between the whining sound and the explosion.

Then there was no interval at all, and we were under the worst kind of friendly fire: huge shell bursts that spewed down jagged shreds of steel in sweeping arcs of destruction. Nobody was standing or sitting now: it was time to dig a hole in the ground and hide. At the base of a large tree, I pawed at the ground, sending pine needles flying. The explosions overhead got so intense that individual bursts merged into an ear-splitting roll of deadly thunder. And I prayed: *Oh, God, please, please make 'em stop. Please God . . .*

Then, very suddenly, there was a terrible silence. It was over, but no one spoke, and bodies rose up like ghosts from a graveyard. Finally, calls were heard from different parts of the hillside: *Medic, over here! Hurry! Help, Medic!*

It was then that I heard, through the scattered calls for help, the one cry that has remained with me all these years. The voice was that of PFC Marks, a rifleman in the 3rd Platoon. Like many of us in the 86th, Walter Marks had been slated to go to college when the war interrupted. I remember him as a smiling person with the impish look of a boy always on the verge of pulling off a great practical joke.

His voice traveled through the woods with a special resonance that overrode the cries for help and sounds of battle.

One word, spoken once. "Mother!"

Curious, I thought. The voice lacked the unmistakable sound of pain, nor did it hold any hint of desperation or even sorrow. It was more like a greeting.

When we were finally marching down to take the town, I chanced to see our company medic.

"Did you see Marks back there?"

"Yeah."

"Wounded?"

"No, killed."

"But I heard him call out."

"So did I, but I don't know how."

And on we went to do our duty.

If I had known Marks better, I thought, *I would try to find his mother when this was over and tell her she was the last thing in her son's heart when he died.* But I hadn't even known his first name, and as often happened, I was unable to continue to deal with death consciously—I blocked out the details in all but my worst nightmares.

Some of our old Company K buddies recently got together to celebrate the golden anniversary of our survival. One of them had been a close friend of Marks'. I asked him about our fallen friend's last moments, and if he'd heard that call. He had.

"He must have seen his mother in his mind's eye and called out to her," I suggested.

"You know, I've often wondered about that," the friend replied, "because Walter never knew his mother. He had never even seen her."

"How's that?"

"She died in childbirth when she brought him into this world."

Austin Goodrich

Baptist Minister

The heart has reasons which reason cannot understand.

Blaise Pascal

I have a cousin who is a Baptist minister. When we were growing up, we only saw each other a couple of times a year. Now we see each other even less.

A few years ago, when I hadn't seen him for some time, I suddenly began thinking about him and his family. I just couldn't get them off my mind. And for some reason, I felt compelled to send him a check for $100. I thought about it for a few days and made more than one aborted trip to the post office. I finally mailed it with a letter saying I hope I wasn't offending him, but I believed the Lord wanted me to do this.

A couple of weeks later I received a reply. My cousin said it never ceased to amaze him how God worked in his life. And now God had once again shown him, through us, that he would always meet our needs. My cousin said the only concern he had was that I had sent too much. All he had needed was $97.56.

Lalia Winsett

Faith

Faith is to believe what we do not see, and the reward of faith is to see what we believe.

Saint Augustine

The fields were parched and brown from lack of rain, and the crops lay wilting from thirst. People were anxious and irritable as they searched the sky for any sign of relief. Days turned into arid weeks. No rain came.

The ministers of the local churches called for an hour of prayer on the town square the following Saturday. They requested that everyone bring an object of faith for inspiration.

At high noon on the appointed Saturday the townspeople turned out *en masse,* filling the square with anxious faces and hopeful hearts. The ministers were touched to see the variety of objects clutched in prayerful hands—holy books, crosses, rosaries.

When the hour ended, as if on magical command, a soft rain began to fall. Cheers swept the crowd as they held their treasured objects high in gratitude and praise. From the middle of the crowd one faith symbol seemed to overshadow all the others: A small nine-year-old child had brought an umbrella.

Laverne W. Hall

Place of Sacrifice

This is the confidence we have in approaching God: that if we ask anything according to His will, He hears us.

1 John 5:14 NIV

Christianity is a farce! I silently raged.

Bending over my little girl's crib, I watched my exhausted baby sleep—my precious little girl, Kim, whose hair glinted gold in the sunlight and whose eyes rivaled the blue of the sky. Tears streaming down my face, I was engulfed by the special fear and terror that only a mother knows when her child is in danger.

First, an overwhelming surge of protectiveness filled my being, then anger hit me in unrelenting waves. Kim and I were trapped, and I felt helpless. There was no escape.

Restlessly, I walked into the living room. Picking up the bill from that morning's visit to Kim's pediatrician, Dr. Rubinstein, I thought: *Endless visits. And for what?*

During that visit I had confronted Dr. Rubinstein and asked for the truth, as much as I didn't want to hear it. "Is Kim going to die? I need to know!"

"I can't answer that question," Dr. Rubinstein said. "She has a good chance, if her body starts responding to treatment."

In the examining room, I had looked at Kim's sweet face, distorted with pain. Her anguish wrung my heart. Holding my crying baby, I turned and faced the doctor. "If, if! That's all I've been hearing for 16 months. Kim has had these painful shots every two weeks since she was born. You can see how she screams and cries. And all you can tell me is, 'if'?"

Understanding the stress and fear behind my outburst, the doctor had not taken offense. "Her white blood cell count is the lowest it has ever been," he said gently, holding the lab report in his hand. "The gamma globulin shots have helped her to survive her bouts of illness, but her own body is not producing white blood cells in large enough quantities. I can't give you a miracle. Kim will either start producing enough white cells or she won't."

The reality of what the doctor told me paralyzed me with fear. Feeling exhausted and defeated, I said, "Kim is always so sick and she gets such high fevers. I'm up every night for weeks. Then, just as she seems to be getting better, the whole cycle starts all over again. And now you tell me that there is no end in sight!"

"You must face this situation," the doctor replied. "There are no guarantees in life. God has placed you in this position. Face it. Do the best you can."

I could hardly keep the anger out of my voice. "Well, if God has placed me here, he can also get me out. I'm beginning to believe he likes to see people suffer, humbled and dependent. I think I've had about enough of such a God!"

Tired and numb, I had returned home. Hearing Kim stir in her crib, I tiptoed in to check on her. In a deep sleep, she sobbed softly as she painfully moved her legs. The shots would bother her for several days.

Returning to the living room, I huddled on the couch. I drew my legs up and hid my face in my arms. I wanted to hide, to be safe. But again, at the thought of my baby's torment, anger and resentment stirred in my heart.

I began pacing the living room. Raising my fists to heaven, I shook them in frustration.

Where are you, God? Why are you so cold and silent? Lord, why are you giving me stone and not the bread that a loving father would give? Have you deserted me? Where is your promised peace and comfort?

Silence was my answer. I felt mocked by God.

Limp as a rag doll, I sat down on the couch again and thought about my unhappy childhood, about my cold, autocratic father and my erratic mother. There had been too many siblings, too little money, too little love.

Though I had gone to church most of my life, God had seemed unapproachable. I thought of him as the Big Policeman in the Sky, ready to punish, but never warm and caring. God was much like my own father, as a matter of fact.

Fathers. Whenever I thought of fathers, my thirteenth birthday stood out in my mind. It had been thrilling to finally be a teenager. Many of the friends that I had grown up with had come to my party. But this day of joy soon turned to one of horror. My father had come stumbling into my party, drunk and disheveled. He always resented when money was spent on anything but absolute necessities.

"You're stupid and ugly," my father had sneered at me, standing in the midst of my friends. "Nobody could ever love you."

As a result of that trauma I became a loner, unable to feel that I belonged anywhere.

Drifting back to the present, I thought: *But that all changed when I found you, Lord. You accepted me just as I am, warts and all. I felt I had come home when I found you! Are you going to betray me, too?*

Stirring out of my reverie, I went to the kitchen and began washing the breakfast dishes. The warm water felt wonderful on my cold hands as I twirled the soap suds, my mind beginning to wander. I was remembering when Kim first became ill.

I wasn't afraid, at first, I thought, as I spoke quietly in my mind to God. *I knew you could heal. There is nothing you can't do. If my baby was ill, you would heal her. Nothing more simple, right? Nothing more simple.*

I reached for the pan on the stove and started fiercely scrubbing it.

Okay, God, so what's the deal? I know I believe and have faith in you. I have prayed. Our church has prayed. The elders have laid hands on Kim. We've studied your word, appropriated your promises and awaited your timing. What do you want? Why won't you heal my baby?

No answer came.

The dishes done, I dried my hands. In utter despondency, I went back to the living room. If my silent God had deserted me, where else was I to turn?

My eyes fell on my Bible on the coffee table. A verse from Genesis 22 slipped into my mind, stunning me with its impact. I quickly opened my Bible to make sure that I had remembered it correctly. I had. The verse read,

> *And he said, "Take now thy son, thine only son Isaac, whom thou lovest, and get thee into the land of Moriah; and offer him there for a burnt offering upon one of the mountains which I will tell thee of."*

I knew then, with absolute certainty, that God was asking for Kim. My mind was suddenly clear as never before, and I realized that I had been placing my love for my little girl above my love for God. I had been asking for my will. My will. Not God's. Not his sovereign choice. A clay pot had been railing at its maker, not falling in submission at his holy feet.

Realizing that I'd been trying to manipulate God, I saw that I'd been doing all the "right things" so he would be required to answer my pleadings. I had never really considered the possibility that he might ask for Kimmie. *Surely, sweet Jesus, you're not asking this of me? Not my baby's life. How easy for you to heal her. Just a touch. Oh, my Lord and my God, not this!*

Even as I spoke, though, I knew the answer. Only total submission to God's sovereign will would do. In my breaking heart I built an altar. Upon this altar I placed my only, beloved child as truly and sacrificially as Abraham had ever placed Isaac on the altar of Moriah.

Oh, my Lord, I place my trust in thee. If you are going to take my baby, take her. I can't fight you any longer. Forgive me, Lord, for my lack of trust and obedience. I don't understand why you are asking for my little girl, but I do love and trust you. Help me in the time ahead.

A profound peace filled me. The battle was over. The victory won. I let go of all the anger and fear that I'd been living with for so many months. I would rest in the perfect will of God for my life.

Six weeks later, Kim and I were at Dr. Rubinstein's office again. Kim had not been ill during all that time. She sat up bright and alert in my arms, radiant with health.

"I've never seen anything like this," said Dr. Rubinstein with a puzzled look on his face. "Kim's white blood cell count is absolutely normal. This is impossible. It couldn't have changed so quickly."

But it had. And in my heart I knew why. As Isaac had been returned to Abraham, so had my little girl been given back to me. My Lord was the Great Physician and a Father to be trusted.

Maybe the time had come for another healing?

When I get home, I thought, *I think I'll call my dad.*

Teresa Anne Arries

Reprinted with permission from Bil Keane.

God, Send Someone!

Listen to my cry for help, my King and my God . . .

Ps. 5:2 NIV

At 4:00 P.M., June 14, my brother Jack was just crawling down into a 10-foot-deep-trench that ran down the center of Washington Street, a main thoroughfare in West Roxbury, Massachusetts.

It was near quitting time. Jack is a welder, and he wanted to finish one particular part of his job before he left. He said good-bye to the other men as they quit, took his welding lead in his right hand, and lowered himself and his electric power cable into the trench. His head was well below the surface of the street.

Traffic above him was heavy. Though Jack could not see the cars and trucks, he could feel their vibrations. Occasionally a pebble would break loose from the side of the trench and fall into it. Jack paid no attention to them.

It was Jack's job to weld the joints of a new water main both inside and out. First he crawled into the 36-inch-diameter pipe, lowered his mask to protect his eyes against the bright welding arc, then went to work. After completing the inside of the joint, he crawled out of the pipe. It was 4:30 P.M. He began to weld the outside. Halfway through the job he stood up to get the kinks out of his legs. Jack stretched, turned toward the pipe, and pulled down the shield again.

Suddenly the bank caved in. Tons of dirt came crushing down on him from above and behind.

Jack was rammed against the pipe with the force of a sledge hammer. He went down, buried in a kneeling position, his shield slammed against the pipe, his nose flattened against the inside of the shield.

He felt his shoulder burning against the red-hot section of pipe he had been welding. He tried to move it back from the pipe, but he couldn't. Then his nose began to hurt. It was bleeding. And he couldn't move his head.

Jack tried calling. Three times he shouted. The sound of his voice died in his shield. He tried to breathe slowly to preserve the supply of oxygen.

It crossed Jack's mind that he might die.

Slowly he began to pray. Going to Mass at St. Patrick's once a week suddenly seemed quite inadequate. My brother continued to pray. He had his eyes open, but everything was black.

Something cool crossed his right hand. He wiggled his fingers and found they moved freely. His right hand had not been buried. He moved the hand again. He tried to scratch around with his hand to open up an air passage down his arm but the weight of the earth was too great. It didn't do any good.

Then it occurred to him that he had been holding the welding lead in that hand. So he fished around with his fingers. He found the rod, still in the holder. He grasped it tightly and moved it, hoping it would strike the pipe. Suddenly his wrist jerked and he knew he had struck an arc—the electric current would be making its bright orange flash. So he kept on tapping the pipe, making an arc, hoping it would draw attention. *That must look like something!* Jack thought. *A hand reaching out of the ground striking an arc against the pipe. That must really look like something!*

He began trying to figure out how long he had been buried, since there was no way of telling time. He wondered how much gasoline was left in the engine-driven welder on top of the trench—whether it would last until dark when the orange arc might draw attention. Then he remembered that it was almost the longest day of the year. Darkness wouldn't fall until nearly nine o'clock. Still, if he had enough oxygen in his little tomb and if the gasoline held out, maybe . . .

He thought of all the hundreds of people passing within a few feet of him up above. He thought of his family and wondered if he would ever see his little grandson again. He thought of Tommy Whittaker, his assistant, out on another job on Route 128.

He figured there wasn't anything to do but lie there and wait and keep tapping flashes, and hope that enough air would filter into the mask to keep him alive. There wasn't anything to do but lie there and pray, "God, send someone."

In another part of Boston, out on Route 128, Tommy Whittaker had quit his work for the day. Tommy was 47 years old, Jack, 41. They had known each other for more than 15 years and were close friends, so close they would sometimes finish each other's sentences. As Jack called out for help, then, it was no wonder that Tommy sensed his prayers.

Tommy did not know that Jack was on the Washington Street job. He got in his truck and started off down Route 128 with the full intention of driving directly home. Route

128 is a main artery, a superhighway that could take him home within minutes.

But as he drove, he began to have the feeling something wasn't right.

He tried to shake the feeling off. He kept driving. The strange and unexplainable sensation grew. He thought that he ought to drive up to the Washington Street job and check it, then dismissed the idea. It meant driving six miles out of his day at the peak of rush hour. Tommy approached the intersection of Washington and Route 128.

Suddenly he turned.

He did not try to explain it to himself. He just turned.

Meanwhile, Jack continued to pray. It was the same simple prayer, "God, send someone." The bleeding in his nose hadn't stopped. The blood ran down his throat and began to clot. "God, send someone." He spat the blood out, but it was getting more difficult. All the while he listened to the muffled sound of his welding motor outside. He wondered if it was dark yet. It seemed an eternity. Things were getting hazy.

Tommy drove along Washington Street. The job was divided into two sections. He stopped his truck at a spot several blocks away from the cave-in and got out. He chatted with an engineer for the Metropolitan District Commission for 15 minutes. Tommy did not mention the gnawing sensation that still would not leave him alone. The time was 5:45 P.M. It was still broad daylight.

Back in the trench, Jack struck some more arcs. He thought it might be dark now. He listened to the welder popping. He hoped someone would come—soon. The clot of blood in his throat was getting harder to bring up. He was a little surprised that he wasn't in a state of panic. Jack just kept praying, "God send . . ."

Up above, a little way down Washington Street, Tommy got into his truck, said good-bye to his friend, and started up again. The gnawing sensation grew stronger. He reached a stoplight. It was his turnoff to get back to Route 128 by a shortcut. If he stayed on Washington Street, he would have to go still farther out of his way. Tommy braked his truck for a brief instant, then continued up Washington.

Underground, Jack finally gave up striking the arc. It was making him breathe too hard. He didn't think he could last much longer. He couldn't get the blood clot out of his throat. He was gagging . . .

At that moment, up above on Washington Street, Tommy arrived at the spot where his friend was lying. Nothing seemed unusual. He noticed the stake-body truck. But it was a truck that Sullivan never used. Tommy thought another man from the shop was down in the trench. Tommy pulled up, got out of his truck, and noticed the welder was running. He thought someone was inside the pipe, welding. Still nothing struck him as unusual.

Then Tommy saw the hand—and saw it move!

"Oh, God!" he whispered.

Tommy jumped down into the trench and dug like a chipmunk with his hands. The earth was too packed. He scrambled out of the trench, looked back at the hand, and shuddered. He shut off the welder and raced through the traffic across the street to a garage.

Underground, Jack heard the pop-pop of the welder stop. It was then that he began to prepare to die. He knew it was over. He was gagging and trying to throw off the mist that had come over him.

Tommy just a few feet away, shouted to the men in the garage. "There's a man buried alive over there! Get a shovel."

Back across the street Tommy raced, carrying a snow shovel. He ran to the place where the hand stuck up, still not knowing it was his friend.

Jack, below, felt an extra pressure on top of his head. He knew someone was above him. He fought to keep from fainting.

The garage men hurried over.

"Send for the police. There's a firebox down the street," Tommy called.

Tommy began to dig. He uncovered a wrist-watch. He thought he recognized the watchband. He kept digging until he uncovered the man's side. He saw the man was still breathing, but his respiration was very weak.

Then Tommy recognized my brother, but by then Jack had fainted. Tommy dug more frantically.

The rescue squad arrived. They applied an oxygen mask to Jack while they were still digging him out. From busy Washington Street, a crowd gathered.

Jack revived slightly when they put him on a stretcher. It was 6:30 P.M. He spied Tommy.

"Who found me?" he asked.

"I did," said Tommy.

With his lips, Jack formed one word.

"Thanks."

There was no more powerful word.

Dick Sullivan

5

ON THE LIGHTER SIDE

To every thing there is a season, and a time for every purpose under Heaven. A time to be born, and a time to die. . . . A time to weep and a time to laugh.

Eccles. 3:1-2,4

Moses at an early age.

How to Get to Heaven

Nothing shows a man's character more than what he laughs at.

Johann Wolfgang von Goethe

Reverend Billy Graham tells of a time early in his ministry when he arrived in a small town to preach a sermon. Wanting to mail a letter, he asked a young boy where the post office was. When the boy had told him, Dr. Graham thanked him and said, "If you'll come to the Baptist Church this evening, you can hear me telling everyone how to get to Heaven."

"I don't think I'll be there," the boy said. "You don't even know your way to the post office."

Brian Cavanaugh's Sower's Seeds

No Parking

A minister parked his car in a no-parking zone in a large city and attached the following message to his windshield: "I have circled this block 10 times. I have an appointment to keep. *Forgive us our trespasses*."

When he returned to his car he found this reply attached to his own note, along with a ticket: "I've circled this block for 10 years. If I don't give you a ticket, I lose my job. *Lead us not into temptation*."

Bits & Pieces

Reprinted with permission from Dave Carpenter.

Irreverent Manipulation

I believe in laughter. I think it's food for the soul.

Tommy Lasorda

Little Benjamin sat down at the desk to write a letter to God asking for a little baby sister. He started the letter like this:

Dear God, I've been a very good boy . . .

He stopped, thinking. *No, God won't believe that.* He wadded up the piece of paper, threw it away, and started again:

Dear God, most of the time I've been a good boy . . .

He stopped in the middle of the line, again thinking, *God won't be moved by this.* So he wadded up the letter and into the trash can it went.

Benjamin then went into the bathroom and grabbed a big terry cloth towel off the towel rack. He carried it into the living room and carefully laid it out on the couch. He smoothed out all the wrinkles. Then he went over to the fireplace mantle, reached up, and very carefully lifted down a statue of the Madonna. He had often seen his mother carefully dust the statue, and he had eyed it many times. On several occasions, his parents had told him that he could look but was not to touch the statue. Now, with all the care he could muster, he had it in his possession.

Benjamin gently placed the statue in the middle of the towel, carefully folding over the edges. He then placed a rubber band around the whole thing. He brought it to the desk, took out another piece of paper, and began to write his third letter to God. It went like this:

Dear God, if you ever want to see your mother again . . .

Excerpted from
Moments for Mothers

Sunday School Lessons

The Sunday school lesson for the day was about Noah's Ark, so the preschool teacher in our Kentucky church decided to get her small pupils involved by playing a game in which they identified animals.

"I'm going to describe something to you. Let's see if you can guess what it is. First: I'm furry with a bushy tail and I like to climb trees."

The children looked at her blankly.

"I also like to eat nuts, especially acorns."

No response. This wasn't going well at all!

"I'm usually brown or gray, but sometimes I can be black or red."

Desperate, the teacher turned to a perky four-year-old who was usually good about coming up with the answers. "Michelle, what do you think?"

Michelle looked hesitantly at her classmates and replied, "Well, I know the answer has to be Jesus—but it sure sounds like a squirrel to me!"

Susan Webber

Wholly Holy Bloopers

Humor is mankind's greatest blessing.

Mark Twain

The tradition of holy howlers popping up in religiously related documents continues undimmed.

Witness the following sampling of bona fide bloopers culled from various church bulletins and orders of service:

- The ladies of the church have cast off clothing of every kind, and they can be seen in the church basement Friday afternoon.
- On Sunday a special collection will be taken to defray the expense of the new carpet. All those wishing to do something on the carpet will please come forward to get a piece of paper.
- Irving Benson and Jessie Carter were married on Oct. 24 in the church. So ends a friendship that began in school days.
- This afternoon there will be a meeting in the south and north end of the church. Children will be baptized at both ends.

- For those of you who have children and don't know it, we have a nursery downstairs.

- The pastor will preach his farewell message, after which the choir will sing, "Break Forth into Joy."

- This being Easter Sunday, we will ask Mrs. White to come forward and lay an egg on the altar.

- The choir will meet at the Larsen house for fun and sinning.

- Thursday at 5 P.M. there will be a meeting of the Little Mothers Club. All wishing to become little mothers will please meet with the minister in the study.

- During the absence of our pastor, we enjoyed the rare privilege of hearing a good sermon when J.F. Stubbs supplied our pulpit.

- Wednesday, the Ladies Literary Society will meet. Mrs. Clark will sing, "Put Me in My Little Bed," accompanied by the pastor.

- Next Sunday Mrs. Vinson will be soloist for the morning service. The pastor will then speak on "It's a Terrible Experience."

- Due to the Rector's illness, Wednesday's healing services will be discontinued until further notice.

- Remember in prayer the many who are sick of our church and community.

- The eighth-graders will be presenting Shakespeare's *Hamlet* in the church basement on Friday at 7 P.M. The congregation is invited to attend this tragedy.

- Twenty-two members were present at the church meeting held at the home of Mrs. Marsha Crutchfield last evening. Mrs. Crutchfield and Mrs. Rankin sang a duet, "The Lord Knows Why."

- Smile at someone who is hard to love. Say "hell" to someone who doesn't care much about you.

- Today's Sermon:
  HOW MUCH CAN A MAN DRINK?
  with hymns from a full choir.

- Potluck supper: prayer and medication to follow.

- Don't let worry kill you off—let the church help.

Long may these bloopers live. Such unintentional levity brings lightness as well as light to many an otherwise dry church bulletin.

Richard Lederer
From Anguished English

Communion

Then I command mirth because a person hath no better thing under the sun than to eat, and to drink, and to be merry . . .

Eccles. 8:15 NIV

Of all the rituals and colorful ceremonies that children see performed in church, perhaps the most misunderstood of all is the sacrament of Communion. Seeing the bread and wine (or grape juice) used in this rite, children often think that refreshments are being served.

- Attending his first Mass, one small boy listened as the altar boys rang the bells for the consecration, and yelled, "Come and get it!" Whereupon those who were to take Communion went and got it.

- A boy of three was intrigued by the Communion rite and watched every move of the priest until he finished by wiping the chalice. Then the boy turned to his mother and said, "He's doing dishes, Mom . . . now can we go home?"

- Kneeling beside his mother at Mass after she returned from taking Communion, a boy asked, "How does that pill taste?" Since she was praying silently to herself, she didn't answer. Then he tried again: "It's the kind of pill that puts you to sleep, huh?"

- After doing her best to explain the ceremony to her daughter, a young mother went to the Communion rail. As she returned, the girl asked, "When will it be my turn to eat lunch with God?"

- Trying to acquaint her five-year-old son with the ritual of the Mass, a mother gave her boy a picture missal so he could see in front of him what was going on at the altar during Communion. The boy watched as the priest opened the tabernacle, removed the chalice, and drank the wine. Then the boy pointed to the tabernacle in his book and asked, "Is that the little refrigerator where he keeps his drinks?"

- While visiting his aunt in Columbus, Mississippi, a second-grader attended the local Methodist Church with her. After they knelt at the altar and partook of the Communion bread and wine, the boy asked, "Aunt Audrey, is that all we'll have to eat up in Heaven?"

- A young married couple who were baptized into the First Presbyterian Church in Hollywood brought along their seven-year-old son, Michael, to see the ceremony. His mother explained in advance about baptism, but she had forgotten to explain that Communion would also be offered to the entire congregation. After the service, she asked him what he thought of the morning's events. "Well," he said, "I didn't think much of the cookies, and there wasn't enough juice."

- Another woman brought her grandson along for Episcopal services. The boy watched as the priest at the altar prepared Communion and said, "Look, Grandma . . . God is making Kool-Aid."

- When his father returned and knelt in prayer after receiving the Blessed Host, a 14-year-old asked, "They got any chocolate ones up there?"

- Not all children are disappointed by what's served at Communion. A teenager's mother tells me he came home after a week at church camp to report that Communion was the only decent meal they had.

- A boy overheard his parents talking about going to the Lord's Supper and told his brother, "I hope we have chicken!"

- The last word on Communion comes from a four-year-old Catholic boy who told his dad what had happened in church that day: "The Father called on some of the people to come down front, and he gave them each an Alka-Seltzer!"

Dick Van Dyke
Submitted by Joanne Duncalf

The board was not pleased with the way you celebrated Youth Sunday, especially the part where you used Pepsi and Fritos for Communion.

Reprinted with permission from Randy Glasbergen.

No Excuse Sunday

*H*umor *is a proof of faith.*

Charles M. Schulz

To make it possible for everyone to attend church next Sunday, we are going to have a special "No Excuse Sunday." Cots will be placed in the foyer for those who say, "Sunday is my only day to sleep in." There will be a special section with lounge chairs for those who feel that our pews are too hard. Eyedrops will be available for those with tired eyes from watching TV late Saturday night. We will have steel helmets for those who say, "The roof would cave in if I ever came to church." Blankets will be furnished for those who think the church is too cold and fans for those who say it is too hot. Scorecards will be available for those who wish to list the hypocrites present. Relatives and friends will be in attendance for those who can't go to church and cook dinner, too. We will distribute "Stamp Out Stewardship" buttons for those who feel that the church is always asking for money.

One section will be devoted to trees and grass for those

who like to seek God in nature. Doctors and nurses will be in attendance for those who plan to be sick on Sunday. The sanctuary will be decorated with both Christmas poinsettias and Easter lilies for those who never have seen the church without them. We will provide hearing aids for those who can't hear the preacher and cotton for those who can.

Author Unknown
From the Joyful Noiseletter

That was a wonderful sermon. Thanks for not mentioning me by name.

Life Begins?

A preacher, a priest and a rabbi were having their usual morning cup of coffee at the local coffee shop. On this particular morning, they were discussing the point at which life begins.

"Life begins at conception," the priest said emphatically.

"No," countered the rabbi. "I believe life begins at birth."

The preacher sipped his coffee as he pondered the question and finally said, "You're both wrong. Life begins when the last child has left home and the dog dies!"

Anonymous
Submitted by Joanne Duncalf

Water Closet

An English schoolteacher was looking for rooms in Switzerland. She called upon the local schoolmaster to help her find an apartment that would be suitable. Such rooms were found, and she returned to London for her belongings. She remembered that she had not noticed a bathroom, or as she called it, "a water closet." She wrote to the schoolmaster and asked if there was a "W.C." in or near the apartment.

The schoolmaster, not knowing the English expression, was puzzled by the "W.C.," never dreaming that she was talking about a bathroom. He finally sought advice from the parish priest. They concluded that she must mean a Wayside Chapel. The lady received the following letter a few days later.

Dear Madam:

The W.C. is located 9 miles from the house, in the heart of a beautiful grove of trees. It will seat 150 people at one time, and is open on Tuesdays, Thursdays and Sundays.

Some people bring their lunch and make a day of it. On Thursdays there is an organ accompaniment. The acoustics are very good. The slightest sound can be heard by everyone. It may interest you to know that my daughter met her husband at the W.C. We are now in the process of taking donations to purchase plush seats. We feel that this is a long-felt need, as the present seats have holes in them.

My wife, being rather delicate, hasn't been able to attend regularly. It has been six months since she last went. Naturally, it pains her not to be able to go more often.

I will close now with the desire to accommodate you in every way possible, and will be happy to save you a seat either down front or near the door, as you prefer.

Author Unknown
Excerpted from The Commencement
Address of Roger Dunker
Submitted by Joanne Duncalf

Saint Peter at the Pearly Gates

Three guys died at the same time and ended up in front of Saint Peter at the Pearly Gates. Saint Peter said to the first guy, "Why should I let you in?"

The guy answered, "I was a doctor and I helped many people get well."

Saint Peter said, "Okay, you may come in."

Saint Peter said to the second guy, "Why should I let you in?"

The guy answered, "I was a lawyer and defended many innocent people."

Saint Peter said, "Okay, you may come in."

Saint Peter then said to the last guy, "And why should I let you in?"

The guy answered, "Well, I was a managed health care professional and I helped to keep health care costs down."

Saint Peter thought about this a moment and said, "Okay, you may come in, but you can only stay three days!"

Author Unknown
Submitted by Joanne Duncalf

Shocking Generosity

The story goes that while Robert Smith was taking his afternoon walk—part of his therapy in recovering from a massive heart attack—the phone rang and his wife, Delores, answered. The call was from the *Reader's Digest* Association Sweepstakes in New York. They were calling to inform the Smith Family that Robert had just won $1,500,000 and that in a few days the certified check would be arriving. Well, as you can imagine, Delores was absolutely ecstatic. Now all those dreams would come true!

But then she remembered her husband was just getting over his massive heart attack, and the doctor had said no excitement over anything. Delores was afraid that if she told him they had just won such a large sum, he would have another heart attack and die. What should she do? After some thought, she decided to call their pastor and ask his advice because he had had some experience in breaking difficult news to families.

Delores dialed. "Hello, Pastor Baldwin . . . this is Delores Smith."

The pastor replied, "Hi, Delores. How are you? And how is Bob?"

"I'm fine, thank you. And so is Bob. He's recovering nicely. But I've got a problem and I need your advice."

"Sure, if I can help, I'll be glad to," the pastor replied.

"Well, Pastor, I just got a call from the *Reader's Digest* Sweepstakes informing me that Bob has just won $1,500,000!"

"That's great!" said the pastor. "But what's the problem?"

"Well, I'm afraid that if I tell Bob, he'll get so excited that he will have another heart attack and drop dead. Can you help me?"

"Well, Delores, I think I can. Hold on, I'll be right over."

So in about an hour, Bob was back from his walk, and he and Delores and Pastor Baldwin were in the den having a nice chat. The pastor leaned toward Bob and said, "Bob, I've got a problem and need your advice."

"Sure, Pastor, if I can help, I'll be glad to," Bob said.

The pastor took a deep breath and went on, "It's a theoretical situation regarding Christian stewardship. What would a person—take you, for instance—do if all of a sudden you found out you had won $1,500,000? What would you do with all that money?"

"That's easy," Bob replied, "I'd start by giving $750,000 to the church."

Whereupon, Pastor Baldwin had a heart attack and dropped dead!

Excerpted from
Moments for Pastors

6

ON DEATH
AND DYING

It is through giving that we receive, and it is through dying that we are born to eternal life.

Saint Francis of Assisi

He Only Takes the Best

God saw she was getting tired
and a cure was not to be.
So he put his arms around her
and whispered, "Come with me."

With tear-filled eyes we watched her
suffer and fade away.
Although we loved her deeply,
we could not make her stay.

A golden heart stopped beating,
hard-working hands put to rest.
God broke our hearts to prove to us
he only takes the best.

Author Unknown

What Was in Jeremy's Egg?

Jeremy was born with a twisted body, a slow mind and a chronic, terminal illness that had been slowly killing him all his young life. Still, his parents had tried to give him as normal a life as possible and had sent him to St. Theresa's Elementary School.

At the age of 12, Jeremy was only in second grade, seemingly unable to learn. His teacher, Doris Miller, often became exasperated with him. He would squirm in his seat, drool and make grunting noises.

At other times, he spoke clearly and distinctly, as if a spot of light had penetrated the darkness of his brain. Most of the time, however, Jeremy irritated his teacher. One day, she called his parents and asked them to come to St. Theresa's for a consultation.

As the Forresters sat quietly in the empty classroom, Doris said to them, "Jeremy really belongs in a special school. It isn't fair to him to be with younger children who don't have learning problems. Why, there is a five-year gap between his age and that of the other students!"

Mrs. Forrester cried softly into a tissue while her husband spoke. "Miss Miller," he said, "there is no school of that kind nearby. It would be a terrible shock for Jeremy if we had to take him out of this school. We know he really likes it here."

Doris sat for a long time after they left, staring at the snow outside the window. Its coldness seemed to seep into her soul. She wanted to sympathize with the Forresters. After all, their only child had a terminal illness. But it wasn't fair to keep him in her class. She had 18 other youngsters to teach, and Jeremy was a distraction. Furthermore, he would never learn to read and write. Why waste any more time trying?

As she pondered the situation, guilt washed over her. "Oh God," she said aloud, "here I am complaining, when my problems are nothing compared with that poor family! Please help me to be more patient with Jeremy."

From that day on, she tried hard to ignore Jeremy's noises and his blank stares. Then one day he limped to her desk, dragging his bad leg behind him.

"I love you, Miss Miller," he exclaimed, loud enough for the whole class to hear. The other students snickered, and Doris's face turned red. She stammered, "Wh—why, that's very nice, Jeremy. Now please take your seat."

Spring came, and the children talked excitedly about the coming of Easter. Doris told them the story of Jesus, and then to emphasize the idea of new life springing forth, she gave each of the children a large plastic egg. "Now," she said to them, "I want you to take this home and bring it back tomorrow with something inside that shows new life. Do you understand?"

"Yes, Miss Miller!" the children responded enthusiastically—all except for Jeremy. He just listened intently; his eyes never left her face. He did not even make his usual noises.

Had he understood what she had said about Jesus's death and resurrection? Did he understand the assignment?

Perhaps she should call his parents and explain the project to them.

That evening, Doris's kitchen sink stopped up. She called the landlord and waited an hour for him to come by and unclog it. After that, she still had to shop for groceries, iron a blouse and prepare a vocabulary test for the next day. She completely forgot about phoning Jeremy's parents.

The next morning, 19 children came to school, laughing and talking as they placed their eggs in the large wicker basket on Miss Miller's desk. After they completed their math lesson, it was time to open the eggs.

In the first egg, Doris found a flower. "Oh, yes, a flower is certainly a sign of new life," she said. "When plants peek through the ground, we know that spring is here." A small girl in the first row waved her arm. "That's my egg, Miss Miller," she called out.

The next egg contained a plastic butterfly, which looked very real. Doris held it up. "We all know that a caterpillar changes and grows into a beautiful butterfly. Yes, that is new life, too." Little Judy smiled proudly and said, "Miss Miller, that one is mine!"

Next, Doris found a rock with moss on it. She explained that moss, too, showed life. Billy spoke up from the back of the classroom. "My daddy helped me!" he beamed.

Then Doris opened the fourth egg. She gasped. The egg was empty! Surely it must be Jeremy's, she thought, and, of course, he did not understand her instructions. If only she had not forgotten to phone his parents. Because she did not want to embarrass him, she quietly set the egg aside and reached for another.

Suddenly Jeremy spoke up. "Miss Miller, aren't you going to talk about my egg?"

Flustered, Doris replied, "But Jeremy—your egg is empty!" He looked into her eyes and said softly, "Yes, but Jesus's tomb was empty, too!"

Time stopped. When she could speak again, Doris asked him, "Do you know why the tomb was empty?"

"Oh, yes!" Jeremy exclaimed. "Jesus was killed and put in there. Then his Father raised him up!"

The recess bell rang. While the children excitedly ran out to the school yard, Doris cried. The cold inside her melted completely away.

Three months later, Jeremy died. Those who paid their respects at the mortuary were surprised to see 19 eggs on top of his casket, all of them empty.

Ida Mae Kempel

I'm Here!

If you conquer, you will be clothed like them in white robes and I will not blot your names out of the Book of Life; but I will confess your name before My Father and before his angels.

Rev. 3:5

The Rogers are devout Christians who have built a strong family. The father has a special interest in the spiritual condition of each of his children and often would quiz them in order to know if they were sure of their salvation. Occasionally he would ask them to share in their own words about their relationship with Jesus Christ.

One day it was seven-year-old Jimmy's turn to express how he knew he had eternal life. Jimmy told his version: "I think it will be something like this in Heaven. One day when we all get to go to Heaven, it will be time for the big angel to read from the big book the names of all the people who will be there. He will come to the Rogers family and say, 'Daddy Rogers?' and Daddy will say, 'Here!' Then the angel will call out, 'Mommy Rogers?' and Mommy will say, 'Here!' Then the angel will come down to call out

Susie Rogers and Mavis Rogers, and they will both say, 'Here!' "

He paused, took a big deep breath and continued. "And finally that big angel will read my name, Jimmy Rogers, and because I'm little and maybe he'll miss me, I'll jump and shout real loud, 'HERE!' to make sure he knows I'm there."

Just a few days later there was a tragic accident. A car struck down little Jimmy Rogers as he made his way to catch the school bus. He was rushed by ambulance to the hospital, and all the family was summoned. He was in critical condition.

The little family group gathered around the bed in which little Jimmy now lay with no movement, no consciousness and no hope for recovery. The doctors had done all that was in their power. Jimmy would probably be gone by morning.

The family prayed and waited. Late in the night the little boy seemed to be stirring a bit. They all moved closer. They saw his lips move; just one word was all he uttered before he passed from this life. But what a word of comfort and hope for a grieving family he was to leave behind. In the clear voice of a little boy, loud and clear enough so all could hear and understand, little Jimmy Rogers said the one word: 'HERE!' And then he was gone to another life beyond this world, where a big angel was reading the names of all those written there.

Excerpted from
Moments for Mothers

Answering The Call

Father John's little desert parish truly loved and appreciated his sincere style and caring ways. During the Sign of Peace, he always called all of the children attending Mass to come up and give him hugs. He did it for himself I'm sure, but he did it for the children, too. Each and every child waited for the time during Mass when he or she could stand next to the altar, be the center of attention and hug the not-so-old, and slightly plump priest.

On one particular Sunday, after all the hugs were thought to have been completed and the "Lamb of God, You take away the sins of the world," had begun, one small voice from half-way back in the church said, "What about me?" Father John stopped his prayer, and held out his arms. The little voice with freckled face, slicked back hair, shiny cowboy boots and shorts, ran down the aisle towards the altar, crying because he thought he had been forgotten. Father John just held out his arms, picked up the little boy and held him very near, and held him very dear.

Three weeks later, I returned to the little desert parish and there was a different priest, one I didn't recognize, saying Mass. I sat next to a woman who silently cried as she held my hand as we all sang, "Our Father, who art in Heaven . . ." It seems that Father John had lost his place in the same part of Mass the Sunday before. He told his parishioners, "As the Lord so taught us to pray . . ." and the parish responded with the Lord's Prayer." And after they were finished, Father John again said, "As the Lord so taught us to pray . . ." and again, the confused, but willing parish responded with the "Lord's Prayer." And for a third time after the prayer was finished, Father John said, "As the Lord so taught us to pray . . ." But then, before his willing congregation could have obliged him for the third time, Father John stopped, and he fainted, and then Father John died. And once again, Father John had stopped his prayer, and held out his arms, and he answered the one who called out to him.

Edward B. Mullen

Jason and Tommy

Jason and Tommy didn't have a typical relationship as brothers. Jason was 14 and Tommy was 10. Jason wasn't just Tommy's older brother, though; he was his best friend in the whole world. While most older brothers wanted nothing to do with their younger brothers, Jason would always try to invite Tommy to participate in his activities. Tommy loved his big brother. They were true pals.

Besides his brother Jason, Tommy didn't have many friends. Tommy often wondered what he would do without his older brother. You see, little Tommy had been born with a cardiopulmonary disease. This had stunted Tommy's growth and had robbed him of his youthful energy. It wasn't that he didn't want to play baseball, tag and all the games that other boys his age played, it's just that he got tired real quick when he did. Knowing this, the other boys never wanted Tommy to be on their team. They would fight over whose team Tommy would have to be on, and he was often labeled as a wimp or sissy by the healthier boys.

But things were different around his older brother Jason. Sometimes Tommy and Jason would play their own game of baseball. Jason was a good athlete and everyone wanted Jason on their team. However, Jason would only consent to play if they would also let Tommy be on his team. If the other boys said no, then Jason and Tommy would both leave and do something together.

School had just ended and it was summer now. Curt, Nathan and Ron wanted to go on an overnighter in the mountains. Naturally, they wanted Jason to come along also.

"Let's go ask him if he can go tomorrow," Ron spoke up.

Curt was quick to respond. "What if he wants Tommy to tag along? It will slow us all down, and we don't want to spend the whole time hiking to the campsite."

Nathan was the first to speak to Jason at his house. "Hey, Jason, the three of us are going on an overnighter up Adam's Canyon. Are you with us?"

"Sure I am!" Jason was excited. "I'll have Tommy's pack and my own ready to go tonight," he said.

The three boys looked at each other, wondering who would tell Jason that Tommy wasn't welcome to come. Finally, Curt spoke up. "Hey, ah, Jason . . . this hike is just for the four of us. Tommy would slow us all down. Nothing against Tommy, but why don't you leave him home this time?"

Jason saw Tommy through the corner of his eye. Tommy was standing by his bedroom door, listening intently to the whole conversation. He was bravely trying to hold back the tears of rejection.

Jason stood up and said, "I'm sorry, guys, but if Tommy isn't welcome, then I'm not going either. You guys have fun."

"Hey, wait a minute," said Ron. "It's okay with me if Tommy comes. We can leave a little bit earlier to give us more time."

The guys agreed on a departing time for the next morning, and left.

Six o'clock came early the next morning. Tommy was ready by 5:30 A.M. This was to be his first real hike.

Within the first quarter mile, it was obvious that Tommy's progress would be slow. He wanted so much to please Jason by walking fast, but the faster he walked, the sooner he would have to rest. The other boys were anxious to get to the campsite, and often found themselves leaving Jason and Tommy behind.

"Here, Tommy, my pack is light. Let me carry yours, too," Jason said, with concern for his brother.

Embarrassed, Tommy gave Jason his heavy burden. "I'm sorry," said Tommy. "I'm doing the best I can."

"I know, Tommy," Jason said as he rustled Tommy's hair.

After two miles, Tommy was struggling with fatigue. He was sweating profusely and fighting for air. His chest felt tight, too. *I'll go a long way before I stop to rest this time*, thought Tommy.

The other boys were out of sight now.

After five more minutes of walking, Tommy fell to his knees. "I gotta stop," whimpered Tommy, with tears of frustration cutting clear streams through the dust on his face.

"That's okay," said Jason. "Take all the time you need." Jason was obviously worried as he saw Tommy struggling for breath.

"Jason! Something is happening inside my chest! It hurts awful bad." Tommy was slumping over on the ground in pain. Jason slipped the packs off his back and rolled Tommy over. Tommy's tense body relaxed suddenly as he looked up into Jason's eyes that had tears now, too.

"I love you an awful lot, Jason." The struggle was over now. Tommy's little body had given up. The tears came freely from Jason's eyes as he tightly hugged his brother.

"I'll miss you, Tommy," Jason softly whispered.

Forty-five minutes later, the tears were still trickling from Jason's eyes when the other boys returned.

"Hey, Jason, we thought you guys got—" Ron stopped short in the middle of his comment. A chill ran down the boys' backs. Jason was supporting Tommy's silent head in his lap, caressing the tear-stained face of his little brother.

"Is he . . . is he dead, Jason?" Ron asked tenderly.

"Yeah," Jason said, as another tear fell quietly from his eyes to Tommy's face. "He was doing his very best for me." Two more minutes passed in silence. "I'll carry him down now," Jason said, as he gently lifted the lifeless body in the cradle of his arms.

Nothing was said for 20 minutes down the mountain trail. Finally, Curt tapped Jason on his shoulder, "I'll spell ya and carry Tommy for a while. You must be getting tired now."

"No," Jason kept walking. "He ain't heavy . . . he's my brother."

Author Unknown

The Greatest Sacrifice

The two caskets lay end to end in the receiving room of the funeral home. Double deaths had come to the Stokes family. Those who occupied the caskets had not come to the funeral home after dying with old age. They were young people, teenagers, just preparing to live. The tragedy of tragedies was that they were brother and sister, and both had been killed in the same tragic automobile accident.

A great crowd gathered to view the teenagers and to greet their grief-stricken parents, The Reverend and Mrs. Paul Stokes. How would they react? What would they say when they viewed not one but two of their precious children, now cold in death?

Each of the children was active in his or her respective school and had many friends. Paul Jr. attended nearby Coastal Carolina College, while Becky, his sister, was in the tenth grade in Aynor High School. Not only were they brother and sister, but they were also good friends.

On the night of the tragedy that led to their deaths, Becky and several friends had a birthday party for Paul Jr. at the First Baptist Church of Aynor, South Carolina, where Reverend Stokes was pastor.

After the party Paul Jr. asked Becky and her date,
Tommy, to go with him to Mullins to get his girl, Barbara,
and they would come back to Aynor. In traveling to
Mullins they had to drive on a highway that passed
through the Little Pee Dee Swamp.

The highway through the swamp was built on a cause-
way, with a canal filled with water on each side of the
road. There were no guardrails on the sides to prevent a
car from going into the canal, and on occasion someone
would run off the road, down the embankment and into
the deep water. Sometimes the person escaped; sometimes he drowned in his car.

No one knew what happened that fateful night after
they had gotten Barbara. They were coming back through
the swamp when something terrible happened. Their car
ran off the highway, down the high embankment and into
the water. The car sank with the brother and sister
drowning in the accident.

It would have been awful enough for one to perish in
the accident, but two, and both from the same family. The
entire student body of Aynor High School, Coastal
Carolina College and surrounding communities were
engulfed in grief. The church community where the
children lived was absorbed in the tragedy. Hundreds of
people were personally involved in the grief process.

At the funeral home, Reverend and Mrs. Stokes arrived
in a grief-worn condition. They went into the receiving
room where their beloved son and daughter lay, cold and
lifeless.

The crowd again wondered what reaction they would
have, or if they would be able to stand the pain.

Reverend and Mrs. Stokes walked and stood gazing
down upon their wonderful children, first one and then
the other. Tears again flooded their eyes as they stood
speechless for moments. Then from deep within his

crushed heart and soul, Reverend Stokes uttered words spoken centuries ago from another man who had lost his family. With tears streaming down his face he uttered the words of Job: "The Lord has given, and the Lord has taken. Blessed be the name of the Lord." With that he fell silent. It was at that precise moment, however, that the strength of the human spirit and supreme faith in God was revealed. The man of God, himself stricken to the heart, utterly human, did not curse his fate or the God that he loved so well. Instead, he and his faithful wife cast themselves and their dead children entirely into the hands of God. Those present knew that the stuff from which the minister and his wife were sewn was also the stuff from which heroes were made.

There was another twist to the story that demanded telling. The real hero of the situation lay in the casket that day. The son, Paul Jr., had indeed gone down with the car into the deep water with his sister. He had indeed drowned on that terrible night. However, Paul Jr., Tommy and Barbara had escaped from the car. He and Tommy had kicked the windshield out of the sunken automobile and three of them had come to the surface. Surfacing, they called to each other in the dark, and Paul Jr. realized that his sister, Becky, was still below, trapped in the car. Without hesitating he took long, deep gulps of air into his lungs and dived back down to the sunken car to help free his sister. Meanwhile, Tommy and Barbara swam quickly to the nearby shore and waited in the darkness for the sounds of surfacing swimmers. Time crawled as they agonized over the struggle that was going on below in total darkness in the black water. Finally, they knew that not only Becky but Paul Jr. also had perished in a tragedy enacted before their eyes.

The whole truth of the ordeal would not come to light for several hours. Paul Jr. had taken a course in senior lifesaving and was an excellent swimmer. Even in the darkness he had located the submerged automobile, but also he had to locate the front windshield to get back into the car. He had done that and had found Becky unconscious in the back seat. However, finding the car, the windshield and Becky in total darkness took time—too much time.

Later, when rescuers found Paul Jr. and Becky in the car, Paul Jr. had his arm around Becky's neck in the lifesaving technique position. In that position he was frozen in death. He had chosen to give his life in attempting to rescue his sister, rather than swim to safety without her. The teenage brother was the real hero, but he came from good stock.

Later, it was learned that Becky had no water in her lungs. She had been dead before she entered the water by either a broken neck or a severe blow to the head in the accident.

What was it Jesus said about such situations? "Better love has no man than this, that he lay down his life for a friend"—maybe even more so for a sister.

A few months ago, approximately 30 years after the accident, as Reverend Paul Stokes lay dying, he referred to Psalm 23 concerning "the valley of the shadow of death." He turned to his beloved wife and said, "I'm going through the valley of the shadow of death right now. Turn off the light so I can go on to our two children up in Heaven; you stay with the other two down here." With those words, he slipped into eternity to be with Paul Jr. and Becky.

The two caskets lay end to end in the receiving room of the funeral home, and in one casket lay a genuine hero who had made the greatest sacrifice.

Ray L. Lundy

Lessons from Lois

Carry each other's burdens, and in this way you will fulfill the law of Christ.

Gal. 6:2

From the moment Lois and I met on a tennis court years ago when our teenagers were babies, I was drawn to her mixture of honesty and encouragement. "Your backhand is better than your forehand," she told me bluntly that first day, which kind of miffed me because I wasn't used to having friends tell me the truth. "But you're okay," she smiled. "Let's play often." We did—and soon our friendship grew beyond the court.

When she was divorced, I was there. When my mother died, she was there. When she remarried, I brought the punch bowl and helped host her backyard reception. When she found out why she couldn't get rid of her cough, she called me. I'll never forget that conversation.

"Got a minute?" she asked when I answered the phone early one morning. She knew me better. I was always running late, but something in her voice made me know I had a minute.

"Sure," I answered. "What's up?"

"I have inoperable cancer in both lungs," she announced, her voice faltering.

I closed my eyes and shook my head in disbelief. "No, Lois . . ." I moaned. "That doesn't make sense." Lois was 43 years old. Her parents were healthy and in their 70s. She had never smoked, she checked ingredients on product labels and she jogged regularly. "What does this mean?" I asked.

"I'll take a leave of absence from teaching and start chemotherapy soon," she answered. "I'll probably get real sick for a while . . ."

"We'll pray, Lois," I vowed in angry determination. "For a miracle!"

"We need one. If the chemotherapy doesn't work, the doctor says I'm in serious trouble." She stopped and I knew she was crying.

"Oh, Lois . . ." I shook my head again, aching for her, and not knowing what to say.

When I hung up, I sank down on my bed and punched the pillow. How could this happen to someone so young, so active . . . so much like me? "Please Lord," I prayed, "give me the strength to walk beside Lois on this journey and don't let my own fears get in the way."

In the beginning Lois was determined to fight, but she also confessed her own fears. "I can't stand the thought of losing my hair," she said sorrowfully one day as she looked in the mirror. "What if I can't drive anymore . . . or get too weak to walk . . . or have to stay in bed all day?"

I didn't have many good answers, but I got her a tennis hat, with "Lois's Lid" embroidered on the brim, to cover her head should her hair start thinning, and I promised to rig up a giant slingshot system to get her out of bed if she felt weak. Mostly I listened to her, not daring to tell her that the thought of her dying scared me too.

After several weeks of chemotherapy, her X rays showed a 45 percent reduction of the tumors, and we rejoiced. She talked about going back to teaching. Her husband, Don, traded in her old car for one with better air conditioning, so she'd be more comfortable on warm days. Together, Lois and Don planned a dream trip to Hawaii.

But in a single day, everything suddenly changed. When I next stopped by, her 15-year-old daughter answered the door. "Mom's having trouble breathing," she said, "and the doctor wants her to go to the hospital right away."

In minutes we were on our way.

An X ray showed a critical buildup of fluid around her heart. "We're going to have to do surgery immediately," the doctor gently told her. "I'll call Don."

Instinctively I reached for her hand as she lay on the bed, but she had a faraway look in her eyes as if she was focusing on something beyond me or the doctor's words. Soon a nurse came and wheeled her to intensive care.

"This is not good," the doctor told me quietly.

The surgery went well, but when I saw Lois again a couple of days later, she was hooked up to a maze of tubes. I stood at the foot of her bed and gently squeezed her toes.

"I don't think we're going to lick this thing," she told me with a half smile. "I've been thinking lots about Jesus in Gethsemane. When he accepted God's plan, God turned his fears into courage and gave him the strength to meet the challenge . . . one step at a time."

A few days later Lois came home and turned a corner in her journey. Instead of fighting to live, she began preparing to die, determined to make the most of the time she had left. For a while, she seemed to have more physical energy than before. She flew to California to visit her parents and did so well that she insisted on following through with her and Don's plans to go to Hawaii.

"How do you like my new wig?" she asked with a giggle as she packed a wad of dark curly hair into her suitcase. Equipped with all sorts of medication, Lois and Don took off. "Having a great time," the postcard said. "Glad you're not here."

When she returned, Lois began sorting through boxes of family photographs and pasting them into albums. She asked me to help her type a detailed family history. She wrote loving letters of motherly advice to her son and daughter and explained how to make the traditional Christmas peanut brittle. With all that done, she asked me to come over and help her with one final detail.

"I'm planning my memorial service and I'd like you to do my eulogy," she said simply, as we sat together at her kitchen table, watching the spring rain drizzle down the window. A bolt of fear shot through me as I tried to imagine standing up in public and talking about Lois on some unknown day in the future, *after* she died.

"I'm—I'm not sure I can handle that," I stammered.

"Sure you can." She grinned and went right on, as if the matter were settled. "I want it to be a service of joy and victory. Here is a list of my favorite Scriptures and songs." She opened a red folder of papers. She talked more about programs and music and finally handed me the whole folder. "I know you can do it," she said, then added with the slightest wobble in her voice, "I don't want Don to have to deal with these details. I'm counting on you."

I nodded numbly. We hugged and I went home.

Later that afternoon, I sat at my desk, staring at the folder. *I can't do this,* I told myself. *But today at least I can write down a few notes about our conversations.* I did that and stuffed the papers into the red folder. "Lessons from Lois" I wrote across the front.

As the weeks passed, Lois grew weaker. When she could no longer walk to the corner, I pushed her around the neighborhood in a wheelchair that we christened "Her Royal Carriage." When she needed to carry her canister of oxygen along, we dubbed it "0-2," like some friendly character out of a science fiction movie. She delighted in our wheelchair walks and so did I.

Though the vitality was being sucked from her body, her spiritual strength seemed to be growing every day. "Sometimes I'm still afraid of dying," she admitted, "but I'm not afraid of *death*. I know where I'm going." Always, I came home from these walks and added more notes to my "Lessons from Lois" folder.

Finally the day came when Lois was no longer able to get out of bed. She became a hospice patient, and a kindly nurse visited regularly to adjust her medicine and keep her free from pain. Her parents came from California. Don began to take more time off work to be with her. We all took turns sitting by her bed. Sometimes I sang songs and read to her when she was awake. She told me I wasn't a great singer, but she liked me anyway.

My last visit with Lois came on a Friday afternoon. I didn't think she knew I was there, but I sat on her bed, my face close to hers, and softly recited some of her favorite verses. "You have fought the good fight . . . finished the race . . . kept the faith . . . well done, good and faithful servant . . ." I moistened her parched lips with a damp swab of cotton.

Without opening her eyes, she reached up and gently touched my face.

"You've done well too," she whispered. "Thanks."

Lois died just before dawn two days later on a summer Sunday morning. "Her journey is over," Don told me quietly on the phone. Even though I expected the news, I suddenly had a hard time connecting the word "death" with Lois. The two didn't go together.

It wasn't until the next afternoon that I pulled out my "Lessons from Lois" folder and began to spread the small scraps of paper across my desk. And as I did, I saw a pattern: clear, tangible evidence of how God gave Lois the strength to meet her challenges. The strength came not *before*, but *when* she got to them. She feared losing her hair, but when she got to that point, she teased about all the dramatic looks she could create with her new wigs. She worried about growing weak and staying in bed, but when that time came she seemed thankful and content. And when she neared the end of her struggle, she grew more and more peaceful about letting go of life here and looking forward to life in Heaven. God transformed her fears into strength one step at a time, just as he did with Jesus in Gethsemane.

As for me, no wonder I didn't have the same courage to face death as she did. Dying was not *my* challenge. Walking beside Lois and meeting her needs was, and God gave me the strength to meet those challenges—one step at a time. Now my challenge was to write her eulogy. I picked up a pencil and began.

Carol Kuyendall

The Miracle of Friendship

There's a miracle called friendship
That dwells within the heart,
And you don't know how it happens
Or how it gets its start . . .
But the happiness it brings you
Always gives a special lift,
And you realize that friendship
Is God's most precious gift!

Author Unknown

The Wedding Dress

It was a beautiful wedding on a crisp December day, a week before Christmas. I felt beautiful in my creamy white satin dress dotted with tiny pearls, accentuating my petite frame and auburn tresses. It was a season of joy and hope.

But joy and hope did not characterize the years that followed. How can one ever understand the mystery, the struggles, the inner life of another? I watched helplessly as my beloved succumbed to the grip of escalating alcoholism and the deceit that abides with it. I felt myself crumbling under the constant rain of emotional abuse, my energies revived only when that abuse began to turn its ugly face toward our two tiny children. Joy and hope were gone; the marriage was in shambles. The wedding dress, carefully packed away in memory of a happier time, became a source of pain.

Pain was also the experience of another woman. At the age of 27, Teresa was dying of cancer. The joy, the hope that should have been hers was ebbing. At her side was her beloved, shattered by the reality that their life together would not be, their wedding day only a dream.

I was no longer the young bride in the satin dress. Now a single parent, I struggled to care for my little ones. I reflected with gratitude upon the education that was mine. The ability to use my nursing skills not only supported my young family, but also provided a ministry of healing that could bless my patients and my wounded self as well. As I sought to lift Teresa's mantle of pain, I gave thanks for the bittersweet blessings of my own life.

As morphine dripped through the intravenous line, Teresa whispered to me, "My fiancé and I have decided that we want to get married before I die. I know that may not make sense, but we want to be one before God, even if only for a short time. I don't know how we would get married here, though."

"Let me talk to our chaplain," I responded.

The next two days in the nursing unit assumed the atmosphere of a party. The wedding chapel at the hospital was reserved, the chaplain counseled with the young couple about the meaning and blessing of marriage, the social worker—a gifted violinist—offered to play for the ceremony, and the hospital cafeteria promised a special reception feast.

"I guess I'll look kind of strange getting married in this hospital gown," commented Teresa. Her funds exhausted, her hospitalization was now covered by state insurance for the indigent. *My dress,* I thought. *My tiny wedding dress. It would be just the right size for Teresa.*

"I have a lovely dress you could wear," I said. "I wore it for my wedding, and I think it would fit you." As I described the dress and the delicate matching veil, Teresa's eyes sparkled.

The wedding day dawned clear and sunny. There was a hush throughout the nursing unit as the medical and nursing staff hurried through their morning tasks. An undercurrent of excitement and joy permeated the environment. The wedding dress hung at the foot of Teresa's bed, ready to be draped gently on the bride. Teresa waited contentedly, a soft smile framing her gaunt face.

At 1:00 P.M., I came into the room to begin dressing the bride. Outside Teresa's room a bridal bouquet of pink roses and baby's breath, donated by the local florist, waited. Entering the room, I glanced first at the creamy white satin dress dotted with tiny pearls, my thoughts on that crisp December day many years ago. I touched the fine fabric, enjoying its smoothness. Picking up the lovely dress, I turned to Teresa, momentarily noting how peaceful she appeared.

"Teresa, are you ready to be a beautiful bride? Teresa? Teresa!" *Oh, no. Please, God, not now. Please don't let her die right now!* Teresa glanced briefly at me, gently smiling her good-bye.

The atmosphere turned from joy to tears. Teresa's fiancé sobbed inconsolably as he threw himself across her frail body. Her mother crumpled at the end of the bed. I held the wedding dress to my own bosom, splashing tears onto the tiny pearls.

Two days later, Teresa's mother and fiancé sought me out, asking if I could spare the time to attend the funeral. "Teresa loved you," said her mother. "We would be honored if you could be with us at the funeral. She wanted so much to be a bride, and you understood."

She wanted so much to be a bride. In life she was denied this joy. "My Teresa would have been beautiful in that lovely dress," said her mother.

If not beautiful in life, why not in death? No, Lord, no. That's too much.

"My purpose is that they may be encouraged in heart and united in love, so that they may have the full riches of complete understanding, in order that they may know the mystery of God." (Col. 2:2, 3 NIV)

"What do you mean, Lord?" I asked.

"Encourage them in heart and show them my love through your love."

With a faltering voice, I asked, "How will Teresa be dressed for her funeral?" Averted eyes—and then, "We haven't decided yet. All her clothes are so old and too big for her now."

"My purpose is that they be encouraged in heart . . ."

"Would you like to dress Teresa in her wedding dress?" I asked.

"But that is your wedding dress," said her fiancé.

"No, it *was* my wedding dress, but it was also to be Teresa's wedding dress. It's her dress. You may have it."

Teresa was buried in the creamy white satin dress with tiny pearls. A filmy matching veil gently covered her face, still delicate in death. I stood at her grave site, trying to understand the mystery of God's ways. *"Oh, the depth of the riches of the wisdom and knowledge of God! How unsearchable his judgments and his paths beyond tracing out! Who has known the mind of the Lord?"* (Rom. 11:33, 34 NIV)

Barbara Frye, Ph.D.
Submitted by Ruby Hinrichs

Helen's Story

. . . I will never leave you or forsake you.

Heb. 13:5

Helen Packer was 17 years old when I met her. A devout Christian and much-loved child, she was entering the hospital for the last time. Her diagnosis was lymphoma and all attempts at remission had failed. Helen shared with me, her nurse, that she could handle everything but the thought of dying alone.

She just wanted a loved one near her to hold her hand and pray with her. Helen's mother would stay at her bedside from early morning to late evening, return home for rest and resume the vigil come morning. Her father traveled in his job but relieved his wife as often as he could.

All of the nurses on the unit realized that Helen was precariously near death, as did she and her family. She began having seizures and lapses of consciousness.

As I was leaving the hospital at 11:00 one night, I noticed Helen's mother heading toward the parking garage as well. Our conversation was interrupted by the loudspeaker. "Outside call, Helen Packer. Please call the operator!"

Mrs. Packer reacted immediately with alarm. "Everyone knows how ill she is!" she blurted. "I'm going back to her room and see who is calling." With that she left me and returned to Helen. The operator reported that the calling party had hung up but left a message: "Tell Helen her ride will be late but is coming."

Baffled, Mrs. Packer stayed at Helen's bedside in anticipation of a mysterious visitor. Helen died at 1:13 A.M. with her mother at her side, holding her hand and praying.

When queried the next day, the operator couldn't remember even the gender of the caller. No other Helen Packer was found, employee or patient or visitor. For those of us who cared for, nurtured and prayed for Helen, there was only one answer.

Sandy Beauchamp

Sweet Good-byes

Truly, I say to you, unless you turn and become like children, you will never enter the kingdom of Heaven.

Matt. 18:3

My daughter, Whitley, was only two when she first met death. It came as a cancer that slowly stole her "adopted" grandmother, "Miss Betty." Whitley's natural grandparents were alive, but "Miss Betty" and "Mr. Bill" were nearby, and because their own grandchildren lived several hours away, Whitley was a welcome addition to their lives. The relationship pleased all of them.

"Miss Betty," an immaculate silver-haired woman, had baby-sat for Whitley when I taught a three-week summer school class, and their bond had deepened. Betty was very active, and the two of them would go on long walks "discovering" the neighborhood flowers. With a twinkle in her eye, she would describe Whitley's daily accomplishments to me just like a proud grandmother. One day Betty mentioned that she had scheduled a doctor's appointment.

"I've had just a little funny feeling in my side," she said. The appointments and tests and surgeries and treatments began soon after that and continued over the next 16 months.

When we went to visit, Whitley couldn't understand why Miss Betty had to sit in her chair all the time. Or why she wore a scarf on her head now. Or why "Mr. Bill" seemed so sad. As Betty's condition moved from bad to worse, we stopped taking Whitley to visit.

The last time I saw Betty alive was in August, and she spoke warmly of Whitley. In a fragile voice, she assured me that Whitley was a special child God would use. Tears streaked down my cheeks as I nodded my head. Betty was dying and yet she was encouraging.

In the midst of the bustle that surrounds a death, Bill, a robust, aggressive man, began to fall apart. Even his children were shocked at the change. With Betty's passing, a man who had always been an indomitable mountain became a hollow shell. Bill and Betty had lived out clearly defined roles. He made the decisions; she agreed. He took the credit, and she was happy for him. Her absence suddenly revealed that he had been the structure, but she had been the foundation.

In the months after Betty's death, my husband and I frequently invited Bill over for dinner. He was the kind of man who had never boiled water, but he had a hearty appetite and savored a home-cooked meal.

He also enjoyed the eager company of Whitley. At first I worried about her many questions. "Is Miss Betty in Heaven?" "Do you miss her?" "Are you ever going to see her again?" But the only topic Bill really wanted to discuss was Betty, and Whitley's questions opened the door for him.

One Sunday afternoon in October, Whitley began to talk about Mr. Bill. She wanted to invite him over for dinner, but we had other plans. I promised we would see him soon, but that didn't pacify her. She was worried about him. "What did he have for dinner?" she asked, her chocolate-brown eyes widening. "What if he's lonely, Mommy?"

The questions continued all evening, and by bedtime she began to cry. "I just wanna talk to Mr. Bill!" To be honest, I was getting a little irritated. In desperation, I suggested she could call him.

When Bill answered the phone, I apologetically explained that Whitley had insisted she speak to him. He was genuinely thrilled and touched by her concern. They spoke briefly about what she had eaten for dinner, her new sleepers and togs.

When I got back on the phone, Bill confided he had been sitting in the darkness and feeling very down. Whitley's call had been like a "burst of sunlight." Yes, he was lonely. I was ashamed it had taken the insistence of a two-year-old for me to make the call.

The next day Bill suffered a massive heart attack. He never even made it to the hospital.

I can't count the number of times I've recalled Whitley's final words to Bill. "Bye-bye. I love you, and I'll see you soon." If only all of our good-byes could be so sweet.

Jeanine Marie Brown

Good Night, Sweet Dreams, I Love You

My dad had been in the hospital for almost three months, suffering from an inoperable brain tumor and from the debilitating effects of the radiation treatment he had received for the tumor. His 76-year-old body just could not tolerate the abuse it had been dealt.

He had been so very weak when he had entered the hospital, but for most of the first two months' hospitalization, he was quite lucid and quite hopeful of recovery and of returning home. He was also afraid though, realizing that death could be near. I believe his fear had more to do with leaving his family than about death itself. But I couldn't know that for sure because we had not and could not discuss it. Though we had our rough times through the years, one thing was always very clear—my dad loved his family more than anything in life.

Toward the end of the second month in the hospital, they found another tumor in his brain. The doctors were not optimistic that his body could tolerate another round of radiation therapy, but left the decision to the family. At this point, my dad was not thinking clearly and could not make this decision for himself, so it was left to my mom (his wife of 52 years), my sister, my brother and me. After many discussions and many tears, we decided not to put him through the pain of the treatment. He had suffered so much already and the prognosis was not good—it would only extend his life by a few months, if he even survived the treatment. We never told him of the second tumor.

During the third month in the hospital, Dad slept a lot and needed help feeding himself. When he did talk, his voice was so weak, we could barely understand him. We tried to get him to write out his messages, and he tried, but he could not write legibly. It was very frustrating for him and for us, also very sad.

My mom spent every day, all day in his hospital room, but went home at night. I went to the hospital almost every night and on weekends when I was not working. I fed him his dinner and just sat with him, telling him news of the family or just chatting about the day's events. He rarely responded, but when he did say something, it was always just a few words that rarely made sense. Yet every night when I left him, he always said, "Good night, sweet dreams, I love you." I could understand these words; words he had repeated to each of his children each night throughout our childhood.

Toward the end of the third month, he slept or stared at the ceiling, not seeming to understand much that was going on around him. The nurses treated the severe bedsores he had developed, but he never complained or even acknowledged the pain they must have caused him.

I tried never to let my dad see me crying, because I didn't want to alarm or sadden him. But one night, when I was alone with him, I couldn't stop the tears. I stood with my back to him, staring out the hospital window, with tears streaming down my face. I was remembering all the good times my dad and I had had together, and was also feeling sad that I had waited too late to tell him how much he had meant to me and how very much I loved him. I also regretted that I avoided discussing the issue of death with him. I know it must have weighed heavily on his mind, but no one mentioned it, not quite knowing how. I knew he would not understand now.

Then from behind me, I heard my father say, in clear, precise words, "Don't cry, honey. I'm not crying. It's time for you to let me go."

Astounded at the clarity of his words and the force of what he had said, I went to his bed and put my arms around him, still visibly crying.

He held me close with the little strength he had and said, "I wish I had been a better father. I wanted to do so much for you, your sister and your brother. And I wanted to be a better husband to Mom."

This miraculous moment gave me the opportunity I thought I had missed. I said, "I don't ever want to let you go, but I understand if you have to. I don't want you to worry about leaving us, even though it will leave a great void in our lives, because you have been the most wonderful father anyone could have ever had. You have loved your family with a rare intensity. And yes, we had some rough times, but we always loved you just as much."

We then shared several stories we remembered, just small incidental things like when he had watched me eating dirt as a toddler. He said I wouldn't eat just any dirt, it had to be just the right kind. I would pick several pieces up and put them down until I found just the right one. He smiled as he recounted this story to me, as he had when he told it so many times before. We talked about the cage he built for my brother and me to keep our horned toads in, and about my brother and me forever annoying my older sister when she began dating. We laughed and we cried over these little pieces of our lives.

He told me he was not afraid, but he hated leaving us. When I asked if I could do anything for him, he said, "Just keep the love and the family together."

After a while, I could tell he was becoming very fatigued and kissed him good night, though I hated to see this moment end. We each said, "Good night, sweet dreams, I love you." His eyes were closed in sleep before I reached the door to the hall.

I left the hospital still amazed at what had just transpired—that we had been able to have a real, meaningful conversation, when he had not been able to communicate for weeks. It was as if he had mustered every ounce of energy and strength left in his body to manage it. It was truly a miracle.

Sometime during that night, my father died peacefully in his sleep. The doctor called us around 6:00 A.M. and told us we should come to the hospital immediately. We were all there within 30 minutes, but he was already gone. Looking at his peaceful face, I felt overwhelmingly sad. But I also knew that I had been granted an extraordinary gift the night before when my dad and I had been able to reach out to each other.

When we reached my mom's house only a few blocks away, a thunderstorm was developing. We were all crying so much, we barely noticed the storm. Then suddenly from the front window, we saw a lightning bolt streak out of the sky and hit the tall pine tree in the middle of the front yard, a tree my dad had watched grow from a sapling. There was an extremely loud pop as flames swiftly blazed out where the lightning hit the tree in an incredible flash. It then extinguished itself just as quickly. It was quite spectacular, and we were all stunned for a moment and stopped crying. Then I knew. Dad was reaching out to us one last time.

As I looked at the tree and at the clouds above, an

overwhelming sense of peace enveloped me as I thought of the conversation I had with my dad the night before, and I calmly said, "Yes, you were special. Good night, sweet dreams, I love you, Daddy."

Marilyn S. Dunham

The Ties That Bind

In my father's house there are many mansions.
I go to prepare a place for you. And you yourself
know the way where I am going.

John 14:2, 4

In 1973 when my dad retired, a new chapter in my parents' lives began. My mom continued to care for the house and tend to her beautiful yard, my dad took care of his backyard garden.

Their past practice of a big meal in the evening changed to an early dinner in the afternoon and a light lunch in the evening. When it was time for their snack, my mom would go into the kitchen, make them something to eat, and set the table for two. She would go into the living room and gently say, "Come on, Pa, coffee's ready," and the two of them would sit down together to eat and converse. Life was good. The two of them continued to enjoy each other, the kids and all the grandchildren, and all that went along with growing old together.

As the years went by and they neared their 80s, a noticeable change was occurring with my dad. We watched

Alzheimer's slowly devour every bit of his life and dignity. But my parents still continued to live and care for each other as they had done for all their married lives. Once again a dark shadow came upon them when my mom had a stroke. Fortunately, she could speak and her mind was still sharp as a tack. After rehabilitation, she walked with a quad cane and came home to her family, still caring for her husband, who most of the time now did not really know who she was. Still, their evening time never changed. Mom would slowly get to the kitchen, set the table for two, prepare a snack and say, "Come on, Pa, coffee's ready," and he would come, not really knowing for what. This went on for over two more years. Although my dad's mind continued to deteriorate day by day, Mom would not even think or discuss the possibility of having my dad put in a nursing home, even though it was all she could do to take care of herself. After all, when you marry, it's through sickness and health, till death do you part.

In the summer of 1995, a short time after their 61st wedding anniversary, my mom's health was failing, and she told us of a vision she had one evening while asleep. There was the most beautifully set table that one could imagine hovering over her bed. She related there was no food on the table, but it was set for two. We thought the table in her dream was set for her and the Lord.

In August, my mom became sick and had to be hospitalized: The day following her admission, my dad took sick and had to be hospitalized also. The family doctor told my mom there was no way she could go on in her condition caring for my dad. It was inevitable: he needed round-the-clock care. A week later, they found a nursing home that would accept Alzheimer's patients, but it was 70 miles away from home. Mom was devastated, but we had no choice. A week after that, my mom went to live with my sister. No more evening snacks together, no more telling him the coffee's ready, no time to sit and enjoy one another's company.

One month later, my mom became very sick. She spent her last week on earth at home with her children, grandchildren and great-grandchildren. They came from near and far to be with the mom and grandma they had loved and cherished. On the night before she passed away, all through the evening she kept thrashing and holding up two fingers. On Friday, September 29, 1995, she went home to be with the Lord. That afternoon, a few of us kids went to the nursing home where my dad was. He smiled and was full of mischief, not knowing any of us. We all agreed it would serve no purpose to take him to the funeral home.

On Monday morning, October 2, 1995, my mom was laid to rest. That evening at 8:00, the nursing home called us to say my dad had passed away. It was now evident that the two fingers she kept holding up had to be that she was telling the Lord that she needed a table for two. Once again, she had gone ahead and made sure that the beautiful table she spoke to us about was set for two, and then called him to say, "Come on, Pa, coffee's ready."

Virginia Jarvis

The Miracle of the Ring

Where there is great love there are always miracles.

Willa Cather

I don't know why that ring, in particular, took on such a significance for me. It's funny, isn't it, after someone dies, which everyday objects take on heightened meaning? But the loss of Ronnie's ring somehow compounded my grief. I guess God knew that.

I bought the ring for my son, Ronald Gene Johnson, when he was 14. It was fashioned from his initials: RGJ. I bought a matching one for my husband, too, so they could have something alike. Ronnie put his on right away. "Thanks, Mom," he said, giving me a big hug. From then on, he never took it off.

Ronnie was a wonderful son. He loved sports—but he also loved to play Beethoven on the piano. He was class president, popular and admired—and he was never embarrassed about hugging me in public. And we were so proud of him when he won a football scholarship to Wichita State.

Then one October evening a friend came to my door to tell me she'd heard on the news that the plane carrying Ronnie's team home had crashed into a Colorado mountain. His body was one of the first recovered, but the ring was gone. I don't remember much about those terrible days. My daughter Vickie Lynn tells me I kept asking, "But where is the ring?" It was impossible for me to grasp that Ronnie was just gone forever, along with all our hopes and dreams.

There were so many moments when I felt Ronnie with me, heard his voice, when I expected to turn and see him. And sometimes I thought I did. But those moments became fewer and the images dimmer as the months wore on.

With time, our grief ebbed but it never went away. Howard stopped wearing his ring, and I understood. It made him feel the loss even more. He put it in a box in the dresser.

Years passed, but still whenever I opened the drawer and my gaze fell on the box that held a solitary ring, I wept, knowing that somewhere there was another just like it, lost forever—like my Ronnie.

What was it about the ring that haunted me? I'm not sure. Maybe it was because it was precious and it had slipped away, like Ronnie's life. The thought of it alone, hidden and buried, troubled me, and the impossibility of finding it weighed me down.

One afternoon, more than 10 years after the crash, I was resting in the living room when the phone rang. The woman on the other end said, "I've been to the crash site on Mount Trelease, and I think I have something that may belong to you."

What? Did I hear her correctly? My eyes filled with tears. "You have Ronnie's ring!" I gasped.

There was a long silence on the other end.

"Yes," she said finally.

Her name was Kathy. "I don't know how to tell you this," she started.

She explained that her husband was an aviation buff whose interest was investigating crash sites. They had taken a hotel room not far from the area and arranged for a guide to take them up the mountain two days later. The first night in the hotel, she said, she was suddenly awakened from a dream, a vision of a young, blond-haired man walking away from her still fresh in her mind.

My heart skipped a beat. Ronnie had blond hair.

The dream disturbed her so much, she convinced her husband to change hotels. But the same thing happened the next night. And this time, she felt compelled to follow the young man in her dream.

In the morning, she drove with her husband and the guide to the base of the mountain. She had no intention of going up there, and had even brought along a book to read while she waited in the van. But when her husband and the guide were about 75 feet up the path, a feeling came over her. *I have to go too,* she thought.

It was a hard climb—it took about three hours. When she sat down on a boulder to catch her breath, she saw by her feet something glinting, poking up out of the ground. Reaching down, she brushed the dirt away and picked up the ring.

"I just knew it belonged to the blond boy," she told me.

"Yes," I said, choking back my tears.

This was so extraordinary—and frightening—to Kathy that she had to know more. So she went to the local television station and looked through footage of the accident. "That's him!" she shouted, when she came to Ronnie's picture. And that's how she found me.

A few days after our conversation, Kathy came to our home. I opened the door to a beautiful, calm face. She smiled sweetly and reached into her purse. I trembled as she placed the ring in my hand. Although the years and elements had left it dull, to me it sparkled brilliantly. In tears, I hugged Kathy, because she was someone Ronnie's soul had touched, and that made her a friend.

I had known for years that having the ring would bring me peace. And it has. I knew it was Ronnie's way of reaching out to me to say, *I'm all right, Mom. And you can be, too.* And it was God's gracious way of reassuring me that he loved me, and cared about a mother's grief, a mother's healing.

Although I will miss Ronnie forever, I knew that in some way, part of my suffering was over. Part of him has now been returned to me. Holding the ring, I watch the light glint off the letters, and wonderful memories come rushing back: all of my first-born's birthdays and holidays, stories he shared, snippets of conversations. I lovingly placed the ring in the box next to Howard's. It's safe now.

Kathy had a marker set at the foot of the mountain in loving memory of Ronnie and the other young lives lost so many years ago, and our hearts were finally healed.

Now, not one day goes by that I don't think of Kathy and her remarkable gift. I wanted so much to visit again with her, but I've never been able to track her down. She seems to have disappeared into thin air. Sometimes I wonder if she was real or if she was an angel on a mission of the heart.

Virginia Johnson
As told to Meg Lundstrom
Excerpted from Woman's World *Magazine*

My Unforgettable Pop

Our work brings people face to face with love. To us what matters is an individual. To get to love the person we must come in close contact with him.

Mother Teresa

After my father died of kidney failure at 35, my mother eventually started dating other men. They showed up loud and jittery, newly barbered and usually smelling too powerfully of cologne. Few of them returned to our house in Philadelphia, and none more than twice. For my two younger sisters and me, they remained only as the butt of jokes or tricks we'd played on them.

One of my mother's dates left his sunglasses in the living room while he had a lemonade in the kitchen. I entertained myself by testing the strength of the frames. They snapped like twigs.

When he returned to the living room, the man pocketed the pieces and abruptly left. My mother said little about what I'd done, understanding better than I the nature of the ill will I harbored in my 14-year-old heart.

Some months later, my sisters came into my room.

"Mom's got a boyfriend," the older one piped.

"What's he like?" I asked.

"He's got a big nose," the eight-year-old said. "That's why his last name is Bananas, because his nose is as big as a banana."

"It's his nickname," my 10-year-old sister added. "He's coming to dinner." None of the other men had been invited to dinner, and I was old enough to know what this meant. My mother was more serious about Al Bananas than the others.

The following evening, a man with licorice-black hair and the facial lines of Roman statuary stood with complete ease in the middle of our living room. *He does have a big nose,* I thought.

"This is Al," my mother said, nervously wringing a dish towel in her hands. "Al Sbarra."

"My real name's Attilio," the man said amicably, "but everybody calls me Al. Good friends call me Al Bananas." He offered his hand, and I awkwardly shook it, mine feeling small and delicate in his calloused plumber's grip.

"We met before," Al said. "I saw you in the hospital when you were a kid. You were in an oxygen tent."

Shortly before my third birthday, I'd come down with severe croup, which so impaired my breathing that I had to undergo an emergency tracheotomy and hovered near death for a week.

"I was a friend of your father's," Al continued. "I gave him a lift to the hospital one day, and I brought you a red fire truck."

"I don't remember you," I told him, unimpressed. But I did remember the fire truck. It was made of steel and had rubber wheels that spun smoothly. I liked that truck so much that I sometimes slept with it, and I can still recall the coolness of its metal against my cheek and the smell of its enamel.

Al returned to the house several times that spring and summer. A year later, not only was he eating dinner at the house every evening, but there was talk of marriage.

I found it difficult to picture Al occupying the same position that my father had, and when I did briefly imagine it, I became irritable.

"I'm never going to call him Dad," I told my sisters.

"Mom says we can call him Pop," the younger one said.

"I'll never call him that either," I answered. To call Al "Pop" would suggest an intimacy that didn't exist between us—nor, I thought, ever would. My father had been distant and often angry, but his presence in the house had been so powerful that I still felt it.

For many years, I regarded Al as merely my mother's friend who showed up at the house around dinner time and who left before ten o'clock. During that period, Al's estranged first wife refused him a divorce. When he was finally able to marry my mother in 1973, I was living in an apartment, going to college and majoring in English literature. Al was neither more nor less than my mother's second husband.

One early summer night after playing softball, I stopped at our house to say hello. I heard a Frank Sinatra tune as I approached the front door and, looking through a window, saw Al and my mother slow-dancing in the kitchen. I'd never seen my mother and father dance, or show any affection for each other, so I didn't have any memory to compare with this picture of Al and my mother. I waited for the tune to end before entering the house.

Al seemed happy to see me. "There's a laborer's job in Jersey at $2.25 an hour," he said, meaning at the construction site where he worked. "If you want it, come with me tomorrow."

I had been looking for a summer job. "I'm very interested," I told him.

The next morning he picked me up at my apartment at seven o'clock, and we rode in the early sunlight into New Jersey. At the job site I was assigned to unload dozens of refrigerators and dishwashers from a trailer.

As we drove home after work, Al asked, "So how did it go?"

"Fine," I told him, too tired to elaborate and doubtful that he was actually interested.

He continued to press, then and later, listening as I talked about the work I'd done. Soon he was asking about more than my work. When I began dating the girl who would become my wife, Al surprised me one day by saying, "Your mother says she's very nice. Tell me about her."

I had no idea he knew about her or cared. But his asking about her broke something in me, and our talks became more open.

Al learned what was important to me, and I, well, I knew what was important to him: work, sports and family.

He'd lived nearly his entire life only a few blocks from the row house in which he was born and raised, and from the houses of his brothers and sisters. That South Philadelphia working-class neighborhood was big and rich enough for him. Our family eventually joined him in South Philly, and on trips through the neighborhood Al proudly introduced me to friends.

"You can never have too many friends," he said during one of our walks. Did he ever desire to live in another place? "Why move away from your family?" he answered.

After that summer ended, Al began to ask me along on side jobs he did once or twice a month on Saturdays. It was a good way for both of us to earn a few extra dollars, and I rarely turned him down, even after graduating from college.

While Al worked, he kept his toolbox within reach and let me perform only the simplest tasks. He seemed to want me to learn his craft by watching and listening. Soon

I was making up the materials list and laying out the tools he needed for a job.

At lunch Al sometimes took me to diners where he seemed to know everyone. Once we shared a table with a group of his buddies, to whom he announced that I was "the kid with the genius hands" he had told them about.

One particular Saturday morning, I told Al that, because of budget slashing, I was to be laid off from my regular work as a library assistant. I wondered aloud, "How am I going to get a job doing what I want to do when I can't even keep a job working at something I don't like?"

Al made no comment until later. "Even if you don't get that job you want, you can always do something to make money," he said. "Don't worry. Everything will work out in the end." He then told me how he'd gotten the name Bananas.

His father, Al said, had peddled bananas in the streets of Philadelphia after he'd lost his job, and he often took Al along with him. Al would run from door to door with a bunch of bananas for sale. Because some of his friends lived behind those doors, they began to call him Al Bananas, a name that stuck.

"My father didn't make much money, but I was sorry when he got another job," he added. "It was nice being with him those times."

I realized then that Al's teaching me a skill and providing me an opportunity to make some money were far less important to him than the time we spent together. Without showing outward affection, Al was fathering me in the only way he knew how, in the way his father had nurtured him. Al had been doing so, really, ever since he'd given me that fire truck when I was a child lying sick in a hospital bed.

Late the following morning, I was feeling feverish. Al came by my apartment to bring me my pay for the work we'd done. "You don't look so good," he said, gazing down at me.

"I don't feel so good."

"I'll have your mother make you some chicken soup. Anything else I can bring you?"

Without thinking, I said, "How about a red fire truck?"

Al looked baffled—then he smiled. "Sure." When he put my wages on the bedside table, I said, "Thanks . . . Pop."

Some weeks later, Pop telephoned to say he was going to the cemetery to visit his parents' graves and asked if I wanted to come along. He knew that my father was buried in the same place and that I had not been there since the funeral, but he made no mention of this.

After some hesitation, I said, "All right."

Later, inside the cemetery gates, Pop gave me a slight nod and started toward the graves of his parents. I watched him head away and then, tentatively, I set off to find my father.

When I located the grave, I stood a long while and simply gazed at my own last name chiseled in the white stone. Beneath the name were the dates that encapsulated my father's brief life. *The most terrible consequence of his early death,* I thought, *was that I had not known him. Who was he? Did he love me?*

I had not moved when Pop joined me at the grave and put his hand on my shoulder. "Your father was a good man," he said. "He would do anything for you." That compliment freed emotions I'd kept locked away since my father died. As I began to sob, Pop held me.

On the quiet ride home, I began to appreciate what Pop had done. He'd asked me along to the cemetery, it seemed, so I might restore part of my life that I didn't even know was missing or important until faced with it—my father's memory. He showed me, by joining me at my father's grave, that there was room in my heart for both of them.

In the summer of 1994, Pop woke up with a severe pain in his back. X rays revealed a lung tumor. This and later news that Pop's cancer had spread to his bones devastated us. He'd never been seriously ill in his life.

Pop showed no bitterness. During all the tests, grim reports and radiation treatments, he never complained or lost faith that the doctors would cure him or that God would intervene. The last time I saw him alive, his smile appeared below the tube that fed oxygen to his lungs, and he said, "Don't worry. Everything will work out."

I held his hand as the day and the last of his life faded, and I pictured him beside my hospital bed when I was a child. I wondered if he'd spoken the same words to my father as they looked at me through the plastic of the oxygen tent. Had he somehow glimpsed himself in my future? I don't know, but he did become a vital part of it. Things had indeed worked out by his becoming my pop.

When it was time to go, I said, "I love you, Pop."

He looked up at me through his morphine haze and, nodding slightly, squeezed my hand. There was that smile. He understood.

"So long, Pop," I said, "See you tomorrow." I went out into the chill autumn dusk, holding back tears.

Pop died in his sleep the following afternoon. When I received the news, I was stunned. I couldn't imagine never hearing his voice again and never placing another tool in his strong hands.

Some weeks after the funeral, I went into my mother's basement for a wrench that I needed to replace a washer in her leaky faucet. I opened the toolbox and removed the wrench, but instead of returning with it to the first floor, I held it tightly against my chest. Trembling with fresh grief, I closed my eyes and remembered the many excursions Pop and I had made, not realizing until that moment how much they'd meant to me, while at the same time being enormously grateful that Pop and I had spent that time together.

My mother descended the stairs with a basket of laundry before I moved. She saw me standing in front of the tools with the wrench clutched in my hands.

"Why don't you take the tools home," she said. "Pop would want you to have them. He wouldn't want them sitting here collecting dust."

"No, neither would I." They still retained Pop's essence, and I wanted to be close to that. "Pop was a good man, Mom, and I'm glad you married him."

That was the first time I'd acknowledged Pop's importance in my mother's life. I'd never quite realized until then that she might have needed to hear it much earlier. We embraced there beside the tools before I headed back upstairs to fix the faucet.

I brought Pop's tools home with me that day, and I will treasure them to my own end. But I will cherish more what Pop taught me—to love without selfishness and to forgive the injuries of the past, for only then will our hearts be fully open.

Albert DiBartolomeo

Dearest Mother

They that sow in tears shall reap in joy.

Ps. 126:5

I have heard of parents who have lost a child and never recovered. Having now been through this most life-shattering of events, I can fully understand how this could happen. That is why I'm so grateful that my precious child, to whom I gave life, gave that same gift back to me.

After having two boys, Michael and Scott, I wanted to dress my little girl in lace. But Michelle was a tomboy, climbing trees and splashing in puddles. She always had such spirit—and her share of scrapes.

So when she began to bruise all the time at 16, I thought it was because she was always being bumped in sports. But then after I hugged her one day, my fingerprints stayed on her arms. Thinking she might have an iron deficiency, I took her to the doctor.

He drew blood and asked us to wait at the office for the results. One hour passed, then two. Something's wrong, I feared. Finally, the doctor came back and said: "I'm afraid Michelle may have leukemia."

I took hold of Michelle's hand. I felt dizzy with despair. "Cancer . . ." I breathed

"Will I die?" she asked.

"No!" I said. But the word was forced. I didn't know. I didn't know . . .

Hospital tests showed that Michelle had acute lymphoblastic leukemia. "It's the most curable form in children," the doctor told us. My hopes rose. Then he said: "But Michelle is no longer a child."

"Don't worry, Mom," she said. "We'll fight this." *My brave baby!* I thought. Looking into her eyes, I saw more determination than fear—and I felt calmer myself.

Michelle immediately started chemotherapy. I worked as a receptionist, and my boss was generous enough to give me the time off I needed—especially since I was a single mom and Michelle had only me. I didn't leave her side for a moment, holding her hand as radiation punished her body. At night, as she slept, I sat by her bedside and prayed, pleading with the deep agony of love. I think the hardest part was when she lost her hair. It was a constant reminder to both of us that she was sick.

Then something wonderful happened. After treatment was over, she threw herself into life and dragged me with her! "C'mon, Mom," she'd say, dragging me away from the sink. "The dishes can wait; let's go see the waterfall!" We waltzed in the kitchen as we made dinner; sang at the top of our lungs to the car radio; laughed until we cried when her wig flew off on an amusement park ride.

Even at the time, I knew this relationship was unusual for a teenage girl and her mother. I knew that our new relationship was a special gift.

Oh, there were times she'd sob, "Why me? Tell me what I did and I won't do it again!" I had to gather all my strength as I took her into my arms.

And there were many times I wasn't so strong. But

Michelle would say, "Mom, if I can do it, you can too! We can beat this."

And for a while, it seemed we had. After two years, Michelle was in remission. "Now I can go to college, be like other girls," she said. I let her go, praying. May she know only happiness.

And she knew real happiness when she met Bill. He was the quiet type, but it wasn't long before he was walking in the rain with her. Michelle's love of life was contagious.

Then one night she called me in a panic. "Something's wrong," she said, her voice shaking. "I don't feel . . . well."

Her cancer was back with a vengeance.

This time, we tried two bone marrow transplants. For the first she received marrow she had donated herself, her older brother Michael's marrow for the second. But it didn't help, and Michelle grew sicker and weaker.

Why now, God? I asked. Why didn't you take her before? Why did you give her hope?

But then I realized she wouldn't have gone to college . . . or fallen in love. These happy years were a gift.

"Mother, I might not make it this time, " she said as her body started to fail her.

"There's a chance you *will*," I said, wanting so to believe. But she slipped farther and farther away.

One afternoon, I saw she was having trouble breathing. Suddenly, with an energy she hadn't had in weeks, she put her arms around me. I knew she was telling me it was time for us to say good-bye. And although I would never, ever be ready, I had to.

"Let go, honey," I said, and started singing a lullaby I sang when she was a baby. "You are my sunshine, my only sunshine . . ." Her eyes fluttered, and she was gone.

For days, I just moved around the house, staring at her place at our table, her favorite spot on the couch, her bedroom. And then one day I walked into her bedroom, quiet and still. There were stuffed animals on the bed and her rocking chair in the corner. How hard it was to stand among so many of her things!

As I sifted through some of her things, a single sheet fell to the floor and I picked it up. *Dearest Mother . . .* it began.

At first, I read it in shock, weeping hard and long after. And then I allowed her words to touch me:

You cried with me and for me, my daughter had written.

> *I was so afraid to leave you. I wasn't always asleep when you thought I was. I heard your prayers.*
>
> *What a wonderful mother you have been. I'll always be with you—inside. I'll see you again, and we will still stay close until then. Mom, being sick taught me how to live. So don't mourn me. Be happy.*

"I promise," I said.

But I'd wake up in the morning and think, I can't do this. How can I just go on? Driving in the car, my eyes would fill with tears, and I'd have to pull over. "Okay, Michelle," I'd say out loud. "I'll pull myself together."

It's a hard promise to keep. And sometimes it hurts so much. But then I take out her letter and hear her voice coaxing me to go out and look up into the sky, to live and be happy. And I go.

I gaze into the expanse of blue sky, full of puffy clouds, and think, *That one looks like a turtle. And that one? Michelle would say it looks like a bird.* And I think of her letter—the part near the end: *It's beautiful up here. . . . You'd love the view.* My tears evaporate and despite myself, I smile.

Lee Kennedy
As told to Eva Unga
Excerpted from Woman's World *Magazine*

THE FAMILY CIRCUS® By Bil Keane

Heaven is a great big hug that lasts forever.

Reprinted with permission from Bil Keane.

7

A MATTER OF PERSPECTIVE

Make it a practice to judge persons and things in the most favorable light at all times, in all circumstances.

St. Vincent de Paul

Escalator Angel

*Live in such a way that those who know you
but don't know God will come to know God
because they know you.*

Anonymous

The crisp February morning chilled the crowd that
waited to catch the MARTA, Atlanta's public rail system.
When the train arrived, I moved with the others toward
vacant seats. Mechanical sounds punctuated the trip: the
humming of electric motors and the loud bell before the
doors slid shut.

As we settled into our parallel journeys, I looked
around. I work at home, and consequently don't often
take public transit at rush hour. This morning I was on my
way into the city for a seminar. The size and diversity of
the crowd on the train surprised me. In our single car,
there were African-Americans, European-Americans and
Asians—a generous representation of world society.

But there was no interaction. Business men and women
had their briefcases open, poring over papers filled with
charts and columns. Casually dressed students studied

books. One young man had on headphones and swayed in a slow dance to his private music. I'm a fiction man, myself. I travel with a novel handy.

But today I didn't open it. I was too busy studying those around me; something felt strange.

I didn't realize what it was until I'd disembarked at Five Points, the connecting point for the east and west trains. In this cavernous space, I joined perhaps a thousand commuters waiting for their trains.

Here I realized what was so eerie: the total silence. One thousand people, packed cheek to jowl, looking straight ahead, pretending the others didn't exist. And I, a 50-year-old white man wearing a blue suit and glasses, was one of them. The only sound two stories under Atlanta's streets was the hum of the escalators.

And then came a woman's voice. "Good morning!"

The greeting echoed through the station. A thousand heads snapped up in unison, scanning the space. The voice had come from a woman riding the descending escalator on the far side of the platform. "How y'all this morning?"

She practically sang her words, punctuating her speech with long vowel extensions. People began to turn toward her.

The petite African-American woman reached the bottom of the escalator and walked purposefully to the edge of the throng. She grabbed a surprised businessman's hand, shook it and looked him in the eye. "Good morning! How ya doing this morning?"

The man looked at the small woman who had him in her grip. He broke into a smile. "Fine, thank you."

Her clothes were a little ragged, but her purposeful smile overcame her stature and appearance as she moved through the crowd, shouting greetings, shaking hands and laughing freely. Finally, she looked across the tracks at the crowd on my side of the platform. "How ya'll folks over there this morning?

"Just fine!" I shouted back. Others answered with me. We surprised each other so much that we broke out laughing. "That's good," she said. She paused and looked around. Now everyone was listening. "God sent me here to cheer you up this morning. And that's the God of the Jew, the Christian, the Muslim and any other religions ya'll brought or didn't bring along."

From where I stood, I could see a twinkle in her eye. Amazingly, the train station came alive with good-natured conversation. As we chatted with each other, few noticed the slight woman quietly ascend the up escalator.

When the northbound train arrived, I squeezed into a car already stuffed with riders. I didn't get much past the door and grabbed a chrome pole that already had hands of every racial color gripping it. My face looked straight into that of an African-American woman about my age. She wore a light yellow business suit. I sensed she didn't like the press of people around us.

Before I could stop myself, I said, "Good morning."

"What?" She seemed surprised.

"Good morning. How are you doing?" A few people watched us.

A smile overtook her. "Fine," she chuckled. "You know, nobody's asked me that this morning. Really, nobody ever says hello."

I grinned and told her about the unexpected visitor back at Five Points, wondering aloud if she might have been an angel. "Isn't that what angels do? They're messengers. That woman demonstrated the goodness of simply greeting each other, sharing our humanity, instead of guarding it."

Others around the pole joined the discussion, and smiles spread through the car.

The woman across from me, now grinning, said, "If it weren't so crowded in here, I'd give you a good hug. You've made my morning."

When the train arrived at my stop, I moved toward the door. "I hope you have a good day!" I called back to my fellow traveler.

"I will, and thank you."

As I looked back into the car, I saw lots of smiles. People were chatting. Someone else touched my shoulder and waved good-bye. I felt happy and alive.

Since then, I've often wondered who that woman was. She didn't have wings; she ascended and descended an escalator and she spoke in a Southern drawl. But silent people who were temporarily buried two stories below Atlanta began to talk and laugh. A chilly February day felt warmer, and a shy guy like me suddenly hasn't been able to keep himself from greeting and talking with strangers on subway trains, elevators and airplanes. But isn't that what a more famous angelic message proclaimed: "Good will to all"?

In other words, good cheer is contagious. Pass it on.

Richard Stanford

An Inch of Kindness

Kindness is in our power, even when fondness is not.

Samuel Johnson

It was the Sunday after Christmas and the seven o'clock Mass was beginning. Chilled latecomers hurried up the side steps and the rear seats were filling up with stragglers, who welcomed the warmth of the radiators that backed the last pews.

The assistant pastor had begun the age-old celebration and the parishioners were very quiet, hardly participating. Each was in his or her own world. Christmas was two days ago and it had taken its toll. Even the children were still. It was a time of rest from the season's whirl, and all were inclined to sit back and rest. As Father John began his sermon, he looked over a most subdued crowd. He began with a pleasant introduction about the holiday time and its true meaning. Then he carried his sermon a little further and talked about charity and love and being good to others all the time. He said we couldn't go wrong by being nice. It was a talk we had all heard before, and we each felt smugly that we had done our part. Then there was a pause, and Father John added a new thought for his flock to contemplate, and we were startled and roused from our reveries.

He talked about the vagrants, the "trolls," the bums and the homeless that were walking the streets of the city and giving testimony to the new poverty. In quiet tones he said that they needed care most of all. Some of us squirmed in our seats and exchanged glances. It was obvious we had some reservations about his statements. Most of us were thinking about the influx of wanderers into the city. Vagrants inhabited the parks, the shopping malls and the downtown area. Most of the petty crime seemed to be blamed on them, and they certainly weren't viewed with charity.

Mrs. Scupp was terrified by their looks and grimy appearance. Last week a dingy stubble-faced man with a blanket wrapped around him had asked her for money. Startled and scared, she dropped all her packages as she squealed, "No." He stooped and helped her pick up her gifts. Then she did find some money in her purse and gave it to him. The experience had unnerved her, and now she shuddered at the thought of repeating it.

Joe Walden's puffy face twisted with a grimace. *Yeah, sure,* he thought. *Show these people an inch of kindness and they'll ruin your business.* At first he hadn't complained about the groups playing violins and guitars in front of his store and asking for donations for their entertainment. But prospective buyers were uncomfortable and passed the shop by. His sales had dropped, and he blamed the street people. What was this priest suggesting? He snorted to himself.

Margaret was so horrified by the ragged-looking bunch down in the grocery store parking lot that she hated to go shopping there, and she cringed at the thought of even being near the homeless. But the store was the closest place to home, so she went at noon when there were plenty of other shoppers.

Al sat back in his pew and was lost in this part of the message. He was deeply involved in reviewing his career as a cop and how it applied. It was his job to round up those that disturbed the peace or interfered with others. The terrible antagonism aroused between the citizens and these wanderers had led to many arrests and "move on" orders. Were they justified? One thought came to mind. *Is there a little extra I could do?* Al pulled his head into the warmth of his coat, stuck his hands into his pockets and dismissed the thoughts.

The priest continued with the sermon, touching on many sore spots. He ended by asking people to be kinder to the less fortunate, to be fair, and to treat everybody the way Christ would treat them. He left the pulpit to continue Mass, leaving everybody in a ruffled mood.

The Mass continued, and at the same time a noise assaulted the solemnity. A cross between a groan and a whistle, it sounded again and again. A snicker ran through the church. It was a snore . . . a mighty one. Anxious looks at the altar proved that Father was unaffected by the noise, but others were. A lady in front with a big red hat was turning one way and then the other, seeking its originator. Three children were giggling. Their father tried to quiet them and at the same time scanned the congregation. Halfway up the middle aisle, to the right, was a hunched-up figure covered with a blanket— the source of the noise. Each time a chord was struck, the gray covering vibrated as the snore escaped its confines.

The snorer was obviously not a member of the church. Maybe he was one of those wanderers on his way south, or somebody who came in from the cold. Maybe he was a bum. One thing was certain, his snoring was offensive.

People coughed nervously and then waited for the next sound.

"Do you think he had a nice Christmas, too, Mommie?" Whispers and hugs identified a little girl in a new pink jacket.

"God loves him too, doesn't he?" Another flurry followed as her father, nodding, picked her up in his arms. She rested her chin over his shoulder and was looking at the inert man. The people moved in their seats. This was a member of the poor that the sermon was about. What an uncomfortable thought!

Father John was saying the final prayers when the little girl spoke to her father in a stage whisper that carried from one end of the church to the other. "Daddy, can't we share our Christmas with him? Can I have some money? I won't wake him up. Promise." There was quiet rustling and movement as she crossed the aisle and laid some bills on the blanket. Al rose to his feet and did the same. Joe Walden strode up with his offering. As Father John finished the Mass, other bills were dropped on the sleeping figure. He watched Mrs. Scupp gingerly place a five-dollar bill on the gray blanket that was now heaped with money. Margaret met Father John's grin as she left her offering.

It was a strange crowd who greeted Father John after services. The man in the blanket had made an impression, and while few words were said, everyone greeted the priest with a special heartiness. It comes with the satisfaction of giving, he thought privately.

When Father John returned to the empty church and walked up the aisle to the man, he saw the green bills nestled in the folds of the gray blanket. There was more money on the floor around the man. Father John gently shook him. The snoring man raised his head and looked vacantly at the priest for a moment. "Oh, I fell asleep, I guess. What's this?" The money cascaded around him as he rose and dropped the blanket. The priest looked with surprise into the face of Chris Gregory, a fireman and paramedic he had known for years. "Gee, Father John, I'm awfully sorry." As Chris gently scooped up and counted the wealth, Father John explained what had happened. Then Chris told his story.

His department had received three calls for fires down in the lagoon and along the railroad tracks. He had been out all night. The last call included a girl who was about to give birth. She was one of those who had sought the warmth of a fire that got out of hand. Before she could be taken to the hospital, he delivered her baby, a boy. Chris went to the hospital and stayed longer than he expected. It had been a long night, and he had stopped to make early-morning Mass before going home to sleep.

There was $600.60 altogether. Father John said, "Suppose we divide it. I'll use my share for the soup kitchen and you take the rest for the new mother. She's going to need it. Now, let's get some breakfast. And fold up that blanket—I don't really think the parishioners want to know who the man in the gray blanket was."

Jeanne Williams Carey

Bobby: When You Can't Be Strong for Yourself

As a physician involved in the care of children I am very fortunate to witness daily the wondrous power, strength and faith of the most physically fragile among us. One such event involves Bobby, a five-year-old child who had been diagnosed with leukemia at age four. Bobby's cancer was in remission—he was free of disease—and he had come to the hospital for a series of diagnostic tests that were a routine part of his treatment plan. Bobby had bright blue eyes and a shy smile that at first glance didn't reveal the wisdom gained through his one-year struggle against cancer.

Bobby had lost all of his hair secondary to his regular chemotherapy treatment. The chemotherapy often left him nauseous and unable to eat. Bobby had experienced numerous painful procedures and treatments and this day was to be no exception. Bobby was undergoing a procedure that was indeed painful. He had been through it before, so he knew what to expect. I explained to him what we were going to do, and why, and the importance of him remaining very still. Bobby assured me that he would be very still, and he promised that the nurses and technologists in attendance would not need to hold him down.

As we began, Bobby asked, "Dr. Brown, would it be okay if I say the Twenty-third Psalm while you stick me?"

"Of course, that would be fine," I said, and we began.

Bobby recited beautifully, no tears, no movement. The procedure went well. Bobby, in his young wisdom, reassured me, "Dr. Brown, that really didn't hurt much." We knew it had. Then Bobby caught me by surprise when he asked, "Dr. Brown, do *you* know the Twenty-third Psalm?"

"Well, sure," I answered him.

"Can you recite it like me?" he asked, a bit doubtfully.

"Well, I don't know. I think so," I said, realizing that I was going out on a limb.

"Let's hear you," said Bobby.

So I proceeded to stumble through it. My performance was quite shabby in comparison to Bobby's, and I didn't have a needle sticking in my back. I noticed all the other white-coated professionals in the room were trying to disappear as they feared being called on next, a prospect more frightening than being asked to perform at grand rounds.

Then beautiful and bald Bobby said to all of us, "You know, you really should learn the Twenty-third Psalm by heart. Because when you say it out loud, God hears you and he lets you know inside your heart that he is being strong for you when you can't be strong for yourself."

". . . for the kingdom of God belongs to such as these."

James C. Brown, M.D.

Erik's Old Man

If you judge people, you have no time to love them.

Mother Teresa

Our family was driving from San Francisco to Los Angeles on Christmas Day. That year Christmas came on Sunday and we needed to be in Los Angeles on Monday morning, having spent Christmas Eve and Christmas morning with my husband's parents.

We stopped for lunch at a diner in King City. I was enjoying a review of the happiness and meanings of the day when my reverie was interrupted. I heard Erik, our one-year-old son, scream with glee in his high chair. "Hi there." (Two words he thought were one.) He pounded his fat baby hands—whack, whack—on the metal tray of the high chair. His face was alive with excitement, eyes wide, gums bared in a toothless grin. He wriggled and chirped and giggled, and then I saw the source of his merriment.

A tattered rag of a coat; greasy, worn. Baggy pants, both they and the zipper at half mast over a spindly body. Toes that poked out of would-be shoes. A shirt that had ring-around-the-collar all over and a face like none other. Gums as bare as Erik's. Hair unwashed, uncombed, unbearable. Whiskers too short for a beard but way beyond the shadow stage. And a nose so varicose that it looked like the map of New York. I was too far away to smell him, but I knew he smelled.

His hands were waving in the air, flapping about on loose wrists. "Hi there, baby; hi there, big boy. I see ya, buster." Erik continued to laugh and call, "Hi there." Every call was answered. I shoved a cracker at Erik and he pulverized it in his tray. I turned the high chair. Erik screamed and twisted around to face his old buddy.

The waitresses' eyebrows were rising. Several diners went "ahem." This old geezer was creating a nuisance with my beautiful baby! Now the bum was shouting from across the room, "Do ya know peek-a-boo? Hey look, he knows peek-a-boo."

The old guy was drunk. Nobody thought anything was cute. My husband was embarrassed. I was humiliated. Even our six-year-old wanted to know why that man was talking so loud. We ate hurriedly and in silence, all except Erik, who continued to run through his repertoire with the bum.

My husband rose to pay the check, telling me to meet him in the parking lot. I grabbed Erik and headed for the exit. The old man sat poised and waiting, his chair directly between me and the door. *Lord, let me out of here before he speaks to me or Erik.*

I tried to side-step to put my back between Erik and any air the old man might be breathing. But Erik, with his eyes riveted on his best friend, leaned far over my arm, reaching out with both arms in a baby's pick-me-up gesture. In the split second of balancing my baby and turning to counter his weight, I came eye-to-eye with the old man. His eyes were imploring. "Would you let me hold your baby?"

There was no need to answer. Erik propelled himself from my arms into the man's and immediately laid his head on the man's ragged shoulder. The man's eyes closed and I saw tears hover beneath his lashes. His aged hands, full of grime and pain and hard labor, gently, so gently, cradled my baby's bottom and stroked his back.

The old man stroked and rocked Erik for a moment, then opened his eyes and looked squarely in mine. He said in a firm, commanding voice, "You take care of this baby."

I said, "I will."

He pried Erik from his chest, unwillingly, longingly, as though he were in pain. I held my arms open to receive my baby, and again the gentleman addressed me. "God bless you, ma'am. You've given me my Christmas present."

Nancy Dahlberg
Submitted by Walfred Erickson

In Jesus' Eyes

We wanted our son to know always that he was adopted. So from the time he was very young, we explained it to him in a way that was simple for him to understand.

"We were told that I could not have a baby in my belly and Jesus knew this, " I said. "Jesus also knew that there was a lady who had a baby in her belly, but she could not be a mommy. From Heaven, Jesus saw this baby on the day he was born. Remembering that we wanted to be a mommy and daddy and that the lady could not be a mommy, Jesus decided that the baby belonged with us. That's how we became a family."

One day on our way home from nursery school, our son asked me if he was born in Jesus' belly. I told him that he was not and once again we talked about how we became a family. After driving a little bit further I asked him if he had any questions.

He said, "Oh no, now I remember. I wasn't born in Jesus' belly, I was born in his eyes!"

Helen Montone

Earth Angels

With a name like Vera Fortune, people often teasingly call me Good Fortune. I feel that way myself, especially when I'm with the 14 grandchildren I've been blessed with.

The kids, ages two to 14, are the lights of my life. I enjoy being there to see everything they do, from 13-year-old Jacob's cross-country races to seven-year-old Danielle and Katie's ballet recitals. Their smiles always make me feel lucky to be alive.

But now I feel even luckier. Because not long ago, when it looked as though my luck had run out, strangers saved me just in the nick of time.

It was raining, and I was rushing from work to my son Rob's house to watch his children—Jacob, Michelle and Matthew. At an intersection, I spotted a Jeep in the opposite lane heading toward me. *It'll stop,* I told myself.

I don't know if the driver failed to see me turning until it was too late, but suddenly I realized the car wasn't stopping.

"No!" I cried in terror as we collided. The crash of metal hitting metal is all I remember before I lost consciousness. I later learned that the impact sent my car spinning out of control and onto a grassy field.

Seconds later I woke up. I felt something trickling down my forehead: blood! But my heart was still beating. *I'm alive*, I gasped with relief.

Then my eyes focused. Through the windshield I saw a lot of water. In horror I realized my car was rolling into a pond.

"No!" I cried again. I slammed my foot down on the brake, but a bolt of pain shot up my leg. *My ankle's broken!* Then I heard a sickening splash, and the car dipped forward. *God help me!* I gasped in horror as water instantly rose above the doors.

Stay calm, I told myself. *It's probably shallow. Even with a broken ankle, you can hobble out of here.*

But when I pulled on the door handle, it wouldn't budge. *Crawl out the window!* a voice inside my head screamed. I rolled it down, but water rushed in, and when I tried to crank it closed, the window stuck.

What am I going to do? I thought, trying to fight the panic squeezing my heart as icy water inched over my knees and swirled up past my waist. As the water crept higher and higher, I realized in horror that I was about to drown.

Someone must have seen the accident, I told myself. *Help must be on the way.* But I heard no sirens, no sounds of people rushing to my rescue—just the rain and water swirling around me.

Frantic to escape, I tried forcing my body through the half-open window. Impossible. But I could stretch my head just above the water's surface.

"Help!" I screamed.

Suddenly, water filled my mouth as the car sank deeper. Choking, I ducked inside and stuck my nose up into the last remaining inch of air. *Don't let me die!* I prayed.

As seconds ticked by, the frigid water numbed my limbs. *How long before I'm too weak to hold my head up?* I worried, my heart filling with despair.

Suddenly the faces of my family flashed before me. I thought of all I'd miss if I left them now. I wouldn't get to see Kelsey and Ellie, both five, start kindergarten. I wanted to be there when 14-year-old Jessica, an aspiring gospel singer, fulfilled her dream.

Little Michelle was about to be tested for her black belt in karate. "You'll be there won't you, Grandma?" she'd asked.

"I can't die!" I cried. "It's too soon!"

While I was sending my prayers up to heaven, Michael Brown, a truck driver, saw the battered Jeep. After checking on the driver, who had only minor injuries, he wondered, *Where's the other car?*

Suddenly he saw a light. Perhaps it was just a reflection on my windshield. Maybe it was a sign from above, telling him where to look for me.

He ran to the water's edge and plunged in, but his work boots pulled him down and he had to head back to shore.

But fate—or perhaps God—stepped in. Patrick Downey, a United Way worker, had taken a different route home that night. And Ken LaPine, a parks director, stayed late at work. It was a blessing that they were both on the road when I needed them.

They saw Michael in the water, and when he yelled, "There's someone down there!" they took off their jackets and shoes and dove in.

Disoriented by fear and cold, I was unaware of the efforts being made to save me. Ken tried the passenger door, but it was locked. Patrick tugged on the driver's door. Miraculously, it opened, and I heard a voice order, "Give me your arm."

I was too numb to move. But like an angel, Patrick reached in and with a mighty yank pulled me to the surface. "I'm free!" I gasped, greedily breathing in deep mouthfuls of air.

Patrick and Ken swam to shore, each holding one of my arms, and paramedics whisked me to an ambulance. At the hospital I was treated for hypothermia, a shattered ankle, a broken rib and head cuts.

"I owe my life to you," I tearfully told my angels when they visited me.

But after I arrived home to my grandchildren's kisses, words didn't seem enough. So I invited my Good Samaritans to a family dinner so they could see how much they'd done for me. As my children thanked Michael, Patrick and Ken, my heroes smiled proudly. But as one by one, 14 children put their small hands into the men's big ones and said, "Thank you for saving my grandma," there wasn't a dry eye.

I believe God placed those men on that road to save me. And thanks to my angels, I now live up to the name Good Fortune. I've been given a second chance at a life with my family.

Vera Fortune
As told to Steve Baal
Woman's World *Magazine*

Wear Out, Don't Rust Out

*A sweet old lady stays active all her life. A
grumpy old grouch sits and rocks.*

Anonymous

"Can you be ready in 15 minutes?" It was my friend
Bardy on the telephone. "I need your help. I'll be by to
pick you up in my car."

"Where are we going?" I asked. "What should I wear?"

"It really doesn't matter. You'll see. Or I should say, I'll
see." Her infectious laughter crackled across the telephone lines, then the dial tone alerted me that she
assumed my willingness to accompany her on some
secret mission. If my hunch was correct, she was probably already out the door, in her car, and headed in my
direction.

For what? I had learned not to try to second-guess my
friend. Bardy is the most interesting person I know—and
the most unpredictable. She had always wanted to be a
registered nurse, so she went back to school and became
one when she was 63 years old. "The real fun started
when I graduated," Bardy had informed me. "When I

applied for jobs, I was told, 'We retire people at your age, Mrs. Bardarson, we don't hire them!'"

Disappointed but not discouraged, Bardy told God that if he didn't want her sidelined, he'd have to help her find her niche. She continued to apply for nursing positions and was finally hired by a retirement home. She was an instant hit with the residents. When they talked with her about their aches and pains, they found a sympathetic ear. After all, she had many of those aches and pains herself. They could tell she loved her work and that she was genuinely concerned for them. When she did retire at age 70, the residents gave her the biggest party in the history of the retirement home.

Soon Bardy was at my front door. "I'm driving today," she announced. "Jump in the passenger's seat."

"Where are we going?" I queried as I locked the front door of my house.

"It doesn't matter," she replied with a Cheshire grin on her face. "Marilyn, you know I had to retire from nursing when it became too much for me to lift the patients. Now I've found a new job. I'm going to travel with blind tourists. I'll get to go to all the places I've wanted to see. I'll be helping others, and I'll even get paid for it! Now I need you to help me prepare. Close your eyes while I drive."

I complied.

"Are your eyes closed? Good!" Bardy said. "I have to practice." She began to describe the scenery of the Seattle streets as she would to a blind tourist. From time to time she would interrupt herself to ask me, "Could you picture that? Was I clear? Did I make sense? Do I sound condescending?"

That day I saw Seattle in a new way. I learned one of Bardy's secrets as well. What makes her such an interesting person is her determination to wear out, not rust out.

Marilynn Carlson Webber

Prayer Is the Key

A missionary was serving as a medic at a small field hospital in Africa. Periodically he had to travel by bicycle through the jungle to a nearby city for supplies. It was a two-day trip so he had to camp out overnight. He had made this trip several times without incident. One day, however, he arrived at his destination and saw two men fighting. One was seriously hurt, so he treated him and witnessed to him and went about his business.

Upon arriving in the city again several weeks later, he was approached by the man he had treated earlier. "I know you carry money and medicine," said the man to the missionary. "Some friends and I followed you into the jungle the night you treated me, knowing you would camp overnight. We waited for you to go to sleep and planned to kill you and take your money and drugs. Just as we started moving into the campsite, we saw you were surrounded by 26 armed guards. There were only six of us and we knew then we couldn't possibly get near you, so we left."

Hearing this the missionary laughed and said," That's impossible. I can assure you I was alone in the campsite."

The young man pressed his point: "No sir, I was not the only one to see the guards. My friends also saw them, and we all counted them. We were frightened. It was because of those guards that we left you alone."

Several months later, the missionary attended a church presentation in Michigan where he told about his experiences in Africa. One of the congregants jumped to his feet, interrupting the missionary, and said something that left everyone in the church stunned.

"We were there with you in spirit," said the man. The missionary looked perplexed. The man continued. "On that night in Africa, it was morning here. I stopped at the church to gather some materials for an out-of-town trip to another parish. But as I put my bags into the trunk, I felt the Lord leading me to pray for you. The urging was so great I called the men in the church together to pray for you."

Then the man turned around and said, "Will all of those men who met with the Lord that morning please stand?" One by one they stood—all 26 of them!

Anonymous
Submitted by Murray Moerman

A Sailor's Christmas Gift

Do what you can, with what you have, where you are.

Theodore Roosevelt

Admiral David L. McDonald, USN
Navy Department
Washington, DC

Dear Admiral,
   This letter is a year late; nevertheless, it is important that you receive it. Eighteen people asked me to write to you.
   Last year at Christmas time my wife, our three boys and I were in France on our way from Paris to Nice. For five wretched days everything had gone wrong. Our hotels were "tourist traps," our rented car broke down; we were all restless and irritable in the crowded car. On Christmas Eve, when we checked into a dingy hotel in Nice, there was no Christmas spirit in our hearts.
   It was raining and cold when we went out to eat. We found a drab little joint shoddily decorated for the holidays. It smelled greasy. Only five tables in the restaurant were

occupied. There were two German couples, two French families and an American sailor, by himself. In the corner, a piano player listlessly played Christmas music. I was too stubborn and too tired and miserable to leave. I looked around and noticed that the other customers were eating in stony silence. The only person who seemed happy was the American sailor. While eating he was writing a letter, and a half-smile covered his face.

My wife ordered our meal in French. The waiter brought us the wrong thing, so I scolded my wife for being stupid. She began to cry. The boys defended her, and I felt even worse. Then at the table with the French family, on our left, the father slapped one of the children for some minor infraction, and the boy began to cry. On our right, the fat, blond German woman began berating her husband.

All of us were interrupted by an unpleasant blast of cold air. Through the front door came an old French flower woman. She wore a dripping, tattered overcoat and shuffled in on wet, rundown shoes. Carrying her basket of flowers, she went from one table to the other. "Flowers, monsieur? Only one franc." No one bought any. Wearily she sat down at a table between the sailor and us. To the waiter she said, "A bowl of soup. I haven't sold a flower all afternoon." To the piano player she said hoarsely, "Can you imagine, Joseph, soup on Christmas Eve?" He pointed to his empty tipping plate.

The young sailor finished his meal and got up to leave. Putting on his coat, he walked over to the flower woman's table. "Happy Christmas!" he said, smiling, and picking out two corsages, asked, "How much are they?"

"Two francs, monsieur." Pressing one of the small corsages flat, he put it into the letter he had written, then handed the woman a 20-franc note.

"I don't have change, monsieur," she said, "I'll get some from the waiter."

"No, ma'am," he said, leaning over and kissing the ancient

cheek. "This is my Christmas present to you." Straightening up, he came to our table holding the other corsage in front of him. "Sir," he said to me, "may I have permission to present these flowers to your beautiful wife?" In one quick motion, he gave my wife the corsage, wished us a Merry Christmas, and departed.

Everyone had stopped eating. Everyone was watching the sailor. Everyone was silent. A few seconds later, Christmas exploded throughout the restaurant like a bomb.

The old flower woman jumped up, waving the 20-franc note. Hobbling to the middle of the floor, she did a merry jig and shouted to the piano player, "Joseph, my Christmas present, and you shall have half so you can have a feast too." The piano player began to beat out "Good King Wenceslaus," hitting the keys with magic hands, nodding his head in rhythm.

My wife waved her corsage in time with the rhythm. She was radiant and appeared 20 years younger. The tears had left her eyes and the corners of her mouth turned up in laughter. She began to sing, and our three sons joined her, bellowing the song with uninhibited enthusiasm.

"Gut, gut," shouted the Germans. They jumped on their chairs and began singing in German. The waiter embraced the flower woman. Waving their arms, they sang in French. The Frenchman who had slapped the boy beat rhythm with a fork against a bottle. The lad climbed on his lap, singing in a youthful soprano.

The Germans ordered wine for everyone. They delivered it themselves, hugging the other customers, bawling Christmas greetings. One of the French families ordered champagne and made the rounds, kissing each one of us on each cheek. The owner of the restaurant started singing "The First Noel," and we all joined in, half of us crying.

People crowded in from the street until many customers were standing. The walls shook as hands and feet kept time to the yuletide carols. A few hours earlier, a few people had been spending a miserable evening in a shoddy restaurant. It ended up being the happiest, the very best Christmas Eve they had ever spent.

This, Admiral McDonald, is what I am writing you about. As the top man in the Navy, you should know about the very special gift that the U.S. Navy gave to my family—to me and to the other people in that restaurant. Because your young sailor had the Christmas spirit in his soul, he released the love and joy that had been smothered within us by anger and disappointment. He gave us Christmas.

Thank you very much.
Merry Christmas

William J. Lederer

Choosing a Good Minister

Dear Abby:

One of the toughest tasks a church faces is choosing a good minister. A member of an official board undergoing this painful process finally lost patience. He'd just witnessed the pastoral relations committee reject applicant after applicant for some minor fault . . . real or imagined. It was time for a bit of soul searching on the part of the committee. So he stood up and read this letter purported to be from an applicant.

Gentlemen: Understanding your pulpit is vacant, I should like to apply for the position. I have many qualifications. I've been a preacher with much success and also have had some successes as a writer. Some say I'm a good organizer. I've been a leader most places I've been.

I'm over 50 years of age and have never preached in one place for more than three years. In some places, I have left town after my work caused riots and disturbances. I must admit I have been in jail three or four times, but not because of any real wrongdoing.

My health is not too good, though I still accomplish a

great deal. The churches I have preached in have been small, though located in several large cities.

I've not gotten along well with religious leaders in the towns where I have preached. In fact, some have threatened me, and even attacked me physically. I am not too good at keeping records. I have been known to forget whom I have baptized.

However, if you can use me, I promise to do my best for you."

The board member turned to the committee and said, "Well, what do you think? Shall we call him?"

The good church folks were appalled! Consider a sickly, troublemaking, absent-minded ex-jailbird? Was the board member crazy? Who signed the application? Who had such colossal nerve?

The board member eyed them all keenly before he replied, "It's signed, The Apostle Paul.'"

Author Unknown
from Dear Abby
Submitted by Jean Maier

Our Mysterious Passenger

Life is short and we have never too much time for gladdening the hearts of those who are travelling the dark journey with us. Oh be swift to love, make haste to be kind.

Henri Frederic Amiel

The midday sun beat down on my wife, Barbara, and me as we walked across the tarmac to the terminal at Loreto International Airport on Mexico's Baja peninsula. We were flying our single-engine plane home to Calexico, California, later that day, ending a week's vacation.

A tall man stood near the terminal, nervously dabbing at his face and neck with a handkerchief. I had noticed him earlier, watching us as we readied our plane.

Suddenly he approached, blocking the doorway. He was in his 40s and looked as if he had spent the night in the terminal. "Excuse me," he said, removing his Panama hat. "Can you help me out? I'm an American and I got bumped from the flight to Los Angeles. I need to catch my connecting flight to Florida."

Trying to muster an authoritative tone, I said, "I'm

sorry, but I've already filed my flight plan with the airport commandant. It only allows me to take my wife out of the country. Why don't you get a later flight?"

"There isn't another flight until tomorrow, and I've got to leave today," he insisted.

"Well, we're only going to Calexico, at the border."

"That's okay," the stranger said. "Let's go to the commandant's office and ask if I can leave with you." He turned to enter the building.

"Wait a minute," I said uneasily. "I don't have an oxygen mask for you, and we're flying at 14,500 feet. You'd feel altitude sickness."

"That's okay. I'm in good shape."

"And there's no room for additional luggage," I added, glancing at his suitcase. "The plane's full."

"I'll hold the bag on my lap."

At this point Barbara asked, "Would you excuse us for a second? I need to talk to my husband."

"Sure." The stranger stood aside to let us enter the terminal.

Barbara, a trial lawyer and the voice of reason in the family, whispered, "Are you crazy? You want to risk our lives by giving a ride to some strange person who could be a fugitive or a terrorist?" Her voice was rising. "What if he hijacks us?"

"Something tells me he's legitimate," I said. "Maybe it's payback time." I was thinking of when Barbara and I had flown to Mexico 10 years earlier. We had ridden a little motorcycle into the desert and lost our way. We were sweaty, sunburned and covered with dust when we finally made it into a town. We met some American pilots and asked if they could take us to our plane, but they walked away. Finally, some California college students got us back to our plane.

"Remember being stranded down here years ago?" I asked. "Let's go to the commandant's office and see what he says. I doubt he'll allow him to go with us, but I'd feel better if we at least asked."

The commandant listened to the stranger's story, glanced at his tickets and quickly changed our passenger number from a "1" to a "2." The entire transaction took about a minute.

Now I had to take the stranger with us. Not knowing what else to do, I wandered off in the direction of our plane. Barbara walked beside me, glaring straight ahead. To break the tension, I turned to the stranger following us and asked his name. "Virgil," he said.

Cruising northwesterly at 14,500 feet, Barbara and I sat in silence, breathing oxygen from our masks. I looked back at Virgil, seated behind her. Strangely, the lack of supplemental oxygen didn't seem to bother him. He nodded back at me and smiled. I was beginning to think things might work out. The drone of the engine had a soothing effect, and an unusually strong tail wind promised to put us in Calexico well ahead of schedule. Virgil's chances of making it to Los Angeles were improving by the minute. Yes, maybe things would work out after all.

Not everyone felt the same way, though. Barbara had her arms folded across her chest and her head hunched down as if she expected a hatchet blow from behind.

Just north of the border, I became more concerned with the weather than with Virgil. The ride grew turbulent, with wind gusts causing our plane, a Mooney 231, to rattle.

Suddenly, we plunged 100 feet in a downdraft. Barbara glanced nervously at me. The radio warned of strong, gusting winds with blowing dust and sand throughout California's Imperial Valley. Visual flight was not recommended.

Looking toward Calexico, I could see a strange, dark-brown cloud spanning the horizon. A sandstorm! In my 23 years of flying, I had never witnessed anything like it.

Calexico is a small field unequipped for instrument approaches. If we couldn't land visually, our depleted fuel and the increasingly turbulent ride would mean flying back to Mexicali on the Mexican side of the border. I shivered as I imagined the air filter clogging up and the engine quitting.

Even if we made it, our unexpected arrival at Mexicali would surely get the attention of some savvy border official. We could be held up for days while our passenger, whom we knew nothing about, was being investigated. Virgil wasn't the only one who had to get back to work.

Whack! Turbulent air jolted me out of my musings, causing the plane to pitch up. *Whap!* Now the nose pitched down, spilling my maps on the floor. I decided that we were going to Mexicali, and probably to jail.

Just as I retrieved the maps from the floor, Barbara exclaimed, "I see Calexico!"

There it was, only five miles in front of us. The sandstorm was swirling all around the airport, but the runway was in the clear.

I banked the plane toward the runway, praying that the hole over the airport would remain open a bit longer. As I eased into our final turn, we encountered wind shear, setting off a wail from the stall-warning alarm. I jockeyed the throttle back and forth. Barbara was frightened, yet her look told me, *You can do it.*

Suddenly the air smoothed out, and we were down. As we turned off the runway, the sandstorm closed in around us. In all my years of flying, this was my closest call.

I looked back at Virgil—and I couldn't believe how calm he was. He was sitting there reading, and of all things, he was reading a Bible. He smiled as he put it away.

Inside Calexico's airport, Barbara sipped coffee and looked out at the sand blowing across the landscape. Finally she said, "Well, what do you make of him?" I still wasn't sure.

Just then Virgil came to the table. I asked him about his prospects for getting to Los Angeles. People weren't even driving in this weather.

"I found a commuter flight leaving from Imperial Valley Airport, a few miles from here. Unfortunately, they don't know when it will take off. On top of that, the flight is sold out. But just in case, I called a cab. Maybe someone will cancel."

I knew the time had come to learn more about this stranger. "What were you doing in Loreto?" I asked.

Virgil stared into his coffee cup. "My wife and I were in a terrible accident in Loreto 10 years ago. We were with another couple on vacation, touring Baja in a rented motor home. The other couple was in the front, and we were in the back. Suddenly the right tire went off the road, and we rolled down an embankment. We were carrying 160 gallons of fuel. The butane tank for the stove exploded. There was a horrible fire. I managed to escape out the back window, and my wife squeezed through the door.

"The other couple was trapped inside, screaming for help. I tried to pull them out through the front window, but I couldn't. It was too late.

"My wife and I were burned pretty badly," he continued, "and my spleen had ruptured. We were several miles from Loreto. We crawled up the embankment and tried to flag down someone to help us. Finally a Mexican fellow pulled over and rushed us to the Health Center of Loreto.

"They saved our lives. But the clinic was poorly equipped. The operating table looked like an old ironing board. I spent the night in a dental chair because there was no bed.

"We were transferred to a burn unit in California. But I vowed that I would come back and give the clinic money to buy proper equipment and medical supplies."

"And your wife?" I asked.

"She had skin grafts, and she's doing fine. I guess I buried the whole experience in the back of my mind. I'm starting my own business—a boat sales company. I hadn't thought about the accident until last Saturday."

Virgil took a deep breath. "I awoke with a start. Something told me I needed to act on that vow I made 10 years ago. I arrived in Loreto yesterday. The health center was still in bad shape—the paint was peeling, the bedsheets were torn, and broken windows were covered with tinfoil. I wrote them a check. It wasn't a large sum, but they were extremely grateful. You should have seen the looks on their faces."

"I'll bet," I said.

"This morning, the flight to Los Angeles was full, and I was left stranded. Then I saw you folks."

We sat in silence for a moment. Then a man approached our table—it was the cab driver Virgil had called. Virgil hurriedly picked up his hat and bag. "Thanks again, folks," he said.

"Wait, Virgil." I handed him a business card. "Let us know if you make it aboard that flight."

I returned home and settled into my routine, still thinking about Virgil and the lesson he had taught me: we were aided by strangers when we were stranded many years before, so we helped Virgil. After the accident, Virgil and his wife were helped by the people of Loreto, so he returned to help them. These were links in a growing chain of kindness, and each kindness we do, I now recognize, always comes back to us, sometimes in mysterious ways.

One day, we received a letter from Virgil, written on the letterhead of his boat sales company: "Just a short note to say thanks once again. I made my flight out of Imperial Valley. The plane was loading as I arrived at the gate. I got the last seat. Love, Virgil."

Ira Spector

8

OVERCOMING OBSTACLES

And Jesus looking upon them saith, With men it is impossible, but not with God; for with God all things are possible.

Mark 10:27

I know God will not give me anything I can't handle. I just wish he didn't trust me so much.

Mother Teresa

The Baby Who Was Born Twice

Faith consists in believing when it is beyond the power of reason to believe. It is not enough that a thing be possible for it to be believed.

Voltaire

Quietly, not wanting to wake her husband, Mike, Rhonda Denis slipped out of bed and tiptoed into the living room of their small duplex in Oakland Park, Florida. Their four-year-old son, Corey, was sound asleep in the second bedroom.

Rhonda, 31, settled into an easy chair and reached for her Bible. A slender woman, she could feel the gentle kicks of the four-month-old life she carried within her. Offering a silent prayer, she summoned courage to face the coming day.

Later that January 10, 1994, she would visit a specialist in high-risk pregnancies. She simply could not believe what other doctors had said: Rhonda's baby was going to die.

The prenatal checkup a few weeks earlier had been routine at first. Rhonda was thrilled to learn she was carrying a little girl. But after examining the ultrasound images again, the doctor's face darkened.

"There may be a problem," he said softly.

"What kind?" Rhonda asked. All he could tell her was that something was wrong with her baby's organs.

Soon after, Rhonda and her husband visited a second clinic, where the picture was even bleaker: the infant had little chance of surviving.

"You could consider terminating your pregnancy," she was told.

"No," Rhonda answered. "I could never do that!"

Stunned by the dire prognosis, Rhonda held Mike's arm as they walked to the hospital parking lot. Raising children had always been Rhonda's dream. When Mike had proposed six years earlier, she had said she wanted a dozen.

Even before Corey was born in 1989, Rhonda had left her job at an employment agency to prepare for full-time motherhood. To support his growing family, Mike worked long hours at his job installing metal support frames in buildings. Their warm, happy home became a gathering place for neighborhood children.

Now the young couple faced the anguish of losing a child at birth. In the car, Rhonda rested her head on her husband's shoulder and cried.

Another sonogram was scheduled in four weeks. "I can't wait that long," Rhonda told Mike that evening. "If something's wrong, I want to know now so we can do something. I'm going to see another doctor."

On January 26, 1994, Rhonda finally got the grim diagnosis. "It's a diaphragmatic hernia," the obstetrician said. He explained that there was a hole in her baby's diaphragm, the muscle separating the chest cavity from the abdomen.

In a fetus, such a hernia allows parts of the stomach, spleen, intestines or liver to float up into the chest cavity.

That crowding prevents fetal lungs from developing properly.

In utero, the baby gets oxygen from the placenta. At birth, however, the baby gasps for breath it cannot draw. In 60 percent of such cases, the baby does not survive.

Four days later Rhonda lay in an examining room in West Palm Beach. Dr. Debra A. Jones, a high-risk-pregnancy specialist recommended by Rhonda's obstetrician, moved the ultrasound probe over Rhonda's womb, examining the baby inside. The sonogram showed that the baby's abdominal organs were compressing the lungs. Worse, the fetal stomach was pushing the tiny heart out of position. *This is bad*, Jones thought.

She remembered two other patients whose babies had the same problem. Both babies had died. Then Jones thought of someone she'd been reading about, someone on the cutting edge of medicine.

"There's a doctor in California who performs surgery on fetuses in the womb," Jones explained. "His center is the only one in the world where this is done. But it's very risky, and you have only a slim chance of being accepted."

"I don't care," Rhonda blurted. "I'm prepared to do anything and everything to have this baby."

Jones was impressed. *What strength and commitment*, she thought. She promised to send a videotape of Rhonda's sonogram to the pioneering California surgeon.

Michael Harrison was a 26-year-old intern fresh out of Harvard Medical School the day he watched a newborn with a diaphragmatic hernia die without drawing a normal breath. He wondered, *If these babies can't be saved after they're born, why not before?* At the time, 1969, the thought seemed so outlandish that Harrison kept it to himself.

Nine years later, as a fully qualified pediatric surgeon, he joined the University of California San Francisco (UCSF) Medical Center. There, he gathered a top research team and began experimental surgery on fetal sheep. Their work proved that once the chest cavity was cleared of abdominal organs, the lungs grew rapidly in utero. But Harrison's research was ridiculed by naysayers who believed fetal surgery on humans to be a fantasy. Nevertheless, Harrison persevered. Even as he maintained a busy surgical practice, he worked in his lab to perfect the delicate techniques needed to save the lives of the smallest patients. Finally he began operating on human babies for whom it was considered the only chance.

In early 1994, when Dr. Jones's letter appeared on his desk, Harrison and his team had completed only a handful of cases. There had been successes, but a number of babies had died, some right on the operating table. The loss of a baby left Harrison devastated. He always met with the family to thank them for their courage, and he never left one of those meetings dry-eyed.

For months he searched for a reason for the babies' deaths. Finally he discovered that when the fetal liver entered the chest cavity, it altered the path of the umbilical vein. Moving the liver back inadvertently created a lethal kink in this critical lifeline.

Studying the snowy images of the sonogram that Dr. Jones had sent, Harrison was relieved to see that the baby's liver would not be a problem. Only a small segment had edged into the chest.

There were other good signs. The infant had no genetic abnormalities that would preclude surgery. She was still undeveloped enough for Harrison to intervene surgically, yet strong enough for the fetal tissue to hold stitches. Finally, according to Dr. Jones, the mother was a stalwart—willing to do anything to save her unborn child.

Rhonda Denis looked like a good candidate for the surgery.

"They'll take me?" Rhonda shrieked into the phone. "I

can't believe it! Oh, thank you, Dr. Jones. Thank you, God!" When Mike arrived home that night, he and Rhonda hugged in celebration. But Mike couldn't help wondering, *What if I lose her?*

Equally agonizing was the realization that he couldn't join Rhonda in California. A grant from the National Institutes of Health would pay for the experimental surgery, but if Mike didn't keep working, family finances would collapse. In the end Rhonda's mother volunteered to go, while a cousin cared for Corey.

On Friday, March 4, in a richly paneled conference room at UCSF Medical Center, Dr. Harrison and his team met with Rhonda and her mother. Harrison didn't mince words: Rhonda faced a harrowing ordeal. There would be two separate surgeries—one to repair her baby's defect; the second, weeks later, for the Caesarean birth. To prevent premature labor and allow her baby time to recover, Rhonda would also have to endure drugs with unpleasant side effects. And in spite of their best efforts the infant could still die. "We offer no promises," Harrison said. "None."

For the first time Rhonda paused. *Maybe I'm not strong enough to get through this*, she thought. She glanced at her mother, Judy Robinson, who had always been her closest friend and inspiration. Back in Florida, Judy had told Rhonda, "God's driving this train. So as long as we stay on it, everything will be all right."

Remembering those words, Rhonda felt reassured. She turned to Harrison. "My baby's name is Maggie," she said. "Could we please refer to her that way?"

Harrison nodded.

Rhonda asked if she could hold Maggie should the child die during surgery. "I'd like to say good-bye," she explained.

"Absolutely," Harrison answered, pleased. He saw what kind of mother she was.

"One final question," Rhonda added. "Do you believe in God?"

Harrison smiled. "Yes," he said, "I do believe in God."

Before the light of dawn on Tuesday, March 8, 1994, orderlies wheeled Rhonda into the operating room. Judy clutched her hand. "Remember, Rhonda," she said, "don't get off the train."

At a little past 6 A.M., Harrison, with his colleague Dr. Scott Adzick at his side, carefully made a six-inch incision across Rhonda's abdomen, exposing the bulging, blue-red tissue of her uterus. The only sounds in the room were the rhythmic hissing of the respirator and the beeping of monitors.

Harrison then cut across the inch-thick wall of the uterus. He listened as Maggie's fetal monitor registered 140 to 160 beats a minute. *Perfectly normal,* he thought with relief.

Keeping the uterus open with stitches and clamps, Harrison and Adzick next exposed the fetal sac, the cellophane-like membrane that held 26-week-old Maggie. Harrison suctioned the amniotic fluid out, while a sterile solution of Ringer's lactate continually bathed the infant.

Using ultrasound to guide the tiny needle, the medical team injected Maggie with a narcotic to erase any pain from the surgery. With his gloved finger Harrison tugged gently on Maggie's left arm, exposing her chest and abdomen. The infant, weighing less than two pounds, was no bigger than Harrison's hand.

Now Harrison began the most technically demanding part. Squinting through lenses that magnified the surgical field fourfold, he made a small incision below Maggie's rib line and another in her chest. He could finally see the hole in her diaphragm—one of the biggest he had ever encountered.

Reaching into the tiny chest cavity with one finger, Harrison gently pushed Maggie's intestines and spleen back through the diaphragm. As he worked, he listened to every beep of the heart monitor. The steady throb never wavered.

Harrison painstakingly stitched a patch of tough, synthetic fiber over the hole in Maggie's diaphragm. It would remain there all her life.

Maggie's organs had not grown in their proper place, and her abdomen was too small to hold them. So Harrison had to attach a plastic bag outside her body to enlarge the abdominal space. Following birth, when her abdomen grew, the bag would be removed.

After the amniotic fluid was replaced with Ringer's lactate and the fetal sac was stitched shut, an ultrasound probe was passed over Rhonda's still-opened uterus. It showed Maggie moving. *Beautiful,* Harrison thought.

After four-and-a-half hours of surgery, Rhonda was wheeled to intensive care. Stirring, she tugged at a nurse. "How's Maggie?" she whispered.

"Your baby's doing fine," the nurse answered.

Smiling, Rhonda closed her eyes.

For Maggie's lungs to develop sufficiently, she'd have to remain in Rhonda's womb as long as possible. Premature labor loomed as a constant threat.

Back in her hospital room and then in a nearby Ronald McDonald House, Rhonda felt encouraged. Gradually, however, the ordeal started taking its toll. Cramplike pains rippled through her abdomen. Terbutaline and magnesium sulfate, drugs to prevent premature labor, made her weak, shaky and nauseated.

Her dragging spirits were buoyed by Tammy Kakazu, a spirited Coloradan who had undergone similar surgery a month before. "It gets better every day, Rhonda," her new friend said.

But then Tammy began experiencing sharp pains. When doctors examined her, they discovered that a shred of membrane from the fetal sac, which had worked loose during surgery, had looped around her baby's umbilical cord, cutting off the oxygen supply. In moments the infant was dead.

"Just because this happened to my baby doesn't mean it will happen to yours," Tammy said bravely. "Keep fighting and keep hoping."

"I will," Rhonda promised, as they locked in a long hug.

A short time later an ultrasound exam revealed that Rhonda's membranes, too, had separated. Harrison immediately moved her to a room directly across from the O.R. and ordered complete bed rest.

Even with her mother close by, the isolation felt unbearable. As weeks dragged by, Rhonda missed Mike and agonized over how Corey was doing. Still, the beeping of Maggie's heart monitor inspired her.

At 9:30 A.M. on April 22, the beeping stopped. Cold fear gripped Rhonda as she saw the wavy line of Maggie's heart monitor go flat.

Within seconds doctors and nurses, alerted by an alarm, burst into the room. "Get her to the O.R.!" one doctor yelled. They hurled tables and chairs aside, clearing a path for Rhonda's bed. Water spilled onto the floor from a toppled flower vase.

"Dear Lord," Judy whispered, "now it's time to unveil this miracle you've been working through us."

In the operating room, Maggie's heart monitor registered a faint 60, less than half the normal rate. *Please keep beating,* Harrison pleaded silently, thinking of Tammy Kakazu's loss. But it had been almost seven weeks since Rhonda's surgery, long enough for her baby's lungs to have developed. If Maggie made it out alive, she could make it all the way.

Obstetrician J. T. Parer opened Rhonda's abdomen and cut through the uterus and fetal sac. Then Parer reached in to grasp Maggie. For the second time in her 33-week life, the infant was carefully lifted from her mother's womb.

Less than 13 minutes had passed since Maggie's monitor had stopped beeping. Parer handed the infant to a pediatrician, who gave her a gentle slap. Come on, Maggie, breathe, Harrison urged.

Drawing in a breath, the three-pound, 11-ounce baby let out a lusty squawk. Harrison's eyes misted as the O.R. team broke into cheers.

One month after the birth of Maggie Macala Denis, she and her mother left the hospital for home. Now age three, Maggie is a happy, healthy child who loves her big brother Corey and enjoys coloring and listening to her mother read stories.

A few months after she returned home, Rhonda sent Drs. Harrison and Adzick a letter from the heart.

"It was through God's love and mercy that Maggie is with us," she wrote. "But that wouldn't have been possible had you not had the knowledge, skill and the will to save lives. I pray for you both."

John Pekkanen

Christmas Mother

Within every adversity lies a slumbering possibility.

Robert H. Schuller

As a kid growing up in Chicago, the winter weather was cause enough to remember a few Noels with a twinge of discomfort. My brother and I, however, had other things working against us as well way back in 1925.

Our dad had died three years before, leaving our mom with only her pride and a strong back.

My brother, Ned, was four years older than me and went to school. It was necessary for my mom to take me with her to the only job she could find—a cleaning lady. In those days, work was scarce and money was scarcer. I remember watching Mom hour after hour scrubbing floors and walls, on her hands and knees or sitting on the outside of a window sill washing windows, four stories off the ground, in freezing weather—all for 25¢ an hour!

It was the Christmas Eve of 1925 that I shall never forget. Mom had just finished working on the near Northside and we headed home on one of the big, red, noisy and cold

Chicago streetcars. Mom had earned her $2.25 for nine hours of work plus a jar of tomato jam as a Christmas present. I remember after she lifted me onto the rear platform of the streetcar, how she searched through her precious few coins for five pennies and a nickel. Her fare was seven cents and mine was three cents. As we sat together on the cold seats we held hands: the roughness of her hands almost scratched my cold hands as she held them tightly in hers.

I knew it was Christmas Eve, and even though I was only five, the past few Christmases had conditioned me not to expect anything more than some extra food, a visit to Marshall Fields' window display of animated toys and snow, and other kids' excitement.

With Mom's hand in mine and the knowledge that our Christmas basket had been delivered by Big Brothers, a charitable organization, I felt a warm sense of security as we headed home.

We had just passed a major intersection where Wieboldts, a large department store, was letting out the last of its shoppers before closing for Christmas Eve. Their feelings of holiday cheer, cries of joy and happiness could be felt and heard through the cold, steel walls and noise of the traveling streetcar. I was insensitive to the joy but as I looked up at Mom I could feel her body racked with pain. Tears streamed down her weathered face. She squeezed my hand as she released it to wipe away her tears with her chapped and cracking hands. I will always remember her hands with the swollen knuckles, enlarged veins, and coarse surface that somehow reflected her sacrifices, her honesty and her love.

The bitter cold struck our faces like a slap as we stepped down from the streetcar and onto the icy, snow-covered street.

I walked close to Mom to stay warm and looked into the front-room windows that framed brightly lit

Christmas trees. Mom walked straight ahead without a side glance, one of her ungloved hands holding mine, the other holding a paper shopping bag which contained her soiled white uniform and the jar of tomato jam.

Our flat was a corner unit in the middle of the block. Each Christmas, Nick, the barber, sold Christmas trees on an empty lot next to his shop. In those days, tree lots were sold out long before Christmas Eve, leaving only broken or dead brown branches covering the ground. As we passed the quiet, emptied lot, Mom dropped my hand and picked up a bundle of broken, discarded pine-needle branches.

Our second-story flat was without heat except for a small pot-bellied stove in the kitchen. Ned and I fed the stove with coal that dropped off railroad cars a couple of blocks away and with wooden fruit boxes that we found in the alley next to our house. It was natural for each of us to bring home anything that would burn.

As we climbed the dingy, uncarpeted, wooden stairs to our flat, I'm sure my relief was only minimal compared with Mom's. We opened the door to the front room that felt like a refrigerator. The still air actually made it colder than it was outside.

There was a front bedroom, off of the front room, and Ned's bedroom, next to the kitchen, which were no warmer. The door to the kitchen was kept closed to keep what little heat there was in the bathless bathroom, the rear bedroom, and the worn linoleum-covered kitchen. Other than two beds and a lion-clawed wood table with four chairs, there was no other furniture or floor covering in the entire flat.

Ned had started a fire and had pulled up close to the stove to absorb what little heat it afforded and fortunately was absorbed in an old issue of *Boy's Life*. Mom unbundled me and sat me next to the stove, then prepared the table for our Christmas feast.

There were few words spoken because the season was about joy, giving, receiving and love. With the exception of love, there was an obvious void in the remaining Christmas features. We sat facing the little wood stove as we ate canned ham, vegetables and bread. Our faces flushed with the heat as the cold attacked our backs.

I remember that my only concerns that evening were having to go to bed early because of no heat and the shock of cold sheets.

As usual, we washed our hands and faces in cold water, brushed our teeth and made a Rambo-like charge to our respective deep freezes. I curled up in a fetal position between the two sheets of ice with my socks and Ace cap still on. A cold draft of air attacked my behind because one button was missing from my thin, second-hand long underwear. There was no great anticipation about what I would or would not receive for Christmas, so I fell asleep fast and soundly.

Because the streetlight was directly opposite my bedroom window and the Oscar Mayer slaughterhouses were only half a block away, it was common for large trucks to wake me up several times a night. But at my age and with the cold, it was no challenge to escape back to my dreams.

During the twilight before dawn, I awoke. The streetlight clearly illuminated Mom's ticking tin clock (with one missing foot). I hadn't heard the milkman rattling bottles or his horses' hoofs in the alley, so I knew I could sleep at least a few hours longer.

However, when I looked over to see my mother sleeping beside me, I realized that she hadn't been to bed yet. Suddenly I was wide awake in a state of panic, wondering if Mom was sick or if she possibly and finally had had enough and left.

The trucks had passed but my panic had not as I lay there staring at the streetlight with my wool cap over my eyebrows and flannel blankets up to my eyes. I couldn't imagine life without Mom.

I lay in the icy stillness, afraid to get up and confirm my fears, but totally incapable of going back to sleep. Then, I heard a grinding, twisting sound coming from the kitchen. It was as constant as a machine: it would stop for a few seconds, then continue, then pause again.

As best as I could tell time at that age, I figured it was about 5:00 A.M. With the darkness of winter there was no assurance of what time it really was, other than it was long past the time Mom should have been to bed.

As much as I feared the truth, I knew I had to find it. I rolled under the covers to the edge of the bed and dropped my stocking-covered feet to the cold, bare wood floor. With the streetlight illuminating the bedroom, I could see my breath as clear as if I were out in the street.

Once into the darkness of the front room, I was guided to the kitchen by a light glowing from under the door which was ajar. The grinding and twisting sound became louder as I approached. The stove had been out for hours and I could see Mom's breath as well as my own. Her back was toward me. She had wrapped a blanket over her head and back for some small insulation against the cold.

On the floor to the right was her favorite broom, but the handle had been whittled off just above the sweeping portion. She was working at the old wood table: I had never seen such total concentration and dedication in my life. In front of her was what appeared to be some sort of a disfigured Christmas tree. As I stared in awe her effort became apparent to me. She was using her broken kitchen knife to drill holes in her broom handle into which she had inserted the branches from Nick's empty tree lot. Suddenly it became the most beautiful Christmas tree I had ever seen in my life. Many of the irregular holes had not been effective in supporting the branches which were held in place with butcher's string.

As she continued to twist and dig another slot for the remaining branches, my eyes dropped to her feet, where a small can of red paint was still open. A wet brush lay next to it. On the other side of her chair there were two towels on the floor that were almost covered with red toys: a fire engine with two wheels missing off of the back; an old steel train with a number of wheels missing and the caboose's roof bent in half; a jack, out-of-the-box, with no head; and a doll's head with no body. I felt no cold, no fears, no pain, but rather the greatest flow of love I have ever felt in my life. I stood motionless and silent as tears poured from my eyes.

Mom never stopped for a second as I silently turned and walked slowly back to my bedroom. I have had love in my life and received some elaborate gifts through the years, but how can I ever hope to receive more costly gifts or more sacrificial love. I shall never forget my mother or the Christmas of 1925.

John Doll

A Place Prepared by God

The Lord *will watch over your coming and going both now and forevermore.*

Psalm 121:8 NIV

The green ceramic tiles of the bathroom floor cooled my baked-out skin. I sat back against the wall, my legs drawn up, clutching my Bible, folding into myself. And I wondered where this fear had come from, consuming enough to send me into the bathroom of a strange motel, hiding my torment from my sleeping sons in the next room.

Until then, I'd been doing pretty well. We'd made it through a sad divorce, and somehow God had given me the strength to move my young sons across the country, to a new house, a new job, a new life. I'd felt capable and even excited.

But now, in the middle of the night, in the middle of nowhere, I saw myself for what I truly was: alone. And in danger.

The danger was not amorphous. It had a name: the Mojave Desert. And it was just outside the door.

So far we'd driven three days across the South, through

sweltering July heat. My little car and I both had miles and experience under our fan belts, but we were still chugging along. Yet the trip, which had started so hopefully, had now turned sour. Perhaps it was the monotony of days of endless driving. During this last day, particularly, all the fears that had dogged me during the past difficult months found long stretches of thinking time to spend with me in the car.

As we neared the Mojave Desert, our final hurdle to our arrival in California, I realized the danger we faced and how vulnerable I was.

I'd heard every horror story—radiators that boil dry, blow-outs, relentless sun that crisps fragile flesh, the sheer isolation of the long asphalt strip that winds its way through the rocky desolation. Hours with no bathroom, no water . . . nothing. No help.

That frightened me the most. If we got into trouble, who would help us? How could I protect my children if the worst happened? They were dependent on *me*, and for the first time in my life, I had . . . nobody.

I lived it all ahead of time, there on the bathroom floor of our motel room.

This is ridiculous! I told myself. *You've got to get to sleep! Your only hope is to be up at five, crossing as much of the Mojave as possible before the arrival of the punishing sun. Pull yourself together. Get a grip!*

But I couldn't. I felt as if all the desert demons were after me.

Noticing the Bible clutched in my hand, I realized I hadn't had time for that day's devotional. Almost mechanically, I opened it to my bookmark, skimming for the verses where I'd left off somewhere in Revelation. *Let's see . . . chapter 12.* I began to read. *Oh, yes, the woman and the dragon.* A familiar passage. A scene of dramatic rescue as the child was snatched up to God and to his throne.

I read on: "The woman fled into the desert to a place prepared for her by God, where she might be taken care of..."

I sat up straight, my heart pounding. *The woman fled into the desert to a place prepared for her by God.*

In a very real sense, I was a woman in flight myself. Looking for a safe place, fleeing into the desert. The words were alive for me, as if I were hearing, not reading them.

Could it be that I wasn't alone? That my Heavenly Father was already out there, in that frightening landscape, preparing a place for me?

In a twinkling the desert was no longer a sinister threat to our safety but a haven to be embraced. The fear in my throat dissipated slowly as I sat there, eyes closed, beside the toilet, embracing my open Bible.

In a short while, I, too, had settled for the night and was fast asleep.

My nerves were steady when the alarm went off. I got the kids up, fixed breakfast from the cooler and loaded up. It would be a long day, 16 hours behind the wheel. I was grateful for the reassurance I'd received the night before. It didn't feel as immediate this morning. But I wanted to believe that the desert was somewhere that I might "be taken care of." I took a deep breath, and off we went.

We drove in the dark for a cool hour. Then the sun rose, full throttle. Not a cloud to be seen. Or another car, for that matter. I looked at the dash, checking dials and gauges one more time. Temperature was holding okay, but my palms were getting a little sweaty.

I laid the back of my hand against the windshield. Hot already! *"Thank you, Lord, for the air conditioning! Please, keep our little car going. Please take care of us. "*. . . a place prepared for her by God, where she might be taken care of . . ." I turned the words over again in my heart.

Almost subconsciously at first, I became aware that a shadow had fallen over the car. No matter the bends and curves in the road, the shadow bent and curved with us. The sky was perfectly blue and clear, except for this one little cloud whose shadow tracked our vehicle like a homing device.

After a couple of hours, we stopped at the one gasoline oasis in that vast expanse. I could see the cloud, like a patient friend, waiting for us at the highway. We resumed our journey, and the shadow cocooned us once more. Under its protection we traveled for another two hours. I relaxed. I laughed out loud with delight at the one who was taking care of me.

As the highway tunneled us back into civilization, our cloud became one of many. It disappeared without me even being aware of it. But its presence remained with me, from that day to this. For I know that I dwell in a place prepared for me, so that I may be taken care of. And I am no longer afraid.

Catherine E. Verlenden

Medicine

Therefore I tell you, do not worry about your life. . . and indeed your heavenly Father knows that you need all these things.

Matt. 6:25, 32

In September of the year that my second child was born, my husband and I moved from a small town to a large city. We were young and had no money, so we rented a mobile home and parked in the woods just outside the city limits. All too soon my son Steve was born, several weeks early and weighing under four pounds. Such tiny babies require special and very expensive care. With the huge hospital bill added to the cost of moving, I wondered how we could ever repay the enormous debt. But I knew that with God's help we would manage somehow.

Our new home was small and isolated but I loved it. The trees were flaunting their glorious colors and our only neighbors were chipmunks and raccoons. I even loved the long walks to the store, although it was a mile to the main road, half a mile farther to the pay telephone and another half-mile to the store, making a round trip of four miles. I would put my babies in the stroller and set off on an adventure to buy milk and bread, never knowing what wild birds or small animals we might see along the way.

One morning in early December, I woke up to a new world. During the night a sudden snowstorm had transformed our woods into a magic delight, where billowing drifts of deep snow completely covered the fences and glittering ice crystals spangled the trees. I hurried to wake up my children and show them the beauty of winter. My two-year-old daughter, Evelyn, was awake and eager to get dressed, but when I touched my tiny son he was burning with fever.

With sudden fear, I realized just how isolated we were. We had no phone, we were over two miles from the nearest person who might help, and, even worse, our dirt road was on private property; the snow plows would not come.

It was not possible to carry two children through such deep drifts of snow. If only I had a sled or a toboggan to take them to a bus stop; if only my husband were here; if only the buses were running; if only ... It was not possible to take my baby to the doctor. There was nothing I could do. I felt the knot of fear pulling tighter and tighter in the pit of my stomach.

I knelt to pray. "Dear Lord," I said, "please help me. I am so afraid for my baby and I don't know what to do." As I waited for an answer, I began to realize that I was seeing the problem the wrong way. It wasn't necessary to take the baby to the doctor, it was only necessary to bring the doctor's knowledge and medicine to the baby. I could telephone him and ask for a prescription for the right medicine. Reassured, I began to bundle up for the long trek to the phone. I was just pulling my boots on when I heard a knock at the door. I could not imagine who it might be. The only person who knew we were there was my husband, and he was out of town. I opened the door, and to my amazement

I saw the man who delivered milk to the convenience store down the road. I didn't know his name, but I had seen him there several times and had spoken to him once or twice in passing. He smiled and said, "Hi, need any milk?"

Speechless I nodded and opened the door wide to let him in. He continued, "I almost didn't come to work today, it's such a mess out there." He waved his arm to include the woods, the snow and the highway beyond. "But I couldn't stop thinking about you and those babies away back here with no milk, so I decided to deliver to the little store anyway. Then I thought I might as well bring it the rest of the way since it wasn't much farther. Mind you, it's farther than I thought with the snow so deep and all. It kind of wore me out. I hope you don't mind if I sit and rest a minute before I start back."

I poured him a cup of coffee and made sure he was comfortable. Then I told him about the baby and finished by saying, "I know that you are the answer to my prayer. If you will stay with the children while I phone the doctor, I won't need to worry. I was afraid to leave them alone, but until you came, I thought I had no choice."

He thought about it for a minute, nodded and said, "I couldn't leave them alone either. You had best get started." He smiled and added, "I'm glad I broke a trail for you."

As I closed the door behind me, I heard Evelyn say her favorite words, "Read to me?"

Even with a trail broken it took me almost an hour to reach the road, with much slipping and falling. I was exhausted by the time I reached the telephone. But the Lord was with me. I reached the doctor on the first try. He remembered the baby and realized at once that this was a serious condition for such a fragile infant. By careful questioning he determined that Steve had an ear infection. He assured me that modern antibiotics would quickly bring this infection under control.

"But," he warned, "you must give it to him as soon as you can. Tomorrow might be too late.

"So," he explained, "I will call the pharmacy and tell them to prepare it for you right away. This is something new and it is quite expensive, but I think in this case it is necessary. What is the name of the nearest pharmacy?"

I told him the name of a large company I had seen in a shopping center several miles away and added, "How much do you think it will cost?"

He named a price so high I was stunned. *Where in the world could I get that much money?* I stammered my thanks and hung up the phone while my mind raced, attempting to discover a way.

I didn't know anyone in the city. I looked in the directory and called several charities, but they all seemed to have the same requirement. Each time I was told, "Come downtown and fill out an application, then we'll see if you qualify. If you feel that you can't wait, take the child to the county hospital." *Where?* On the other side of town, of course.

By this time I was ready to panic. I only had one coin left for the phone and I still had no idea where to get the money or what to do. Then it occurred to me that there was a way to get the medicine without paying for it. I could wait until the store closed, break in the back door and steal the medicine. I couldn't get the wrong one since it would have my baby's name on it.

I had never stolen anything before. I knew stealing was a sin, something God had specifically commanded us not to do. But I had to get the medicine if my baby was to survive. Surely God would forgive me.

I prayed, "Dear Lord, please guide me. I don't want to steal, but I have tried everything, and there is no other way."

Then I heard a voice, as calm and clear as if someone was standing beside me.

The voice said, "Unless they give it to you . . ."

Give it to me? The idea was so ridiculous I almost laughed out loud. But I only said: "Yes, Lord, I will ask them."

I did not believe for one minute that a large drugstore would give an expensive medicine to a total stranger, but until I asked them, I could not say honestly that I had tried everything.

So I used my last coin and I called the drugstore. When the pharmacist answered, I told him who I was and asked if he had received a prescription from my doctor. He confirmed the order and added that it was ready. I took a deep breath and prepared myself for rejection.

"You don't know me," I said, "but I live a few miles away in a trailer parked on Sovereign Road. I don't have any money but my baby is very sick. If you would let me have the medicine now I will pay you when I can."

The pharmacist said, "That's fine. Can you pick it up or would you like us to deliver it?"

"You can deliver it?" I asked in astonishment.

"Oh yes," he replied. "We have a young man here who came to work today in a Jeep with four-wheel drive. I wondered why he brought the Jeep today, but now I know."

"Thank God!" I cried.

"Yes," the pharmacist agreed. "We do that here quite often." After I thanked him and hung up the phone, I just stood there, hip deep in snow, filled with awe and wonder, and praising God. I believe I had just experienced what is called "Amazing Grace."

This was the first time I was aware of God's hand on my life, but it was certainly not the last. I did not have an easy road to travel, but every time I reached the point where trouble was so deep that I thought I could go no farther, someone came along to help me through the deepest drifts. I didn't always know who these people were, but I always knew who sent them.

Jeanne Morris

Most Richly Blessed

I asked God for strength, that I might achieve,
I was made weak, that I might learn humbly to obey.
I asked for health, that I might do greater things,
I was given infirmity, that I might do better things.
I asked for riches, that I might be happy,
I was given poverty, that I might be wise.
I asked for power, that I might have the praise of men,
I was given weakness, that I might feel the need of God.
I asked for all things, that I might enjoy life,
I was given life, that I might enjoy all things.
I got nothing I asked for—
but everything I had hoped for.
Almost despite myself, my
unspoken prayers were answered.
I am, among all men,
most richly blessed.

Anonymous Confederate Soldier

Mrs. B's Thanksgiving Surprise

Todd Zimmerman was not altogether happy to be working on Thanksgiving Day. As one of a skeleton staff of five manning the State of Maryland's EBT Help Desk (the state's alternative to food stamps), the morning seemed to stretch on. As lunchtime approached, it was hard not to fantasize about the feast his family was preparing, and the laughter and stories that would be told.

Before his lunch break, a call came in from an elderly woman who was obviously distressed.

"I was at the grocery store buying food, but my purchase didn't go through!" she said. "The clerk said the transaction was denied."

Todd knew the questions to ask, and it wasn't long before he diagnosed the problem: the woman's temporary card had expired. Apparently she hadn't understood that she needed to obtain a permanent card.

"Oh, but . . . but I hadn't collected my $10 from October, either! I purposefully left it on account to put together with this $10 for a Thanksgiving dinner."

"I'm sorry," Todd said sympathetically. "Do you have any food in the house?"

"No . . . not really, I was saving up for today, you see. My family thought they were going to be able to come, and I wanted to have a nice meal for them. But something came up, and they can't make it." There was a catch in her voice. "I guess it's just as well."

After she hung up, Todd couldn't get her off his mind. He realized that because of the error this woman, whom he knew only as "Mrs. B," would not only be alone, she'd also go hungry on Thanksgiving Day, all for want of $20. Determinedly, Todd called the grocery store where the woman's transaction had been denied, his own credit card at the ready.

Sorry, they said, no phone orders. And they didn't deliver, and couldn't make an exception today of all days. They also had a skeleton crew and more customers than they could handle.

Lunchtime came. Todd suddenly didn't care that he was eating cafeteria food. Two of his coworkers, Kim Twito and I, took lunch with him, and together we vowed to do whatever we could to solve Mrs. B's problem.

Back at the help desk, we let our compatriots, Julie Simon and Mark Liessmann, in on the dilemma. Working together, we felt we could surely staff the phones while finding a Thanksgiving dinner for Mrs. B.

Unfortunately, by then, virtually every grocery store in Mrs. B's county was closed or closing. None would deliver.

Exhausting the Yellow Pages, one of our coworkers thought of Chesapeake Beef, a grocery store with which EBT had a high volume of business and a good relationship.

Chesapeake Beef was closed for Thanksgiving.

"The owners, Stas and Mary Witezak, are very nice people," I said. "They might know of a local store that's open. I bet they wouldn't mind if I called them at home, even if it is a holiday."

"I'm sorry," said Mary, "I can't think of any open stores.

But you know what? I have a better idea. It sounds like Mrs. B lives about 15 miles from here. We've finished our dinner, but we still have plenty left! Let us bring Thanksgiving to her. I'll put the kids to work making a special card while Stas and I get together a meal. Oh—but please let her know someone is coming. We're unexpected strangers, and we don't want to frighten her."

This was easier asked than accomplished. E.B.T. didn't have Mrs. B's phone number, which was unlisted. However, the telephone operator was willing to call Mrs. B and ask her to return a call to Todd at the Helpline.

When a confused Mrs. B called back, Todd simply told her that friends were coming with a surprise.

Several hours later, Stas Witezak called in. "Thanks so much for giving our family the opportunity to make a difference in someone's life," he said. "Mrs. B very much appreciated the food, but what really touched her were the cards the children made. She nearly cried when she read them. Her response was to ask if she could hug them—and they happily let her."

Mrs. B called back, too. She thanked everyone involved in her Thanksgiving surprise.

When our shift ended, the five of us who had reluctantly come to work that Thanksgiving bade each other farewell with a smile. Though we didn't say it, we were all recalling Mrs. B's words: "I've always been a Christian—but now I know for sure there is a God!"

"Happy Thanksgiving!" said Todd as we parted ways. And in fact, it had been the happiest Thanksgiving of all.

Suzanne L. Helminski

Now This Is Music!

*The Lord is my strength and my shield; in Him
my heart trusts so I am helped, and my heart
exults, and with my song I give thanks to Him.*

Ps. 28:7

I had such wonderful plans laid out for my life, and they
all seemed to be right on track. In fact, on that day in
March of 1988, it seemed nothing could possibly go wrong.
I never suspected that within a month, that day would
seem like a different life, lived by someone else altogether.

"My kids" were obviously nervous as they streamed off
the bus for the music competition at the Orange County
Performing Arts Center. We'd worked so hard for this day.
It was to be the shining hour of their musical year, and my
"blaze of glory" farewell.

In a way it was a miracle in itself that we were here.
Vocal music had long been my life, but for years I'd felt
called to be a teacher as well. When I was hired at San
Clemente High School as the choral music teacher, it
looked to be a challenge to say the least: there were 18
students enrolled in choir classes.

Through dedication and persistence, our ranks had swelled to 150. Lots of "cool kids" joined, and singing was suddenly an "in" thing to do. The music room became a place kids wanted to be; a place they belonged. They recognized how much I cared about them and showed their appreciation by voting me Teacher of the Year.

As much as I loved my kids, 1988 was to be my last year at San Clemente. I was engaged to be married in the spring and would join my new husband in Denver after the wedding. I happily made plans to continue to teach in Colorado. It was as a final tribute to my students that I entered our choir into this competition.

We knew it wasn't any ordinary festival. Dr. Howard Swan, known as the grandfather of choral music, would be rating the participants. He was known to be a tough judge.

We were shown to the large room where we robed up and vocally prepared. "Brahms?! But it's so heavy!" My students had whined when I first told them of my musical selection for the upcoming competition. "Besides, it's in German. C'mon, Miss Lacouague, give us a break!" I explained to them that though they didn't always get to choose the songs, if they'd put their trust in me, they would surely be singing beautiful music.

I selected Brahms because it's emotional and passionate, complex yet simple. It flows then swells, it's loud then soft. It's a melodic love song, and it would push our choir to its limits; it would test our talent, so Brahms it was.

We worked long, hard, disciplined hours, and we had fun. Our goal of earning a good mark from Dr. Swan couldn't be reached without everyone together. Our relationships with each other grew stronger. After months of practice, it was now time to show our stuff.

Thousands of guests filled the rows of seats beyond the blinding lights. The theater grew silent and the hushed whispers finally ceased. Dressed in solemn black robes, the choir watched me expectantly from the stage, and I could tell they were nervous. Just the day before, we'd decided to change the tempo of the Brahms to more fully communicate the passion of the song. We hadn't had much time to rehearse. Standing in front of them, I tried to show them with my eyes that everything would be okay if they followed me.

In my humble opinion, they gave their best performance ever. They absolutely nailed it! Yet we didn't dare risk elation until we received our ratings from the judges. The kids headed toward the safety of the bus in a frenzy of excitement while I waited behind, nervously awaiting the results.

When I finally boarded the bus, the kids were overcome with anticipation. "What's it say, Miss Lacouague? How'd we do? What'd we get?"

My stomach fluttered as I opened the rating sheet.

It merely read, "Now *this* is Brahms!" The rating next to the comment was SUPERIOR—the highest ranking.

We all squealed with delight. Hugs, kisses and high fives went all around.

What a wonderful send-off. If only my wedding and job search would go as well!

One month later, on a Sunday evening, I got up from my kitchen table after preparing lessons for the upcoming week. I was happy but exhausted: I'd spent all day directing the choir and orchestra in a musical. On top of that, I had all my planning to do for the wedding, the impending move and many farewells.

Around 2:00 A.M., I woke up mid-air, falling out of the foot of my bed onto my head. As I hit the floor, I heard my neck crack. I found myself flat on my back with my feet in the closet, and my head up against the dust ruffle. *How did I get here?* I asked myself sleepily as I tried to roll over and sit up.

It didn't work. Instead, I heard another *craaaaaack* and felt a burst of pain. Resolutely, I tried to roll over to my other side. *Crrraaccck.* That shot of pain took my breath away. I was way beyond tears. I knew now I couldn't get up—I needed help.

I tried to yell out to my roommate, Dorothy, whose room was upstairs. My shout came out as a breathy whisper. I couldn't even talk!

"She'll never find me! I'll lie here until morning!" I tried not to panic.

Amazingly, within minutes the door opened and Dorothy walked into my room, turning on the light. "Renee?" she asked, "Are you all right?"

"My neck is killing me," I whispered. "Call the paramedics."

Seeing the distress in my eyes, she ran for help.

When I awoke in the hospital's intensive care unit, I was groggy and uncertain. The doctor's deep, dark eyes had a serious look in them. He wasted no time mincing words.

"Renee," he said, "your neck is broken. You're paralyzed from the neck down. You're a quadriplegic."

"A what?" I asked, unsure of what he meant.

"You'll never be able to walk, sit up, or move your arms or legs for the rest of your life," he explained. "And I'm sorry, but you'll never be able to sing again either."

I was crushed. All I had done was go to bed. I couldn't be paralyzed! Was I dreaming?

It's hard to stay in denial when faced by such overwhelming physical evidence. Next I tried to grasp the impact of the injury on my life. Or what used to be my life! It was clear my plans were all as shattered as my vertebrae: I couldn't teach, I couldn't sing and certainly I couldn't expect Mike to marry a quadriplegic when he'd proposed to a healthy woman!

My life was over. It was over. "God," I whined, "this is not what I had in mind for my life! I can't do it! Why? Why couldn't you have given me an easier path?"

And then I heard that still, small voice: *You may not always get to choose the songs, but if you put your trust in me, you'll surely make beautiful music.*

Did I have the same faith I required of my students?

My answer was hard-wrung. "Yes, Lord, I'll trust you, I'll trust you."

The first "song" he gave me was incredibly precious. My beloved Mike insisted on becoming my husband. He strengthened the resolve I had to teach again. The fight I might not have been able to make for myself became easy when I thought of God, and Mike, and my future students. I even vowed to sing again.

It's been nine years since then, and God has been good. The teaching I've done hasn't been at school but at church, where I've been able to form three youth choirs. I've made a recording of songs for people who need courage, strength and hope like I did. I've been able to give concerts where I sing and tell my story to prisoners, teenagers, church and women's groups.

No, my life is not at all what I'd planned. But every now and then I see the sweet harmonies and sweeping cascades of God's arpeggios all around me, and I think: *Now this is music.*

Renée Lacouague Bondi

A Healing Place

"Chris collapsed on the football field." Kristina Bean heard the coach's strained voice say. "Collapsed?" Kristina repeated, trying to grasp his words. Though small for his age, her 16 year-old son, Christopher, had always seemed healthy. Oh God, please don't let it be serious, Kristina prayed as she sped to the hospital near their Auburn, California, home.

But it was. Chris's color was gray, and he barely had the strength to nod to her from the stretcher. "Chris has a hole in his heart," the doctor told Kristina and her husband, Jim. "He's probably had it since he was born. But we can correct it surgically."

As a child, Chris had sometimes seemed to be out of breath, but she'd told herself it was because he played so hard. She bent down to her son, who was in an oxygen tent to help him breathe. "The doctors can fix this," she reassured him.

"I just want to be like everybody else," Chris said. "Let's do it!"

Only two months later, Chris was mid-sentence when he gasped, "Mom, my heart's racing."

In a panic, Kristina reached for the phone. Soon Chris was back in the hospital. *This can't be happening again,* she told herself. But tests showed Chris's heart was beating 300 times a minute, nearly three times the normal rate.

"We didn't realize it before, but your son has tachycardia," the doctor told them. "A nerve in his heart is misfiring, causing episodes of rapid heartbeat."

"Could it . . . kill him? Kristina blurted. *Please say no,* she begged silently.

The doctor paused. "His heart will become more and more damaged over time," he admitted, "We could try to treat it with tranquilizers."

Chris objected. "But I want to play football!" he said. "I want to ski and hike."

"We'll take this one day at a time," Kristina told him. *But what if his days run out?* She wondered. *The pills will work,* she vowed. *They have to.*

But on the medication, Chris had only enough energy to get through school, with none left over to play sports. He had to skip a pill just to stay up to attend a game with friends. When he did, Kristina would worry. What if he had an attack while crossing a street? What if next time they couldn't stop the attack?

"There must be something we can do!" she cried to Jim. Desperate, they saw another cardiologist who suggested using a laster to sever the nerve that was misfiring.

"Maybe it's the cure we've been praying for," Kristina told Jim. But when the doctor appeared in the waiting room, he was pale and shaken. *Oh God, no . . .* she thought.

"Chris's heart wasn't strong enough to withstand the procedure," the doctor began. "We had to stop."

"We'll try again," Kristina said. But the next attempt failed, too.

"We can try once more," the doctor suggested.

Chris wouldn't hear of it. "No more surgery!" he cried.

Dear Lord, Kristina despaired. *Look at him. He's lost 35 pounds. He's so thin and tired. He's had enough of the pain and frustration. But, oh, I don't want to lose him!*

Over the next few months Kristina was alone with Chris much of the time as Jim had to travel for his job. She watched helplessly as her son became more and more withdrawn. He stopped calling his friends, broke up with his girlfriend and announced that he was dropping out of school.

"I have no future," he told Kristina. She heard his unspoken message: why plan for anything if I'm just going to die?

Chris stubbornly refused to consider another operation. Kristina understood, but asked herself. *Wouldn't it be better to try again than live in a haze of medication—or constant fear?*

Dear God, Kristina prayed. *I don't know how to give him back his will to live! We've tried everything. I just can't say good-bye to him this way.*

One day, a crazy impulse seized her, "We're getting out of here," she announced to Chris. *A change of scenery might do us both good,* she thought. *What have we got to lose?* "Chris," she said, "We're going to get in the car and drive."

Chris didn't ask why. Surprising her, he replied, "Mom, I've heard Montana's really beautiful."

"Montana?" She opened her mouth to object. It was so far away. But there was a light in his eyes she hadn't seen for months—or was it years?

So they drove. Through California, Nevada and Idaho. As they left the crowded freeways behind and entered Montana, Kristina looked over at Chris. He couldn't seem to get enough of his surroundings—the deer drinking from a clear stream, the mountains stretching toward the sky—everything captivated him.

In the Bitterroot Valley near Missoula, Chris asked suddenly, "Mom, can we live here?"

With Jim's job requiring so much travel, we could live anywhere, Kristina thought, *and if it makes Chris happy* . . .

Soon the Beans were living atop a mountain rim that overlooked rivers Chris said he wanted to fish, near trails he said he wanted to hike, near a town where people stopped and said hello.

"I'm going to climb that mountain," Chris said one day, gazing upward. Then he turned to her. "One more operation," he said.

He was meant to live here, Kristina thought. *And he will.*

This time after surgery, as Chris came out of the anesthesia, Kristina and Jim could tell him, "Now you can hike that mountain!" The procedure had worked.

"Once he thought he had no tomorrows," Kristina says. "Now he wants to build his own log house here."

She turns her eyes to the setting sun that splashes the sky with color. "I used to think God lived in heaven. Now I think he lives in Montana."

Chris McGonigle
Excerpted from *Woman's World Magazine*

The Story of Raoul Wallenberg

God helps the brave.

J. C. F. von Schiller

I'm a professional photographer. My offices in New York are only three blocks from the United Nations, where signs designate "Raoul Wallenberg Walk." Those who know of Wallenberg think of him as someone who saved nearly 100,000 lives in Budapest, Hungary, in the last fierce days of World War II. To me, Raoul Wallenberg not only *saved* lives, he also left a mark on those he saved. I know. He left a deep mark engraved in my heart and mind, one that has shaped my thoughts and actions ever since.

I first met Wallenberg on October 17, 1944, when I was a young man. By then, the Nazis had "cleansed" the Hungarian countryside of Jewish people; more than 430,000 men, women and children had vanished, at the rate of 12,000 a day, never to be seen again. Now, in the closing days of the war, the Nazis prepared to exterminate the last large population of Jews alive in Europe, those in Budapest.

Raoul Wallenberg, a young Swedish architect, had been sent to Budapest in July for the sole purpose of saving lives. He worked through the Swedish Legation, although he'd never been trained as a diplomat. He'd been in the import-export business and knew his way around Europe. His weapons were his wits, determination and a belief in the worth of each human life to the point of risking his own in exchange.

I'd grown up learning photography from my father. He was the court-appointed photographer to the Hapsburgs, the personal photographer of the Hungarian regent, Admiral Miklos Horthy, and the top society photographer in Budapest. Admiral Horthy gave us a personal exemption from the existing laws imposed on the Jews. On October 15, when the Arrow Cross—the Hungarian Nazis—took over the government, all exemptions were canceled. Through my father I knew one of the Swedish diplomats, Per Anger. Knowing my life was in immediate danger, I headed for the Swedish Legation. Against all odds, I made it through the crowds of people seeking help, and was admitted.

I told Per the bind I was in. "Let me introduce you to someone," he said. He leaned out the door. "Raoul?"

Raoul Wallenberg came in, a young man, early 30s, slim with brown hair. His air was down-to-earth, a center of calm in a world gone mad. Per said, "This is Tom Veres, a photographer, a friend of mine. He could be useful."

Wallenberg said, "Good. You'll be my photographer. You will document the work we are doing. You'll report directly to me." They made out official papers on the spot.

Much of my time was spent taking pictures for *schutz-passes* (passports) that Wallenberg then issued by the thousands. They stated that the bearer was approved to move to Sweden after the war, and was already under the protection of the Swedish government.

But the day I found out what it really meant to be Wallenberg's photographer was a month later, on November 28, when his secretary handed me a piece of paper with his instructions: "Meet me at Jozsefvarosi Station. Bring your camera."

The Jozsefvarosi train station was a freight depot on the outskirts of town. I took my Leica and got on the tram, not knowing what to expect. To tell you the truth, everybody, especially those on the Nazis' hit list, thought lying low was the best plan. Keep quiet, keep out of sight. Don't get involved. Yet here I was, on a raw November morning, heading for Jozsefvarosi Station.

I found the station surrounded by Hungarian Nazis and gendarmes from the countryside. Anyone in his right mind was trying to get out. Wallenberg expected me to find a way in. I shoved my camera into my pocket and went to one of the gendarmes. Using the world's phoniest Swedish accent, I spoke in a mixture of broken Hungarian and German. "I'm a Swedish diplomat! I must go in to meet Raoul Wallenberg!"

The gendarme stared at me incredulously but let me in. The scene inside the station was harrowing. Thousands of men were being loaded onto cattle cars. Wallenberg was there, as were his Studebaker and his driver, Vilmos Langfelder. When Raoul saw me, he walked over and whispered slowly, "Take as many pictures as you can."

Pictures? Here? If I were caught, I'd be on that train myself, legation or no legation. I climbed into the backseat of the car and took out my pocketknife. I cut a small slit in my scarf and positioned the camera inside it. I got out and walked through the trainyard as calmly as possible, snapping pictures.

Wallenberg had his black ledger out. "All my people get in line here!" he called. "All you need to do is show me your schutzpass!"

He approached the line of "passengers." "You, yes, I have your name here. Where is your paper?" The startled man emptied his pockets, looking for a paper he never had. He pulled out a letter. "Fine. Next!"

Men caught on at once. Letters, eyeglass prescriptions, even deportation notices became passports to freedom. In his ledger, Raoul and his assistants carefully checked off, or added, each name in the book. I tried to become invisible, snapping away, trying to catch the atrocity of what was going on.

"Tommy! Tommy!"

I heard my name and turned around. Had I been recognized?

"Tommy!" In line, almost on the train, was my best friend, George. George and I had known each other for years. We'd been assigned a seat together in first grade and had sat together by choice every year since. He was brilliant academically, the valedictorian of our gymnasium. Now he was in line to die. I had only a split second to think.

I walked over to him, grabbed him by the collar and said, "You dirty Jew, get over there!" I pointed toward Wallenberg's line. "I said go! Are you deaf?" I kicked his backside. He understood and got in line.

Wallenberg had pulled hundreds of men out of line when he sensed the Nazis losing patience. "Now back to Budapest, all of you!" he said.

The new "Swedes" walked out of the station to freedom. Wallenberg turned back to the captors. He began to lecture them in measured tones about health conditions, crowding on trains, anything to take their attention off the departing men.

As soon as they had a good head start, Raoul and I got back into the car where Vilmos waited. The danger we'd been in didn't hit me until then. This man, a Swede, who could have waited out the war in safety, was marching into trainyards—and asking others to do the same!

When we got back to town, I found George, took him to one of Wallenberg's protected houses and took his picture for a schutzpass. "Now stay here until I get your papers!" I said.

The next day, work came: more deportations from Jazsefvarosi Station. Again I was asked to come. It was a ghastly repeat. Gendarmes with machine guns, thousands of men being herded onto trains. Wallenberg with his table and his black "book of life."

This time my Leica was already hidden in the folds of my scarf. As Wallenberg started calling off common names that many men might answer to, I started snapping photos.

That day, my cousin Joseph was among those marked for death, as was one of Hungary's great actors. I pulled them out of line to join Wallenberg's hundreds.

It was then I saw my chance. I walked around the train, inches from the armed guards. On the other side, the side away from the station, I climbed onto the already filled car. The train hadn't yet been padlocked from the side. I jumped, pushing all my weight onto the bolt that held the door shut. The spring clicked. The long door slid back in its tracks.

The men inside, who a moment ago had stood prisoner in the darkness, now blinked in the November sky. "Move, quickly!" I said. Men started jumping off the back of the train, running to the line where Wallenberg continued to give out passes.

Inside the station Wallenberg clearly saw that his time was up. "All of you released by the Hungarian government, back to town! March!" At the same time a Hungarian police officer saw what I was doing. He pointed his revolver at me. "You! Stop what you're doing!"

Raoul and his driver got into their Studebaker and they

drove around to my side of the train. Raoul opened the door and leaned out. "Tom! Jump!"

I didn't have a moment to think. I made the longest jump of my life.

Raoul pulled me inside and Vilmos stepped on the gas. Raoul smiled and looked back at the train station. "I don't think we'll come back here for a while!" he said.

A couple of days later, at Wallenberg's Ulloi Street offices, George's mother came to see me. She was crying. George had tried to slip out to see his fiancée in a house two corners away. Two Arrow Cross thugs arrested him within those two blocks. I never saw my best friend again.

By January the Soviet Army was pressing close to the city, but the Nazis and Arrow Cross still ran Budapest. Wallenberg was in a pitched battle to keep the 30,000 people in protected houses from being added to the 70,000 people already locked in the Central Ghetto. He was doing everything he could to stop the program to finish the ghetto off.

By now there was constant bombing day and night, so hundreds of us lived in the Ulloi Street offices. On the night of Monday, January 8, a pounding came at the legation door. Within moments, the Arrow Cross burst in, shining blinding flashlights from face to face.

The Arrow Cross didn't know that Edith Wohl was at the telephone switchboard upstairs and that she made a quick call. "Everybody line up!" the officer yelled at us. "At once! Or we'll shoot you on the spot!"

It was finally happening. I was standing under guard in line, about to be marched to my death.

"All right, everyone. It's time for a walk to the river!" one soldier spat. He turned to a couple of his buddies sitting nearby. "It's your turn to take them."

"We just got back from taking the last group!" one of them complained. "There's still snow on our boots!"

Just then the door burst open. There stood Wallenberg. "What are you doing? These are Swedes! You've made a very serious mistake! Let them go!"

The Arrow Cross turned, stunned, to find a truckload of Budapest Police filling the room, guns drawn.

Raoul Wallenberg stared down the Nazi captain. "You heard me. Let them go. Now!"

The captain stared at the machine guns surrounding him. He stared at the Swede. The captain let us go.

The war was within days of being over when the bad news came. Everyone, Jews and Christians alike, who lived in my family's apartment house had been marched away by the Arrow Cross because they'd found the huge hidden food stocks kept by the well-known Zserbo Confectionery stored in the building's basement. My parents were taken as well; they were taken straight to the Danube and shot, their bodies thrown into the river. It was too late for Raoul to save them.

But it wasn't too late for thousands of people whom Raoul had pulled out of trains or off marches. It wasn't too late for the people in the ghetto whom Wallenberg and his accomplices had saved from the final pogrom, even as the firing squads were assembling.

The last time I saw Raoul Wallenberg, he and his driver, Vilmos Langfelder, were getting ready to leave for Debrecen to meet with the newly established provisional government about setting up reconstruction programs. He asked me if I wanted to come, but I had yet to find out the whereabouts of my parents. The two men left on January 17 with a Soviet escort. Before reaching Debrecen, they were taken into custody by the NKVD, a precursor of the KGB. Neither man has been seen outside Soviet prisons since.

I've thought often about how the timing of my parents' tragic deaths kept me from disappearing along with

Wallenberg. Sometimes I think my life was spared so that I could tell his story.

What happened to Wallenberg is shrouded in mystery to this day, but what he did for thousands of men and women and children will always be bright and clear. It's been said, "Greater love has no one than this, that one lay down his life for his friends" (John 15:13). They were not literally his friends, these people whose lives Wallenberg saved, they were simply his fellow human beings, and as such, he felt responsible for them. He wasn't some super-human, although his actions were heroic. He was an ordinary person who dared other ordinary people to do what he did.

So here, I tell his story.

Tom Veres

The Voice of an Angel

Among the U.S. Marines who fought against the Japanese in World War II was 21-year-old Corporal William Devers, who considered himself an agnostic. No amount of arguing, Bible-quoting or coercion by his fellow Marines or the chaplain could sway him. During the company's first major encounter with the Japanese, a number of the unit were killed and the chaplain was wounded. In great pain, the chaplain called to Devers, "My . . . left pocket . . . take it . . . please . . . Last night I had a dream. In the dream an angel appeared and told me that I had to make you take the Bible. Take it, son . . . please." Devers shoved the Bible into his shirt pocket to satisfy the wounded man.

Twenty minutes later, Corporal Devers' squad stumbled right into a Japanese patrol, and before he knew what had happened he was on the ground, his mind fading into the darkness, certain he was dying. When he came to, he felt a ripple of pain shoot through his chest, but there was no blood.

The bullet had torn into the Bible he carried in his pocket, ending its journey at the book of Psalms, which read: "A thousand shall fall at thy side, and ten thousand at thy right hand; but it shall not come nigh thee."

James Pruitt

An Old Irish Blessing

May the road rise to meet you:
May the wind be always at your back,
The sun shine warm upon your face,
The rain fall soft upon your fields,
And until we meet again
May God hold you in the hollow of his hand.

Author Unknown

More Chicken Soup?

Many of the stories and poems you have read in this book were submitted by readers like you who had read earlier *Chicken Soup for the Soul* books. We are planning to publish five or six *Chicken Soup for the Soul* books every year. We invite you to contribute a story to one of these future volumes.

Stories may be up to 1,200 words and must uplift or inspire. You may submit an original piece or something you clip out of the local newspaper, a magazine, a church bulletin or a company newsletter. It could also be your favorite quotation you've put on your refrigerator door or a personal experience that has touched you deeply.

To obtain a copy of our submission guidelines and a listing of upcoming *Chicken Soup* books, please write, fax or check one of our Web sites.

Chicken Soup for the *(Specify Which Edition)* Soul
P.O. Box 30880 • Santa Barbara, CA 93130
fax: 805-563-2945
To e-mail or visit our Web site:
www.chickensoup.com

You can also visit the *Chicken Soup for the Soul* site on America Online at keyword: chickensoup.

Just send a copy of your stories and other pieces, indicating which edition they are for, to any of the above addresses.

We will be sure that both you and the author are credited for your submission.

For information about speaking engagements, other books, audiotapes, workshops and training programs, please contact any of the authors directly.

Passing it On!

It has become a tradition to donate a portion of the net profits of every *Chicken Soup for the Soul* book to several charities related to the theme of the book. Past recipients have included the American Red Cross, The Wellness Community, the Breast Cancer Research Foundation, the National Arbor Association, the American Association of University Women Educational Foundation, and Literacy Volunteers of America.

We have selected the following nonprofit organizations to receive a portion of the proceeds from this book:

The Bosnian Orphanage Relief

The Bosnian Orphanage Relief, one of the works of charity administered by the non-profit Catalyst Complex, provides physical and spiritual care for needy orphaned children of war-torn Bosnia. You may contact this organization at: Bosnian Orphanage Relief, 3726 Birchwood Road, Kettle River, MN 55757 or call: 218-273-6232. Web site: www.kettleriverusa.com

Feed The Children

Feed The Children is an international, nonprofit Christian organization providing food, clothing, medical equipment and other necessities to people who lack these essentials because of famine, drought, flood, war or other calamities all over the world. Feed The Children was formed by Larry Jones in 1979 and has distributed over 280 million pounds of relief commodities. Today, Feed the Children programs supplement 123,000 meals per day.

For more information on them please write: Feed the Children, P.O. Box 36, Oklahoma City, OK 73101-0036.

Habitat For Humanity

Habitat For Humanity International works with people around the world, from all walks of life, building houses and developing communities in partnership with those in need.

Habitat For Humanity helps meet the universal necessity for a safe, decent place to live. This basic need is what compels Habitat to improve the human condition; and in so doing, build God's kingdom on earth, one house, one family at a time.

For more information on them please write: HFHI, 121 Habitat Street, Americus, GA 31709-3498.

Covenant House

Covenant House is the largest privately-funded child-care agency in the U.S. serving over 400,000 youth in the last 25 years. It was incorporated in New York City in 1972 and has since expanded to New Orleans, Houston, Fort Lauderdale, Orlando, Los Angeles, Anchorage, Newark, Atlantic City and Washington, D.C. It has also established programs in Guatemala, Honduras, Mexico and Toronto, Canada.

Providing food, shelter, clothing, crisis care, health care, education, vocational preparation, drug abuse treatment, prevention programs, legal services, recreation, mother/ child programs, transitional living programs, street out-reach and aftercare to homeless and runaway youth.

Last year they provided residential and non-residential services to over 44,000 youths. Their Covenant House Nineline (1-800-999-9999) received almost 88,000 crisis calls from youngsters all over the country who needed immediate help and had nowhere else to turn.

For more information on them please write: Covenant House, 346 W. 17th Street, New York, NY 10011.

Who Is Jack Canfield?

Jack Canfield is one of America's leading experts in the development of human potential and personal effectiveness. He is both a dynamic, entertaining speaker and a highly sought-after trainer. Jack has a wonderful ability to inform and inspire audiences toward increased levels of self-esteem and peak performance.

He is the author and narrator of several bestselling audio- and videocassette programs, including *Self-Esteem and Peak Performance, How to Build High Self-Esteem, Self-Esteem in the Classroom* and *Chicken Soup for the Soul—Live.* He is regularly seen on television shows such as *Good Morning America, 20/20* and *NBC Nightly News.* Jack has coauthored numerous books, including the *Chicken Soup for the Soul* series, *Dare to Win* and *The Aladdin Factor* (all with Mark Victor Hansen), *100 Ways to Build Self-Concept in the Classroom* (with Harold C. Wells) and *Heart at Work* (with Jacqueline Miller).

Jack is a regularly featured speaker for professional associations, school districts, government agencies, churches, hospitals, sales organizations and corporations. His clients have included the American Dental Association, the American Management Association, AT&T, Campbell Soup, Clairol, Domino's Pizza, GE, ITT, Hartford Insurance, Johnson & Johnson, the Million Dollar Roundtable, NCR, New England Telephone, Re/Max, Scott Paper, TRW and Virgin Records. Jack is also on the faculty of Income Builders International, a school for entrepreneurs.

Jack conducts an annual eight-day Training of Trainers program in the areas of self-esteem and peak performance. It attracts educators, counselors, parenting trainers, corporate trainers, professional speakers, ministers and others interested in developing their speaking and seminar-leading skills.

For further information about Jack's books, tapes and training programs, or to schedule him for a presentation, please contact:

The Canfield Training Group
P.O. Box 30880 • Santa Barbara, CA 93130
phone: 805-563-2935 • fax: 805-563-2945
To e-mail or visit our Web site: *www.chickensoup.com*

Who Is Mark Victor Hansen?

Mark Victor Hansen is a professional speaker who, in the last 20 years, has made over 4,000 presentations to more than 2 million people in 32 countries. His presentations cover sales excellence and strategies; personal empowerment and development; and how to triple your income and double your time off.

Mark has spent a lifetime dedicated to his mission to make a profound and positive difference in people's lives. Throughout his career, he has inspired hundreds of thousands of people to create a more powerful and purposeful future for themselves while stimulating the sale of billions of dollars worth of goods and services.

Mark is a prolific writer and has authored *Future Diary, How to Achieve Total Prosperity* and *The Miracle of Tithing.* He is coauthor of the *Chicken Soup for the Soul* series, *Dare to Win* and *The Aladdin Factor* (all with Jack Canfield) and *The Master Motivator* (with Joe Batten).

Mark has also produced a complete library of personal empowerment audio- and videocassette programs that have enabled his listeners to recognize and use their innate abilities in their business and personal lives. His message has made him a popular television and radio personality, with appearances on ABC, NBC, CBS, HBO, PBS and CNN. He has also appeared on the cover of numerous magazines, including *Success, Entrepreneur* and *Changes.*

Mark is a big man with a heart and spirit to match—an inspiration to all who seek to better themselves.

For further information about Mark write:

P.O. Box 7665
Newport Beach, CA 92658
phone: 949-759-9304 or 800-433-2314
fax: 949-722-6912
Web site: *www.chickensoup.com*

Who Is Patty Aubery?

Patty Aubery is the vice president of The Canfield Training Group and Self-Esteem Seminars, Inc. Patty came to work for Jack Canfield in 1989, when Jack still ran his organization out of his house in Pacific Palisades. Patty has been working with Jack since the birth of *Chicken Soup for the Soul* and can remember the days of struggling to market the book. Patty says, "I can remember sitting at flea markets in 100 degree weather trying to sell the book and people would stop, look and walk to the next booth! They thought I was crazy. Everyone said I was wasting my time. And now here I am. Fourteen million copies have been sold of the first 11 books, and I have coauthored two of the books in the *Chicken Soup* series!"

Patty is the coauthor of *Chicken Soup for the Surviving Soul: 101 Stories of Courage and Inspiration from Those Who Have Survived Cancer.* She has been a guest on over 50 local and nationally syndicated radio shows.

Patty is married to Jeff Aubery, and together they have a two-year-old son named J.T. Aubery. Patty and her family reside in Santa Barbara, California, and can be reached at The Canfield Training Group, P. O. Box 30880, Santa Barbara, CA 93130, or by calling 1-800-237-8336, or faxing 805-563-2945.

Who Is Nancy Mitchell?

Nancy Mitchell is the director of publishing for The Canfield Group and manager of all copyrights and permissions. She graduated from Arizona State University in May of 1994 with a B.S. in Nursing. After graduation Nancy worked at Good Samaritan Regional Medical Center in Phoenix, Arizona, in the Cardiovascular Intensive Care Unit. Four months after graduation, Nancy moved back to her native town of Los Angeles. Her sister and coauthor, Patty Aubery, offered her a part-time job working for Jack Canfield and Mark Victor Hansen. Nancy's intentions were to help finish *A 2nd Helping of Chicken Soup for the Soul* and then return to nursing. However, in December of that year, she was asked to continue on full time at The Canfield Group. Nancy put nursing on hold and became the director of publishing, working closely with Jack and Mark on all *Chicken Soup for the Soul* projects.

Nancy says that what she is most thankful for right now is her move back to Los Angeles. "If I hadn't moved back to California, I wouldn't have had the chance to be there for my mom during her bout with breast cancer. Right now my priority is to be there for my mom and for my family." Out of that struggle Nancy coauthored *Chicken Soup for the Surviving Soul: 101 Stories of Courage and Inspiration from Those Who Have Survived Cancer.* Nancy has recently relocated to Santa Barbara with The Canfield Group and can be reached at The Canfield Group, P. O. Box 30880, Santa Barbara, CA 93130, or by calling 1-800-237-8336, or faxing 805-563-2945, or via e-mail at *www.chickensoup.com.*

Contributors

Many of the stories in this book were taken from books we have read. These sources are acknowledged in the Permissions section. Some of the stories and poems were contributed by friends of ours, who, like us, are professional speakers. If you would like to contact them for information on their books, tapes and seminars, you can reach them at the addresses and phone numbers provided below.

Many of the stories were also contributed by readers like yourself, who, after reading other volumes of *Chicken Soup for the Soul*, were inspired to submit a story out of their life's experience. We have included information about them as well.

Rhonda Adams graduated from The Columbus College of Art and Design in Columbus, Ohio, in 1979. The creator of hundreds of greeting cards for numerous manufacturers over the past decade. Rhonda specializes in humerous illustrations. Fast becoming recognized nationally, her cartoons are printed on t-shirts, posters, postcards, clocks and soon to be seen in a 1998 wall calendar Let Us Laugh. For more information, you can reach Rhonda on the Internet at *http://www.infr.com/pcf/illustrators/rhonda_adams.html* or by e-mail at *rhonda@infr.com*.

Joan Wester Anderson is a bestselling author and is recognized around the world as an authority on angelic and miraculous intervention in everyday life. Over 2 million copies of her books have been sold. She can be reached at P. O. Box 1694, Arlington Heights, IL 60006.

Teresa Anne Arries is a researcher, speaker and freelance writer published in Christian and secular magazines. A former contributing editor for *Bible-Science Newsletter*, Terry's research and nationwide contacts made possible a program for ABC's *20/20* on "Death Education in the Public Classrooms." She can be reached at P. O. Box 4433, Pagosa Springs, CO 81157, or by calling 970-731-2525.

Steve Baal is an award-winning freelance writer with numerous national, regional and local credits for articles on a wide variety of subjects. Steve can be reached at P. O. Box 162, Indian Rocks Beach, FL 33785.

Aaron Bacall is a New York cartoonist whose work appears in magazines, books and advertisements. He has worked as a pharmaceutical research chemist and a university educator before turning to full-time cartooning. He can be reached somewhere in cyberspace at *ABCARTOON@JUNO.COM* or via fax at 718-370-2629.

Sandy Beauchamp is a career nurse and cancer survivor of 18 years. In her practice, she has come to identify the necessity of soul nurturing as well as physical care for the maintenance and attainment of health. Sandy has published 5 articles. A proponent of healing touch, Sandy can be reached at 129 Timbers Dr., Slidell, LA 70458.

Anne Bembry lives with her husband, Dan, in Live Oak, Florida. Together they have seven children. Anne currently is a shift supervisor with Corrections Corp. of America. Andy works as an officer in the correctional field, as well as being a national guardsman.

Bits & Pieces, the magazine that inspires the world, has motivated and amused millions for almost 30 years. For your free issue, call 1-800-526-2554. Available in English, Spanish and Japanese.

James C. Brown, M.D., is the husband of Justine and the father of Ryan and Sally. He is a physician involved in the care of children, and a faculty member at Creighton University School of Medicine in Omaha, Nebraska, where he enjoys teaching. Dr. Brown is an author, bronze sculptor, coach, and with his wife, Justine, he raises and trains Belgian draft horses. He can be reached at Creighton University Medical Center, Department of Radiology, 601 N. 30th St., Omaha, NE 68131-2197, or by calling 402-449-4753.

Jeanine Marie Brown is a freelance writer who lives in Placentia, California. She is a graduate of Azusa Pacific University and taught high school English and speech for seven years. Jeanine specializes in personal narratives and short fiction. She can be reached at 2300 W. Worth Ave., La Habra, CA 90631.

Jeanne Williams Carey raised eight children and numerous foster children. It has kept her happily busy. She ventured into education and took delight in teaching. She was a principal for a short time. Jeanne now writes stories about the vivid courage, bright hopes and joy of people who know it is a great life.

Rebecca Christian is a playright, travel writer, speaker and columnist raised in Dubuque, Iowa. Her work has appeared in over 100 magazines and newspapers. She can be reached at 641 Alta Vista St., Dubuque, IA 52001, or by calling 319-582-9193.

Charles W. Colson was former special assistant to President Richard Nixon and pled guilty to Watergate-related offenses in 1974, serving seven months in prison. Currently he is president of Prison Fellowship, located in Reston, Virginia. He has authored numerous books, which include the bestselling *Born Again.*

Reverend Nancy Dahlberg is currently serving the United Church of Christ as an Interim Minister. She continues to write, speak and lead seminars on topics which motivate and inspire Christian service and leadership. She can be reached at P.O. Box 3100, York, PA 17402

Jenna Day is a poetess, writer and educator who lives in western Maine with her family. She has published several poems and is currently at work on a collection of short stories about growing up in rural Maine. She can be reached at R.R. #1, Box 364, Brownfield, ME 04010.

Paul Della Valle has been a journalist for 20 years. The New England Press Association named him best columnist in 1995 and 1996 and best humorist in 1993. He is the author of two books, as well as being a university teacher and editor/publisher of *The Lancaster (MA) Times*, a weekly newspaper in his hometown.

Albert DiBartolomeo is the author of two novels, *The Vespers Tapes* (*Blood Confessions* in softcover) and *Fool's Gold*. He has published a number of short stories, memoirs and commentary pieces in publications such as *Italian Americana, Reader's Digest* and the *Philadelphia Inquirer*. He lives in Philadephia, Pennsylvania, where he teaches at Drexel University.

John Doll and his wife, Lanie, presently live in the middle of a twenty-five acre orange and avocado grove. Before his retirement in 1987 he did international marketing for one of Times Mirror's corporations. He is a freelance writer with a number of short stories published. His forte is nostalgia and memories. Originally he wrote material for Laurence Welk. He can be reached at 2377 Grand Ave., Fillmore, CA. 93012. Phone 805-524-3821.

Dave Dravecky is the author of *Worth of a Man* and president of Outreach of Hope, a ministry of encouragement that offers hope through Jesus Christ to those suffering from cancer or amputation. His mission is accomplished by providing ongoing contact, prayer support, public speeches and presentations, resource referrals, materials and curriculum and distribution of literature. You can contact Dave at 13840 Gleneagle Dr., Colorado Springs, CO 80921 or by calling 719-481-3528.

Colleen Edwards is a ghostwriter for **Renée Lacouague Bondi's** story "Now This Is Music!". She is an inspirational writer part time and a marketing executive in Orange County, California full time. Her next goal is to spread the message of love and kindness through her own newspaper column. Editorial/publisher inquiries welcome. Contact her at 107 W. Avenida Valencia, San Clemente, CA 92627. Phone 714-498-0657.

Vera A. Fortune lives in Madison, Wisconsin where she works for the state of Wisconsin full-time. She has 4 children and 11 grandchildren with one on the way. Vera was involved in a terrible auto accident on May 14, 1996 where she underwent emergency surgery to reconstruct her ankle, had a metal plate and 8 screws required. Since then, her life has been almost completely devoted to recuperation and coping with the subsequential repercussions.

Barbara Frye is an associate professor of international health and program manager of the graduate program in maternal child health at Loma Linda

University School of Public Health. She consults internationally in the areas of maternal and child health, traveling extensively in Africa, Southeast Asia and Latin America.

Marilyn Dunham Ganch is a native of Houston, Texas who graduated from the University of Texas at Austin with a degree in English and Journalism. She is currently an office manager for a medical clinic and mother of a teenage daughter. An aspiring writer, she has written short stories, personal essays and poetry. She may be contacted at 9703 Harrowgate, Houston, TX 77031.

Randy Glasbergen has more than 20,000 cartoons and illustrations published by magazines and newspapers around the world. He is also the author of many books. When you are online, be sure to visit *Todays Cartoon by Randy Glasbergen* at *http://www.norwich.net/~randyg/toon.html* or via e-mail, at *randyg@norwich.net.*

Austin Goodrich served as an infantryman (gravel-clutcher) in World War II before pursuing consecutive careers in journalism and espionage. Currently he leads a semi-domesticated life writing stories, speeches, scripts and research papers, for which he gets considerable satisfaction and a non-negotiable two bits a word. Call him at 414-427-1030.

Laverne W. Hall has done major radio, TV and newspaper interviews and has published one book of poetry. She can be reached at 3994 Menlo Dr., Atlanta, GA 30340, or by calling 770-491-8887.

Malcolm Hancock was a freelance cartoonist who was published internationally. A paraplegic following a tragic accident at the age of 17, Malcolm spent his life communicating the humor in human existence. Malcolm died in 1993 after a valiant fight against cancer.

Wilma Heffelfinger is an herbalist who publishes a monthly newsletter focusing on simpler lifestyles and growing your own medical herbs. She also won an Editor's Choice Award in the national poetry contest in 1996. She can be reached at Sunny Meadows, P.O. Box 33, Greenwood, MO 64034, or call her at 816-331-4934, fax: 816-322-5181; e-mail at *Sunnymdw@sky.net.*

Beverly Hulsizer works as a staff assistant for Procter & Gamble Company in Cincinnati, Ohio. She and her husband, George, have been married for 34 years and have two daughters, Amy and Beth. Beverly was raised in Bethlehem, Pennsylvania.

Reverend Dr. Bruce Humphrey pastors Trinity Presbyterian Church, which has grown from 250 to 650 members during his 10 years of leadership. The author of five books, Bruce is known as a storyteller-preacher. With two earned doctorates, Bruce speaks at seminars, camps, retreats and renewals. He can be reached at 630 Park Ave., Prescott, AZ 86303.

Virginia Jarvis (Ginny) resides in Bay City, Michigan, and is married and the mother of three children. She enjoys bowling and golf. For 15 years she has worked for the Veterans Administration Medical Center in Saginaw, Michigan, and is an Accredited Record Technician. This is her first article, and she is very proud to have it published in *Chicken Soup for the Christian Soul*.

Virginia Johnson knows that many people have experienced miraculous occurences with their deceased loved ones. If you'd like to share your experiences with Virginia, you may contact her at 816-587-6054. It is an enormous step in the healing process. Thanks to Meg Lundstrom, Ron continues to touch many lives as he did in his time on earth.

The Joyful Noiseletter is a monthly newsletter of the Fellowship of Merry Christians and has provided clean jokes, holy humor and cartoons to pastors and church newsletter editors for 11 years. The newsletter has won awards for excellence from the Associated Church Press, the Catholic Press Association and the Evangelical Press Association. For information about "The Joyful Noiseletter" and the Fellowship's other holy humor resources, call 800-877-2757 or write FMC, P.O. Box 895, Portage, MI 49081.

Ida Mae Kempel has been widely published in Christian magazines. She is also the author of three books. The latest, *What Was in Jeremey's Egg? and Other Stories*, is a compilation of some of her work. To order books or to request an interview, write to Nascent Press, 2137 Otis Dr. #302, Alameda, CA 94501, or call 510-523-8741.

Edward Koper is not an internationally recognized speaker, but is a happily married man with a wonderful wife, Diane, and two terrific daughters named Emily and Rachel. Ed feels fortunate to have had his life touched by God in a small way and hopes everyone learns to recognize God's hand in their lives. Ed can be reached at 908-566-3130.

Priscilla Larson is the author of *STRANGER DANGER* (Tyndale House, 1991) and numerous articles for many publications. Her favorite assignments are interviews that demonstrate how faith sustains someone in difficult times. She can be reached at 117 Lincoln St., Lexington, MA 02173, or by calling 617-862-8918.

Richard Lederer has published more than two thousand articles and books about language, including his blooper series *Anguished English, More Anguished English* and *Fractured English*. He has been elected International Punster of the Year and profiled in *The New Yorker* and *People* magazine. His weekly column, *Looking at Language*, appears in newspapers and magazines throughout the United States. He makes 150 speaking appearances each year and is a regular language commentator for public radio. He can be reached at 9974 Scripps Ranch Blvd., Ste. 201, San Diego, CA 92131, or by calling 619-549-6788 or via e-mail at *richard.lederer@pobox.com;//www.pobox.com/~verbivore*.

William J. Lederer is a graduate of the U.S. Naval Academy in Annapolis, Maryland. He is the author of 16 books including, *The Ugly American, A Nation of Sheep* and *All the Ships at Sea*. He was a Nieman Fellow at Harvard University and a Far East correspondent for *Reader's Digest*. William is now working on a book, *How to Become a Successful Author*, based on interviews with 51 world-famous writers.

Elizabeth Leland writes for *The Charlotte Observer*. For copies of her book, *A Place for Joe: A True Story of a White Southern Family, a Black Man, Their Lifetime Together and Their Love for One Another*, write Down Home Press, P. O. Box 4126, Sheboro, NC 27204, or call 910-672-6889, or fax 910-672-2003. The cost of the book is $19.95 plus $2.50 shipping and handling.

Sharon Linnéa has been a book editor and a staff writer for four national magazines. She and her husband have a son, Jonathan, and another child arriving shortly. She speaks often at Writers Conferences, as well as to schools about a kid's needs for heroes. Autographed copies of either of her two latest books—the young adult biographies *Raoul Wallenberg: The Man Who Stopped Death* (JPS) and *Princess Ka'iulani, Hope of a Nation, Heart of a People* (Eerdmans)—can be purchased by sending $15.00 made out to Sharon Linnea, c/o Shimersbrook, 290 River Rd., Montague, NJ 07827.

Meg Lundstrom lives in New York, is the coauthor of *The Power of Flow: Practical Ways to Transform Your Life with Meaningful Coincidence*. (Harmony, 1997).

Ray L. Lundy is a minister, poet and inspirational speaker who writes magazine articles and a weekly column for a local newspaper. He has also written an inspirational book entitled *Special Heroes*. Ray may be reached at P.O. Box 217, Fair Bluff, NC 28439, or by calling 910-649-7178.

Paula McDonald is a bestselling author who has sold over a million copies of her books on relationships and gone on to win numerous awards worldwide as a columnist, inspirational feature writer and photojournalist. She is a highly regarded national lecturer on relationships and family communications, as well as being a popular inspirational speaker, both in the United States and abroad. Paula is available as a speaker or a writer and can be contacted through Creative Consultants, 417 W. San Ysidro Blvd., Suite L724, San Ysidro, CA 92173. Tel/fax: (Rosarito, Mexico): 011-52-66-313173, or e-mail: *102526.356@compuserve.com*.

Chris Caldwell McGonigle has a Ph.D. in English from the University of Washington and has been writing for the women's magazines for 10 years, specializing in real-life dramas. Her first book, about surviving a spouse's chronic illness, will be published in 1998 by Henry Holt. She lives in Montana.

Andrea Nannette Mejia is a published author, entrepreneur, actress and mother of three wonderful children whom she home-schools. She founded Andrea's Heavenly Baked Goods and Chocolates and has won many awards at the Los Angeles County Fair. You can contact her by e-mail at *TNT4GOD@juno.com*.

Warren Miller has been providing sports films for almost 50 years. Currently he is writing for newspapers and giving speeches that reflect his life spent lurching from one near disaster to the next.

Helene Montone has been married for 16 years and has been a registered nurse at a center city hospital for 21 years. She has never written anything before. She is grateful to both Jesus and her son's birthparents for giving her family such a great joy. Helene hopes this story will bring a smile, touch a soul or mend an aching heart.

Jeanne Morris was born in Norfolk, Virginia, and grew up on Chesapeake Beach. She attended high school in Picton, Ontario and later enrolled in the U. of H., still living in Houston, Texas where she and her husband maintain a prayer garden for their church, the Aldine United Methodist Church. The garden offers special services to survivors of homicide victims. She is also an active member of Parents of Murdered Children. You can reach Jeanne at 1905 Bennington Rd., Houston, TX 77093.

Edward B. Mullen is a wildlife biologist who works in Santa Barbara, California. He is currently writing a series of nature-related inspirational stories. He can be reached at 816 State St., Santa Barbara, CA 93101 or call 805-984-8899.

Judith E. Peitsch has been writing poetry along with music composition for the past 25 years and is an accomplished pianist. She's married, with one son in college, and is a secretary in advertising. She can be reached at 32456 Ridgefield, Warren, MI 48093.

Daniel Rosandich is a professional cartoonist who is "on call" to illustrate any of your publishing projects. He will illustrate under your art direction and will fax "roughs" to you to approve. Call Dan at 906-482-6234.

Helga Schmidt is a wife, mother, grandmother of eight and a registered nurse. She lives in rural Newton, Kansas with her husband, Archie. She works in a local clinic and enjoys writing in her spare time. Helga can be reached at 10408 N. Anderson Rd., Newton, KS 67114 or by calling 316-367-2325.

Randy Shaver teaches debate and speech and is a nationally recognized speech coach. He is an inspirational speaker and writer and is privileged to be Anderson and Sarah's dad. He can be reached at 245 Hampton Rd., 2-C, Asheboro, NC 27203, or by calling 910-629-0429.

Gary Smalley is an internationally recognized speaker/author on family relationships who has sold 9 million copies of his books and videos. He is the president of *Today's Family*, based in Branson, Missouri. Gary's catalog and seminar schedule is available through calling 800-84-TODAY or *http://www.GarySmalley.com*.

Ira Spector, is an author whose latest work, *Last Chance*, tells the story of a ruthless downsizing expert who has a change of heart and hires the homeless to work at a gambling resort. Ira Spector may be reached through Arius Publications, 121 Edelen Ave., Los Gatos, CA 95030 or via e-mail: *ira_spector@msn.com*.

Richard Stanford is a Presbyterian minister and recently became a full-time writer. He has had several articles and stories published. He currently has a novel and two short stories under consideration for publication. You can write to Richard at 1219 Mohican Trail, Stone Mountain, GA 30083, or e-mail to *Richard_Stanford@msn.com.*

Barbara Stith has been a writer for *The Post-Standard* and the *Syracuse Herald-Journal* for seven years. She was a reporter and editorial writer before becoming a senior writer/editor in 1996.

Dawn Stobbe is grateful for each day, her family and friends, and her life. She is a cancer survivor and she believes in prayer and miracles. She and her husband, Rich, share seven children. Dawn and Rich are co-creators of Miracle Crafts (rock and wood crafts with miracle theme). You can reach Dawn at P.O. Box 5412, Grand Island, NE 68802.

Tom Suriano is the son of Jim and Evelyn Suriano of Martins Ferry, Ohio. He is a high school guidance counselor and football coach; and he and his wife, Kim, have two daughters, Susan and Stephanie. A 41-year-old educator, Tom, who holds a master's degree in counseling and has 20 year's experience in education, feels blessed by his newfound Christianity through a strong faith in Jesus Christ.

Tom Veres was asked by Raoul Wallenberg to document how two Swedes made an extraordinary rescue of thousands of Hungarian Jews from Adolph Eichmann's Einsatzkommando in 1944. Tom did so, often at the risk of his own life. Two of his photos form the basis of the 1997 U.S. stamp honoring Wallenberg. He works as a commercial photographer in New York City. More of his story is told in the young adult biography *Raoul Wallenberg: The Man Who Stopped Death,* which can be ordered from JPS at 800-234-3151. Veres is currently working on his own autobiography.

Catherine Verlenden is a lay counselor, short-term missionary and freelance writer of articles for Christian publications.

Linda Vlcek lives in Sierra Madre, California. She has been married 30 years and raised three sons. She has been an employee of Huntington Memorial Hospital of Pasadena for 30 years. Above all, she is a very strong believer in Jesus Christ and continues to witness his miracles in her friends' and family's lives.

Arnold Watts is first and foremost a Christian, then an American, then a veteran, then a husband, then a father, then a grandfather, then a mason, then a lion and last but not least, then and now and always, a poet. He places all of these in high regard.

Marilynn Carlson Webber is an award-winning author of the bestseller *A Rustle of Angels* and other books. An inspirational speaker, Marilynn ministers to women's clubs and churches large and small. She has been interviewed on hundreds of radio and TV shows. She can be reached at 275 Celeste Dr., Riverside, CA 92507, or by calling 909-784-4313.

Kathleen Weber and her husband have raised five children in Boston, New York. She is a Catholic school librarian and also works at Weight Watchers. Kathy is active in many church and community organizations and enjoys poetry as well as the arts.

Jeannie S. Williams is a prolific author/lecturer and a master storyteller. She is a member of the Fellowship of Christian Magicians and has been entertaining audiences for years with her creativity. Jeannie shares the magic of working with children in her newest book, *What Time is Recess?* She can be reached at P. O. Box 1476, Sikeston, MO 63801.

©1997 by *Guideposts*, Carmel, NY 10512.

In His Mother's Footsteps. By Davida Dalton, as told to JoEllen Johnson. ©The Church of Jesus Christ of Latter-day Saints. First published in April 1994 *Ensign.* Used by permission.

Hands Poem. Reprinted by permission of Wilma Heffelfinger. ©1997 Wilma Heffelfinger.

My Mother's Hands. Reprinted by permission of Beverly Hulsizer. ©1997 Beverly Hulsizer.

Hands. Reprinted by permission of Judith Peitsch. ©1997 Judith Peitsch.

Out of a Job. Reprinted with permission from *Guideposts* Magazine. ©1980 by *Guideposts*, Carmel, NY 10512.

The Two Sides of Love. Reprinted by permission of Gary Smalley. ©1997 Gary Smalley.

Don't Let It End This Way. Reprinted with permission from *Guideposts* Magazine. ©1979 by *Guideposts*, Carmel, NY 10512.

The Halfhearted Gift—A Dog for David. Reprinted by permission of Priscilla Larson. ©1988 Priscilla Larson.

Andy's Dream. Reprinted by permission of Anne Bembry. ©1997 by Anne Bembry. Excerpted from *Woman's World* Magazine.

Safety Blanket. Reprinted by permission of Reverend Dr. Bruce Humphrey. ©1996 Reverend Dr. Bruce Humphrey.

My Father. Reprinted by permission of Tom Suriano. ©1997 Tom Suriano.

The Bible. Reprinted by permission of Universal Press Syndicate. Excerpted from *Dear Abby.* All rights reserved.

Home for the Holidays. Reprinted by permission of Linda Vlcek. ©1996 Linda Vlcek.

God Calling. Excerpted from *Where Miracles Happen: True Stories of Heavenly Encounters* by Joan Wester Anderson. ©1995 by Joan Wester Anderson. Published by Brett Books, Inc. Reprinted by permission.

Invisible Guardians. From *Where Wonders Prevail* by Joan Wester Anderson. ©1996 by Joan Wester Anderson. Reprinted by permission of Ballantine Books, a Division of Random House, Inc.

A Reason to Heal. Reprinted with permission from *Angels on Earth* Magazine. ©1995 by *Guideposts*, Carmel, NY 10512.

Expect a Miracle. Reprinted by permission of Dawn Stobbe and Meg Lundstrom. ©1996 Dawn Stobbe and Meg Lundstrom. Excerpted from *Woman's World* Magazine.